FAITH IN THE AGE OF SCIENCE

– Atheism, Religion, and the Big Yellow Crane –

MARK SILVERSIDES

Sacristy Press

Sacristy Press
PO Box 612, Durham, DH1 9HT

www.sacristy.co.uk

First published in 2012 by Sacristy Press, Durham

Copyright © Mark Silversides 2012
The right of Mark Silversides to be identified as the author
of this work has been asserted by him in accordance with
the Copyright, Designs and Patents Act 1988.

All rights reserved, no part of this publication may be reproduced
or transmitted in any form or by any means, electronic,
mechanical photocopying, documentary, film or in any other
format without prior written permission of the publisher.

Sacristy Limited, registered in England & Wales, number 7565667

British Library Cataloguing-in-Publication Data
A catalogue record for the book is available from the British Library

ISBN 978-1-908381-04-0

www.marksilversides.com

Contents

Introduction v
Atheism in Crisis 1
The New "F-word" 29
The Appliance of Science.. 53
Daftness and Beyond... 68
Mr Charles Darwin had the Gall to Ask 77
The Evolutionary Enigma 85
The Blind Project Manager 99
The Golden Grain... 108
Narrowing the Odds 126
Quantum Quirkiness... 141
Harold from Cowley Reveals All 159
A Pause for Reflection 172
The Big Yellow Crane... 182
Return to the Philosophical Forum 202
The Theological Theme Park..................................... 211
Significance 223
Glossary... 227
Bibliography 237
Index 240

Introduction

To borrow a cliché from sports commentators, my adult working life has been a game of two halves. For the first half, lasting about sixteen years, I was a Church of England clergyman. For the second half, lasting roughly the same length of time, I have been working in what is broadly known as "digital media".

Normally the "spiritual" type of mid-life crisis happens the other way around. People with little apparent religious leaning get to middle age and find that intimations of mortality can no longer be ignored. A search for "spiritual values" gets underway, and before they know it they're writing to bishops about taking up a "late vocation" to the priesthood or ministry. I presume that similar things happen in other faiths—but what do you do if you've already been there and "got the T-shirt", as they say?

I moved out of the Vicarage, but not out of religion, although I did drift into a rather weakened version of Christianity. In some ways I became what's known as a *deist*. The idea behind deism is that God created the universe then went for an extended lunch. That's very different from the view known as *theism*—or *monotheism* when there is only one God involved—the belief that God not only did the creating but also takes a continuing interest in what's going on, even extending to some current concerns about us mere mortals. I hovered between the two views, but then along came *The God Delusion* by Richard Dawkins.

Having long ago read Dawkins' seminal works *The Selfish Gene* and *The Blind Watchmaker* I was inclined to listen to the arguments in *The God Delusion*. Yet, as I proceeded through the book, doubts began to creep in. As you can probably imagine, I've rubbed shoulders over the years with a wide cross-section of religious people—indeed, I can be one myself on good days. As I read *The God Delusion* the nagging question that started coming to mind was, "Why had I been so unaware of the wickedness all around me in these religious institutions?"

Religion has great imperfections, and Dawkins points these out with his customary, and welcome, incisiveness. Yet, looking at my own practical experience in both the pulpit and the pew, I just couldn't see the all-pervading darkness that Dawkins perceives enshrouding the whole religious enterprise. In his more recent book *The Greatest Show on Earth* and his television series *The Genius of Charles Darwin* space is also made for atheist invective within otherwise brilliant narrative. All in all, though, *The God Delusion* remains a flagship, and Dawkins is certainly the chief spokesman for atheism today.

My plan in this book, therefore, is to get to grips with Dawkins' views—this seems to be a mandatory first step in considering the place of faith in a scientific culture. At the same time, however, his work links in with other atheist writers and with broader aspects of philosophy, science, and religion. I hope to make some salient points in each of these areas, to respond to a broader agenda than that put forward by Dawkins alone, although he is my starting point.

However, before tackling the main issues, it's necessary to attend to one particular delusion, namely, the belief that important books are bought by everyone, and that they are read by all who buy them.

A Bluffer's Guide to Dawkins and the *New Atheists*

Charles Darwin (1809–82) published his *Origin of Species* in 1859. Now it is true that evolution has from time to time been a source of disagreement between some scientists and some conservative Christians, but the idea that there was a uniform bipartisan conflict immediately after Darwin published his work is a caricature. There was strong debate, but many prominent scientists, not just religious leaders, raised questions about evolution. The main protagonists are generally portrayed as T. H. Huxley (1825–95) and Bishop William Wilberforce (1805–73). Yet John Lennox in *God's Undertaker: Has Science Buried God?* shows convincingly that the famous debate between Huxley and Wilberforce in 1860, although undoubtedly significant, was not considered critical at the time.

Indeed, the "conflict thesis" so eagerly promoted in the last quarter of the nineteenth century by the likes of Andrew Dickson White (co-founder of Cornell University) and John William Draper (co-founder of New York University Medical School) is now almost entirely discredited, despite the eminence of its main propagators and the fact that it was slavishly repeated for a long time. Authoritative historians of science such as Colin Russell, David Lindberg, and Ronald Numbers now regard the Draper-White methodology as deeply flawed, verging on fabrication. Nevertheless, this supposed conflict is taken as almost unquestionable fact in the writings of Dawkins and his like-minded associates, who are commonly grouped together as the "new atheists".

Conflict did take off in the USA in 1925 when John Scopes was convicted of teaching evolution in a publicly-funded educational establishment, contrary to Tennessee State Law. Controversy rumbled along for 80 years until the famous *Kitzmiller v Dover Area School District* federal trial of 2005, which concluded that the idea of *intelligent design* was a religious view akin to *Creationism* and therefore should not be taught in state schools.

Nothing disturbs the "new atheists" more than Creationism. In its most extreme form this is the belief that God created human beings relatively quickly, rather than through a protracted process of evolution. Some go so far as to say that the earth itself is very young, typically about 6,000 years old. Others—often referred to as "old-earth" creationists—admit that the earth is old, as geologists and cosmologists argue, but still maintain that mankind was created directly by God. Others accept the general thrust of evolution but argue that at certain stages there must have been some kind of intelligent design at work. Many in this latter group would reject the "creationist" label.

However, there are many convinced theists who see no conflict between evolution and their beliefs, a position known as *Theistic Evolution*. Within Christianity, this is the majority view outside the United States, but within the United States these various views are much more evenly balanced, with significant numbers of creationists and upholders of intelligent design. Some wish to reverse this trend by the promotion of less extreme religion, others, like Dawkins, want to reverse it through the promotion of atheism. He is particularly associated with Daniel Dennett, the late Christopher Hitchens, Sam Harris, and A.C. Grayling in this aspiration.

Apart from his strong conviction, though, there is no particular reason for Dawkins to write or broadcast about religion—in fact, in many respects, he lacks the qualifications to do so. Others with greater knowledge than mine have drawn attention to the poor nature of Dawkins' sources throughout *The God Delusion*. John Cornwell in *Darwin's Angel* points out Dawkins' lack of relevant references to anyone who might not totally agree with him. Moderate forms of religion are particularly neglected.

The distinguished literary critic Terry Eagleton put it this way (Review of *The God Delusion* in *London Review of Books*, 19th October 2006):

> Card-carrying rationalists like Dawkins, who is the nearest thing to a professional atheist we have had since Bertrand Russell, are in one sense the least well-equipped to understand what they castigate, since they don't believe there is anything there to be understood, or at least anything worth understanding. This is why they invariably come up with vulgar caricatures of religious faith that would make a first-year theology student wince. The more they detest religion, the more ill-informed their criticisms of it tend to be.

Dawkins is not, then, flavour of the month everywhere. It is perhaps also worth noting in a preliminary way that, even within the scientific field, he is not unanimously supported in all the views that he proclaims so dogmatically. His outlook is strictly *neo-Darwinist*, an outlook that holds evolution to be almost entirely driven by a slow process of mutation and natural selection. His argument with the palaeontologist Stephen Jay Gould is particularly well known in the trade, and there are others who would also significantly modify his approach. Ultimately he believes that natural selection in some form is relevant to cosmology and to cultural development, a view which appears to amount to an article of faith.

The Delusions

In essence the "new atheists" regard belief in God as the biggest mistake ever made by the human race. This alleged error leads on to one delusion after another. It is perhaps acceptable to use the word "God" in some kind of poetic manner, and it may be *relatively* harmless to believe in a God who kicked things off then retired from the scene. As I said earlier, this is the deist's view, but anything more specific is almost infinitely damaging.

Dawkins classifies religions in a rather rough way. There are monotheistic religions (mainly Judaism, Christianity, and Islam) that developed from belief in the "Abrahamic" God, and the rest (polytheism and "philosophies of life" like Buddhism). It is the monotheists who cause all the problems, because theirs is a vengeful God, as we can see from the early books of the Old Testament. The main monotheistic religions are different from each other, but those differences are unimportant compared to their common theme, that the God of the Bible is a sadistic ogre.

In Christianity, Jesus, if he existed, had some good moral teaching, but the early Christians fouled it all up. Dawkins sees Christian belief as mere hair splitting about a non-existent being, and those who have given their lives to this pursuit, sometimes literally, have done so in vain. The real founder of Christianity was probably the Apostle Paul, and he was obsessed with the idea of atonement—an idea which just takes us back to the vengeful bloodlust of the Old Testament God. No improvement shown.

So much for the unreasonable nature of all supposedly revealed religion. Although Dawkins and the other "new atheists" comment most often on Christianity, their criticisms extend equally to Judaism and Islam. Sometimes they seem to notice little difference between them.

Isn't it possible to take a more reasoned view, even a *scientific* view of things, and hold to religious beliefs, as do many scientists? The answer given by Dawkins is a resounding "No!" A reasoned approach to religion is based on formulating arguments for the existence of God, but these are fatally flawed, and some are simply, in his view, ridiculous.

The Heart of the Matter

Dawkins consistently claims that there is almost certainly no God. Chapter 4 of *The God Delusion* is a pivotal exposition of his whole scheme of thought—no type of belief in God can be justified by the evidence available to us in the universe. The chapter falls into two major parts, of which the first deals with the development of life on earth, and the sufficiency of natural selection to explain that development. No God seems to be required. In fact, the whole impression of design that we see in the natural order is an illusion. Dawkins is here restating in summary form his thoroughly worked out and eloquent books *The Selfish Gene, The Blind Watchmaker, The Extended Phenotype,* and *Climbing Mount Improbable.* The same ideas are also explored in *River Out of Eden* but with some reworking around the central metaphor of a river of digital information flowing down the millennia, the information being coded into DNA. *The Greatest Show on Earth* restates the case in a fresh form, but with little substantive addition.

The second major subject of Chapter 4 of *The God Delusion* is the probability, or otherwise, of a planet such as ours coming into existence at all, so that the whole process of the inception and evolution of life could take place. Natural selection is of no use to Dawkins here, because planets, stars, and galaxies don't mutate and replicate like living organisms. When we consider that we need *very* precise conditions for the earth to exist in just the way it does, it might seem as if a divine guiding hand were required. Yet here again such a supposition would be a mistake. Given the scale of the universe even the very improbable is not that surprising.

In the Dawkinsian view, then, there is no rational way of justifying religion. The irrational approach produces fundamentalism, which corrupts politics, education, and society in general. It is highly influential in our current culture and therefore causes untold damage. The only way of avoiding this is to demolish the whole religious enterprise and create an atheistic culture. Such moral and aesthetic elements as are beneficial should be kept, but appreciated for themselves, free of unnecessary superstitious baggage. This dimension is expounded most fully in *Unweaving the Rainbow.*

For Dawkins, religion can be adequately accounted for without the existence of a God. Unsurprisingly, he leans towards neo-Darwinist explanations of religion, with his own particular spin. The idea of *memes* (which for now we can simply regard as units of memory) often pops up in this connection. In general, though, his thought here is not particularly original, following familiar refrains of the disgusting character of God in the Old Testament and the equally disgusting idea of atonement in the New Testament. Worst of all, wars have been fought so often in the name of religion. People like Stalin and Hitler may have been atheists, but at least they did not fight in the name of atheism. In any case, we have to admit that to a great extent they were influenced by the moral climate, the *zeitgeist,* of the time.

Fundamentalism is particularly blameworthy in Dawkins' view. It subverts science, suppresses sexuality, causes suffering by opposing abortion and euthanasia, corrupts education, and stifles thought. (Oh, and by the way, don't you moderate religious-types think you can escape criticism: in Dawkins' view it is moderate religion like yours that provides a breeding ground for extremists.)

Some of Dawkins' statements are famously offensive, such as the claim that religious education amounts to child abuse. My main concern, however, is with the substance of what Dawkins and the other "new atheists" have to say. If the substance is correct then lapses into exaggeration can be overlooked, perhaps even justified. To be distracted by such things carries the risk of missing the main point—and the main point, whether or not we should believe in God, is fairly important.

In this book I aim first and foremost to be true to the facts, although I trust that a little passion will be excused from time to time. I hope that most of what I have to say will be of interest to atheists, agnostics, humanists, and the followers of many religions, since the fundamental question at stake is relevant to us all. Most of my more specific material relates to Christianity and particularly Protestant Christianity, but that should not be taken as implying that I believe other versions of Christianity or other faiths are unimportant. Rather, I do not want to comment on areas where my knowledge and experience are minimal, which is likely to be not only misguided, but also insulting to those who hold to other beliefs with great integrity.

Underpinning

I currently live in the north-east of England, the land of my birth. Occasionally, as in other former mining areas, a mysterious hole will appear in the ground, or a building will develop alarming cracks. The only answer to these problems is to underpin—dig down and pour in a large amount of concrete. In the case of Dawkins and his colleagues, that which is to be underpinned is atheism, and the equivalent of the concrete is anything that can be pressed into service. Often it appears that the material chosen is more like expanded polystyrene than concrete, and I shall point this out from time to time.

There are no doubt many reasons for Dawkins' determined style, and he certainly believes the views he proclaims with such vigour. I have come to feel, however, that there is also an underlying motivation behind the underpinning exercise, for all is not well in the atheist camp. Dawkins and his "new atheist" colleagues look around at our cultural landscape and its difficulties and pronounce on the root cause of them all. Apparently there is an elephant in the room, and its name is religion. Well, I agree there is an elephant in the room, but its name is not religion.

Atheists have a major problem that they seem unwilling to acknowledge, a problem of self-contradiction. *This* metaphorical elephant has made itself very comfortable, yet atheists prefer to skirt around it and admire the wallpaper, rather than address issues raised by the unwelcome intruder. To investigate the nature of this proboscoid presence is the purpose of my first chapter.

CHAPTER 1

Atheism in Crisis

There have been atheists throughout western history, starting from the pre-socratic philosophers of the sixth century BCE, but generally as a very small minority. Until the eighteenth century the almost infallible rule was that people would follow the religious belief into which they were born, or convert to a different faith, voluntarily or under duress.

The atheist viewpoint had greater freedom to develop with the onset of the Enlightenment during the seventeenth century, so that in the eighteenth and nineteenth centuries atheism became more of an option. This modern phase is generally held to start with Baron d'Holbach (1723–89) and a handful of others in the second half of the eighteenth century. D'Holbach was one of the *materialists* (we shall consider this philosophy in more detail later) who provided the intellectual groundwork for the French Revolution. Julian Baggini in his book *Atheism: A Very Short Introduction* gives greater detail of what he calls "the birth of avowed atheism" at this time and connects it across the centuries with the pre-socratics as part of an ongoing story, although, as he himself admits, not all authorities would agree with him on this point.

Baggini's book is an excellent introduction to atheism, both concise and constructive, and he may be correct in making a theoretical link with the ancient Greeks. There was also some medieval discussion concerning atheistic views, for example in the works of Peter Abelard (1079–1142). However, for modern readers, atheism in our western culture originated in eighteenth-century Europe.

Atheism Today

I suspect that Baggini would not support the belligerence of the extreme Dawkinsians as he seems to be more interested in promoting useful philosophical discussion. In a similar vein, Lewis Wolpert is a card-carrying atheist, but is more conciliatory than aggressive in tone. Martin Rowson, a piercing humorist and author of *The Dog Allusion: Gods, Pets and How to Be Human* thinks it would be better just to pat religion on the head and leave it alone in its basket to gnaw on its leg. Hopefully, this might keep it out of politics, a wish also expressed (at least most of the time) by commentators such as the late Christopher Hitchens. Like *The God Delusion* their writings often draw insufficient distinction between types of religious belief, and show little real engagement with the content of those beliefs. Margaret Wertheim labels herself as a "pinko-liberal-feminist atheist"—hardly a religious fanatic—yet castigates Hitchens, along with Sam Harris, for an attitude of blanket condemnation and undiscerning invective. The same criticism could be brought against other popularising atheists.

Victor J. Stenger appears to be the latest proponent of the aggressive "shoot first" tendency, which is unfortunate because his physics in *God: the Failed Hypothesis* is thought-provoking, compared to his general attacks on faith, which have been doing the rounds for centuries and are getting rather tired. Likewise, I fear Dawkins' atheist successor at Oxford, Marcus du Sautoy, may go the same way—brilliantly presented mathematics, but with the odd snipe at religion popping up for no obvious reason. On the other hand, the physicist Brian Cox enjoys dialogue with religious individuals and does not see the value of attacking religion as such, making an understandable exception for creationists.

Modern atheism, then, is a very mixed bag—I almost said "broad church". For Dawkins, any peace-brokering with religion is betrayal. Tolerant sceptics like Michael Ruse, who has even had the nerve to point out areas of congruence between Darwinism and Christianity, and palaeontologist Stephen Jay Gould, are associated with 1930s politician Neville Chamberlain as mere "appeasers". A somewhat similar hard line attitude emerges from *The Brights,* an internet-based network for those who do not believe in the supernatural, of which Daniel Dennett is a founding member. Yet there are others who are more tolerant.

Long-standing bodies like the *British Humanist Association*, *National Secular Society* and *Rationalist Association* are of course not always belligerent. Bertrand Russell, the favourite uncle of modern atheism, was certainly an activist but seemed content to build an argument rather than throw up dust. Such clarity is often difficult to find, because many organisations and networks admit agnostics—the "don't knows" of the faith world—as well as atheists, therefore it is hard to know whether their statements represent a distinctively atheistic viewpoint. Sometimes the word "humanist" is used in a broad sense to mean something like "atheist with a heart" but that doesn't help much. In fact, it seems that almost all atheists claim to be humanists, although not all humanists claim to be atheists.

It is difficult to say, then, that there is a specifically atheistic line on practically anything, apart from the claim that there is no God and therefore all religion is mistaken. The general attitude is to follow the hallowed principle known as *Occam's Razor,* which states that explanations are not to be multiplied unnecessarily. If it is not necessary to believe in a God then we should not do so, any more than we should believe in fairies. Because of the strength of this assumption, the typical assertive atheist feels he has made his case if he mounts a good attack on any supposed evidence for God's existence. It is also *de rigeur* to assume that science is the most valuable source—probably the only source—of knowledge.

However, even with their common starting point, atheists often disagree on the logical implications. For example, they are divided on the American presence in Iraq, as Tina Beattie analyses with great perception in *The New Atheists*. The general tenor of much current atheist output is consistent enough: religion (radical Islam) is responsible for "9/11", and religion (American fundamentalism) is responsible for the war in Iraq. The difference arises as to whether or not it is a good thing to set a thief to catch a thief. Using one group of religious fanatics to get rid of another could be seen as rather clever. The underlying hypothesis tends to be that religion is the root of all evil, so that ultimately any form of conflict, including terrorism, is caused by religion. Of course, all religions are held to be basically the same in that respect. This is not a well-founded view, but popular atheism is not always precise.

Atheists' lack of precision is particularly clearly seen in this example, for the great majority of terrorism has always been politically and nationalistically motivated. Suicide attacks in the last two centuries go back to nineteenth-century Russian nihilists, the Japanese Kamikaze, the Viet Minh in Vietnam, the PKK in Turkey, and the Tamil Tigers in Sri Lanka, who first devised the suicide bomber's vest. Using the "root of all evil" methodology we could say that atheism (revolutionary socialism) was primarily responsible for this modern trend. However, that seems to be overlooked in favour of the assumption that religion is the driving force behind all such horrors, even though none of these movements were religious. Intriguingly, Aditya Chakrabortty writing in *The Guardian*, in the wake of Osama bin Laden's death, cites much evidence that even Islamist suicide bombers are not primarily driven, for the most part, by religion. Nationalistic idealism, often coupled with a sense of cultural or ethnic humiliation, seems to be far more important.

Atheism is not a solid movement with a long development. Denial of the existence of God is clearly of the essence, frequently followed by attacks on religion, adulation of science, and selective use of historical facts to bolster the cause. There is, of course, much that is justifiable in attacks on religion, much that is praiseworthy in science, and much that is ambiguous about history. The flaw is in the one-sidedness, although this is less pronounced in the more tolerant members of the atheist community. As always, though, the less tolerant tend to have the loudest voices.

Much of this book is concerned with science, so I shall not say much about it in this chapter. My main concern at present is to tackle the question of what atheism is, what its effects have been and what its weaknesses are.

Some History: Lisbon, 1755

An earthquake occurred in Lisbon on All Saints' Day (1st November) 1755. By all accounts it was a severe quake followed by a tsunami, which devastated the city and killed 30–50,000 men, women, and children, with some estimates even higher. The psychological impact on Europe was immense and is difficult for us to understand today, even though our contemporary media bring us heart-rending images of similar, and sometimes even greater, catastrophes.

Amongst what we call the "chattering classes" the effect of the earthquake was dramatic, for the general mood had been one of optimism. Things were moving forward, particularly in science and philosophy. Sir Isaac Newton (1643–1727) and Gottfried Leibniz (1646–1716) had reduced the apparent mysteries of physics to a few simple laws and developed calculus to help with the sums. Empiricist philosophy tied in well with the ever-developing science which seemed able to explain, at least potentially, the secrets of the universe. Suddenly, with the Lisbon earthquake, everything was called into question. How can this be the "best of all possible worlds" (a phrase coined by Leibniz in his philosophical mode) when suddenly so many men, women, and children are destroyed, without reason or warning?

News of the earthquake eventually reached a grumpy philosopher with the pen name "Voltaire" (1694–1778), who responded initially with a poem and then, four years later, with his short novel *Candide,* the best known of his works. It tells how the youthful and optimistic Candide travels from his home, the castle of the most-noble Baron of Thunder-ten-tronckh, which is the best of all possible castles. His optimism is derived from the teaching of Dr Pangloss, the greatest philosopher in the province and therefore in the world.

There follows a whirlwind global tour, in the course of which Candide meets a variety of beliefs and religions. Those encountered include Jesuits, Dutch Protestants, Anabaptists, Jews, and Turks. It is fairly clear that the effect of the earthquake was to confirm Voltaire's cynicism about all types of religion and religious philosophy, leaving what I think we could call a kindly humanitarian deism. It's a rattling good read—here's a tiny snatch from the opening chapter that gives an excellent insight into the teachings of Dr Pangloss:

> Master Pangloss taught the "metaphysico-theologo-cosmolonigology". He could prove to admiration that there is no effect without a cause; and that, in this best of all possible worlds, the Baron's castle was the most magnificent of all castles, and my lady the best of all possible baronesses.
>
> "It is demonstrable", said he, "that things cannot be otherwise than they are; for as all things have been created for some end, they

must necessarily be created for the best end. Observe, for instance, the nose is formed for spectacles, therefore we wear spectacles. The legs are visibly designed for stockings, accordingly we wear stockings..."

Voltaire was not an atheist, but a deist, like many of his fellow *philosophes*. This is the philosophy of the absentee God, the creator who set the universe going and then simply left it to its own devices. After all, if he were concerned about us, earthquakes and all the other afflictions we suffer wouldn't happen. As I put it earlier, this God is always out to lunch. Voltaire had an intense dislike of d'Holbach and his atheistic philosophy, but even so, once God was pushed away to a respectable distance it became much easier to cease believing in him at all. The trend is perfectly understandable, particularly when large, powerful ecclesiastical structures appeared to have been indifferent to much that was wrong in the world.

Although there were certainly other causes, I think it is highly likely that the Lisbon earthquake, the general public reaction to it, and Voltaire's brilliance combined to place the problem of suffering right at the top of the agenda for atheists, agnostics, and many religious believers alike. As we shall see, it often occupies that position today, with Leibniz in the background playing the role of naive optimist, particularly in the minds of atheists.

The Best of All Possible Colleges

It would be wonderful at this point if one could show an atheist train of thought that developed in a humanitarian direction despite the upheavals of the French Revolution, the Napoleonic wars, the great movements of industrialisation and empire, and on into the twentieth century. Eventually we should arrive at Bertrand Russell (1872–1970), whose influence is well known—as is his criticism (partially justified) of religion. This positive view would lead us to consider the happy development of atheistic humanitarian institutions in the twentieth century and their effects today. Unfortunately, the atheist cause is not as coherent as its defenders would like it to be.

I happened to be attending a meeting recently at University College London, which I later found considers Jeremy Bentham (1748–1832) as its "spiritual" founder. During the lunch break, in search of sustenance, I noticed nearby the pub named after Bentham, with a plaque outside quoting his maxim for morals and legislation, "the greatest happiness for the greatest number". I also learned that his mummified body is kept on display in University College, but with a wax head, the real head having been damaged in the embalming process and later locked away for safe keeping. Apparently it used to be regarded as quite a jape among students to purloin Jeremy's head.

I'm not sure how this gruesome presence (requested by Bentham himself) contributes to the greatest happiness for the greatest number, but it's hard to deny the attractiveness of that principle. Sometimes it's called *utilitarianism*, and was also followed—and developed—by John Stuart Mill (1806–73). Now of course the religious person could claim that the greatest happiness for the greatest number is always procured by following some version or other of a divine law, but this is not the route taken by the utilitarian. Rather, because utilitarianism focuses on outcomes, it is a branch of *consequentialism*. This is the principle that human actions should be governed, not by some claimed "higher law", but solely by their consequences. Naturally most atheists support this principle, since the danger with a higher law is that it so easily suggests a higher Being.

It seems difficult to offer any comment on atheistic belief as such because of its all-embracing basic principle. Religious belief generates whole libraries, atheism doesn't. What can you say about a non-existent God? There are many ways of existing, but only one way (as far as I can see) of not existing. Some might say there are an infinite number of ways of not existing, but that hardly improves matters.

At first sight, then, atheism might seem to be impervious to criticism. However, any culture needs an ethical system in order to enjoy stability, and it has generally been the role of religion to provide this. Atheism can hardly claim to supplant religion if it has little to say on this front, and in my opinion this is its first great weakness.

The problems with developing an atheistic ethic are many, even when consequentialism is amended to include other principles. Baggini recruits Aristotle (384–322 BCE) to the cause. From "the philosopher" we may derive the principle that we should conduct ourselves so that life goes well. Being in the grip of vice (or, for that matter, compulsive "do-gooding" or religious activity) goes against this and therefore should not be part of the wise person's life, for it will not produce happiness. Practical wisdom, consisting largely of enlightened self-interest, involves steering between the various extremes to find a virtuous "golden mean". Baggini also invokes the principle of "universalisability" that was propounded by Immanuel Kant (1724–1804). According to Kant we should always ask ourselves, "What would happen if everyone behaved in this way?" or "How would I feel if this were done to me?"

These ideas are part of ethical debate down the centuries, but they do appear inevitably to raise the question of why either the golden mean or consideration of others should be regarded as important. The utilitarian is bound to answer that they are conducive to the total aggregate of human happiness. Such a claim, however, does not impinge on the very fundamental question of what constitutes human happiness in the first place. Some people are happy with a coffee and a sandwich, while others regard champagne in a chic environment as a basic essential of life. Some visit art galleries, museums, and opera houses, others go to football matches or bingo. Some, even when there is no compulsion, follow a religion, others do not. Some are happy in the pursuit of sporting achievement, others prefer to exert unbridled aggression.

Mill's answer to this problem sounds today unbearably elitist. He claims that those who have experienced both "refined" and "vulgar" pleasures generally prefer the former and should be heeded in preference to those who have experienced only one or the other. Well, I beg to differ. I can appreciate Beethoven's late quartets, *Grosse Fugue* and all. I can also appreciate contemporary "pop" music, and would be hard pressed to say which gives me greater happiness. I should certainly not like to claim that there is some kind of moral difference between the two that would justify sanctioning one more than the other. Nor do I believe that substituting some other word such as "contentment" in place of "happiness" alters the basic problem.

Even if we accept the validity of all forms of happiness it would appear difficult to make the quantitative evaluations required to estimate the aggregate of human happiness. Measuring the happiness potential of a burger as against a banana would be much more difficult than simply weighing up nutritional values. Moreover, happiness cannot be considered in isolation. Aldous Huxley rightly pointed out that happiness is generally a by-product of other things. If that is so, then almost anything in life can be a source of happiness in the right context.

The most that can be said is surely along the lines of a *via negativa*, that there are some things that almost always act *against* happiness. The list is short and simple: illness, poverty, isolation, starvation, insecurity of person or property, humiliation, and purposelessness would probably suffice. To make the removal of such things a measure of utility seems eminently sensible, and does not require elaborate assessment of the thoughts or feelings of others. A less negative slant can be achieved by listing positive equivalents such as good health, material sufficiency and so on. These can be built into a "rule-based" utilitarianism, which holds that keeping to the rules will ultimately produce happiness with greater sureness than trying to evaluate every human act in its own right.

Mill tended in this "rules-based" direction, but even if such thinking is valid we still have no reason, from within utilitarianism itself, to give any value to these aspirations. Significantly, even though Mill was an agnostic and possibly atheistic, he admitted to the utility of religion in producing morality.

Unpredictability

The second great difficulty of any form of consequentialism is that of knowing what the consequences of an act will be. As I was drafting this section a good example was spotlighted on the morning news. The British government is to spend many millions of pounds on vaccinating 12–14 year old girls against cervical cancer and its precursors, which stem from the human papilloma virus (HPV). Will this produce a net benefit? Or will it signal to adolescent minds that it's now acceptable to do whatever they like, thus leading to escalation of other sexually transmitted infections (STIs) such as Chlamydia—already a huge threat to public health?

This is nothing to do with trying to frighten teenagers into not having sex. I agree with Sam Harris that such a policy is probably not effective. But I do not agree with him that the solution lies in education—the line frequently taken by governments. There is a growing realisation that sex education (coupled with free contraception) is not producing the anticipated outcomes. Teenage abortions and STIs are on the increase. Sex education may decrease teenage *angst* but does not dramatically affect behaviour. In addition, reputable non-religious organisations such as the NSPCC, Girlguiding UK, and the Mental Health Foundation are now drawing attention to the effects of normalising under-age sexual activity. As well as intensifying peer pressures, this trend has opened the way for increasing manipulation of young people by commercial interests. As if to confirm such misgivings, it was recently announced that record numbers of children in the UK are being prescribed the contraceptive pill at the age of eleven.

Other examples of such contrariness are not hard to find in various fields. Does imprisonment of minor criminals reduce recidivism, or give them a training ground for more serious crime? Will increasing the minimum wage make the poor better off, or will it increase unemployment as employers shed staff? Do legal restrictions in areas such as gambling protect the vulnerable or create vicious "underground" alternatives? Even with regard to the immediate act, what (to use the jargon) will be the disbenefits? As an example, the huge amount of money spent on the vaccination plan will no longer be available for other purposes such as kidney transplants, heart surgery, stem cell research, or the treatment of breast cancer.

The fundamental problem here is the connectedness of things. The same applies particularly to those choices traditionally tagged "moral". Dawkins illustrates the point himself with his rather meagre attempt at constructing a new morality, particularly when he says we should enjoy our own sex lives as long as no harm is caused to others. We should also allow everyone else to do the same, he claims, whatever their inclinations may be.

Yet how can we be sure that no harm will be caused to others? Sex is (still) most often part of an emotional relationship. *Any* such relationship has its effect on other relationships in the present and in the future, and these relationships hold together families, communities, and societies in an intricate web. Moreover, even sexual behaviour *outside* relationships still affects those relationships in which people do get involved. It is inherently impossible, therefore, to predict that no harm will be caused by sexual activity once we step outside some fairly narrow boundaries. Relationships seem to be a particularly difficult area in which to apply consequentialism.

The problem can also be seen as one of *individuality*—any action intended to produce the greatest happiness for the greatest number can be defeated by individual behaviour, as self-interest becomes less enlightened and more exclusively self or group orientated. This difficulty applies equally to particular acts and to any general set of rules drawn up on a pragmatic basis.

Consequentialism with a utilitarian flavour is, then, always likely to involve a multiple guessing game. What really creates the greatest total happiness? If that can be answered, will any proposed law, policy or initiative deliver such happiness more effectively than the alternatives available?

There would seem to be only one way out of these quandaries, which is to try to create some kind of model as to how human beings work in social groups such as those in which we want our ethic to apply. If our model can somehow indicate the total amount of happiness in the system, then so much the better for the application of utilitarian thinking.

Go With the Flow

Bill Phillips (1914–75) was a remarkable person, a New Zealander decorated for his courage as a POW during the Second World War, then becoming a student of sociology at the London School of Economics. After switching to the study of economics he built the "Phillips Machine" in 1949. You may have seen the old footage which gets an airing from time to time. The machine is an arrangement of transparent tanks, pipes, and sluices, the whole thing containing coloured water. The purpose of the machine is to demonstrate how money flows in a modern economy—we tweak this interest rate or alter that ratio and the results are shown. Phillips became a professor at the LSE and an eminent economist, and about a dozen of his machines were built. They were used for conceptualising and teaching economics, although mainstream modelling rapidly became transferred to computers.

The problem is that despite the ingenuity of Phillips and his successors, in real life the "Law of Unintended Consequences" so often pops up, which makes economic forecasting demonically difficult. It is impossible to predict the outcome of a huge number of complex choices, or to foresee the outcome of a small number of perverse choices.

Consequentialism seems to require a human-behavioural version of the Phillips machine—preferably incorporating a graduated measuring cylinder labelled "total happiness". Then we could evaluate all outcomes beautifully. Unfortunately, such a machine has never been built. The only alternative would seem to be to appoint experts of various sorts. Some would have to predict the unpredictable results of human actions, while others would have to assess which individuals were being too individualistic—surely a recipe for totalitarianism.

This is not to say that paying attention to consequences is entirely wrong. There is a strong belief in Christianity, for example, in the concept of prudence—the view that we *should* take into account the consequences of our actions. There are always hard cases where the lesser of two evils may have to be decided upon. However, without an absolute moral code it is easier to put two and two together and make five, especially when contemplating a morally dubious act. For example: "No one can foresee all consequences. No one can predict what will make a person happy. Anyway, perhaps there are good consequences I haven't foreseen. And, after all, I'm entitled to some happiness as well. If people don't like it, perhaps that's their problem more than mine . . ." In effect, we can easily adjust our perception of what is reasonably foreseeable to suit our own ends, and we can easily take a rather biased view of what makes other people happy.

In other words, the problems of assessing the aggregate of happiness on the one hand, and of predicting outcomes on the other, create a fatal subjectivity. That's not to deny the presence of subjectivity in many situations even when there is held to be an absolute ethic, but belief in an absolute will generally constrain behaviour within certain boundaries. When the boundaries are crossed, as in the "hard cases", at least we know we are doing that, and we can form responsible judgements with awareness and consultation.

Bentham, and those that came after him, were not unprincipled; quite the opposite. However, in a subjective system, there is little to prevent a despot from judging that unhappiness caused to inferior races or tribes is less important than the potential happiness of the dominant race or tribe. This can ultimately become a route to genocide.

In theory, declaring oneself in favour of reason as the only source of knowledge might lead to a land of clear air, obvious truth, and unimpaired vision. I accept that a good dose of reason never comes amiss in the criticism of religion, whether delivered by atheists or others. Scepticism from a Baggini, a Ruse, or a Wolpert is important in situations of gross superstition or ecclesiastical pomposity, and the threat of such things is never far away. From that point of view, atheism can perform a valuable service, because religion is not of necessity against reason, as many notable thinkers have pointed out, and the application of reason should therefore be welcomed.

Yet if we look at the overall picture, and if we are to be good consequentialists, surely we are bound to ask a basic question: what has been the main consequence of atheism? It is hypocritical for the upholders of any principle to demand that others be judged by that principle, but not they themselves. If the majority of atheists uphold the principle of consequentialism then my question is hardly unfair.

The common response to this question from non-atheists is simple: the main consequence of atheism was the most horrific war and oppression ever seen, inflicted by Nazism and Communism. Put in such a stark form, of course, this is a cheap shot, not to be accepted uncritically—but there may be within it at least a grain of truth, and I should now like to examine that possibility.

The Spirit of the Age

The first line of defence against this accusation is obviously to point to the *zeitgeist* or "spirit of the age" and Dawkins follows this route, expending most of his energy on discussion of Nazism. He claims that even if Hitler were an atheist, the actions of the Third Reich were to some extent understandable from a purely political point of view, therefore atheism itself should not be blamed for what happened.

What Dawkins does not discuss, however, is where the spirit of that particular age in Germany was most nurtured. We might note initially that from 1904 to 1907 Namibia (then a German colony) was the scene of the first twentieth-century genocide. The strategy was to drive over 70,000 members of the Herero and Nama tribes into the desert and then poison the wells. It is difficult not to see in this a foreshadowing of things to come.

Of course, in the era of imperialism, slaughter was often the order of the day, but generally with a view to winning a battle or subduing rebellious tribes who didn't want to be ruled by the British, French, Belgian, Dutch, or any other imperial power. "Ethnic cleansing", as we now call it, is a lot more, being based on the view that a certain race or class is not worthy of life, and indeed may be impeding the fulfilment of a higher plan. From where did this new view arise?

One factor was the dialectical philosophy of Georg Wilhelm Friedrich Hegel (1770–1831)—the concept of history as inexorable progress through thesis, antithesis, and synthesis. This is a hugely complex story with endless debate among different European philosophers in favour of some aspects of Hegel and against others. From it all a significant development was the nineteenth-century philosophy of Friedrich W. Nietzsche (1844–1900) with his famous declaration that *God is dead*, and his concept of the *superman*. The new is born out of conflict within the old order—you can see why Nietzsche was approved reading for members of the German National Socialist Party. Here's a sound-bite from Nietzsche's best known work, *Thus Spake Zarathustra* (Part IV: *Of Higher Man*):

> Up and on, ye Higher Men! Only now travaileth the mountain of man's future. God is dead; now *we* will that the Superman live! ... The most anxious ask today: "How is man to be preserved?" But Zarathustra, alone and first, asketh: "How is man to be *surmounted?*"

It all makes sense if you play some Wagner very loudly. Nietzsche was a close friend of Richard Wagner until 1888 when he disagreed with the composer publicly about the latter's anti-Semitic attitudes. Nietzsche was not himself anti-Semitic, but his concept of the "higher man" was easily distorted by those who were. Without this striding forward, life, the universe, and everything is just a monotonous *eternal recurrence,* an endless repetition of what has gone before. Unfortunately, shortly after the break with Wagner, Nietzsche entered a twelve year period of insanity lasting until his death in 1900, and was not able to control the manner in which his thought was interpreted. His attitude to religion was actually complex, but simplified and one-sided interpretations often carry popular appeal. One notable proponent of such interpretations was Nietzsche's sister, Elisabeth, who lived until 1935, was a member of the Nazi party, and was well known to Adolf Hitler, who attended her funeral.

For Nietzsche the good-natured utilitarianism of Bentham was anathema, since in his view people don't need to be happy so much as powerful, in order to survive. *The Will to Power*—a collection of various Nietzsche fragments—was published posthumously, in a highly prejudiced and corrupted form, by Elisabeth. Her compilation reflected her virulent anti-Semitism, which was shared by her husband, Bernhard Förster (1843–89), who had committed suicide while trying to set up a model Aryan state in Paraguay.

The Thule Society, which was a strong upholder of the mythology of an Aryan super race, coupled with elements of occultism drawn from Mme Helena Blavatsky (1831–91) and others, was an influence on Nazism in its early period. The anti-Semitism of such movements flowed together with that of Nietzsche's sister, some of the Wagners and many others in the intellectual elite, while the occultism affected some Nazi elements, notably in the developing SS. The Thule Society was part of what is commonly designated the *völkisch* movement, which generally believed in a kind of romantic nationalism. It was not, however, a homogeneous movement, more a conglomeration of many associations and groups.

With all this in the background it's easy to see how arguments about the injustice of the Versailles treaty and the legitimate borders of Germany could be inflamed into a general campaign against the so-called non-Aryan races. They were *destined* to be on the losing side.

Nietzsche also acted as a conduit for the idea of "survival of the fittest", a phrase coined by the political theorist Herbert Spencer (1820–1903) and then adopted by Charles Darwin himself, and for the early theories of eugenics developed by Francis Galton (1822–1911), Darwin's half cousin. These ideas gradually penetrated the German intellectual and military elite, as witnessed to by the wonderful *Headquarters Nights* by the American Vernon Kellogg. The professor was based at German Supreme Command in Brussels during the First World War, prior to American entry into that conflict. He was a pacifist neutral engaged in humanitarian work, but eventually advocated American entry because of the brutality that had developed. In some cases the cruelty approached that of the Namibian atrocities, and occurred during the invasion of Belgium and the later deportations to forced labour camps in Germany. Kellogg is utterly clear that "survival of the fittest" was the driving philosophy.

Counter Arguments

In order to deflect blame away from atheism and towards religion, Baggini and other atheists bring in some counter arguments, and we shall look briefly at four.

First, it is true that Italian fascism was supported by the Catholic church. However, it was not unreasonable at the time to think that fascism would be a beneficial bulwark against Russian strength, especially as there had been attempted communist uprisings all over Europe since 1916. The fascist Oswald Mosley received significant pre-war support in the UK, and even Churchill supported Mussolini until 1937 because of the communist threat. Hungary fought as an axis power against Russia, yet protected its Jewish population and sued for peace with the allies, until invasion by Germany in 1944. Sometimes it seems that the lesser of two evils is the best we can do. Italian fascism, incidentally, was not initially anti-Semitic, being supported by many Jews. It became anti-Semitic later because of the need to please Hitler.

Second, it is also true that the majority of German church leaders complied with Hitler during his rise to power—and I would not for one moment deny that the Christian churches were hopelessly wrong footed by the rise of Nazism, which grew with such force that rapid decisions needed to be made without the benefits of hindsight that we enjoy. In fact, with the exception of a few of the "old guard" in Germany and other European nations, almost everyone in leadership made the same mistake.

We should remember that the true horrors of Nazism only gradually became clear. I'm not sure that many of these, albeit compromised, leaders would have taken part in the setting up of the "final solution", and compromise was not the whole story. The heroism of many in the "confessing church" is well known, and the first concentration camp, Dachau, had a special block for religious leaders, accommodating about 3,000, of whom about one-third died. Catholic priests were the largest group. It may be that in an ideal world more should have taken the heroic route; yet while failure to do this may make a person weak in some way it does not make him or her into the *initiator* of the evil. Complicity is not the same as constructing the whole apparatus of mass murder in the way that Nazism did. That rather obvious point seems to be lost on many critics.

Pope Pius XII has attracted particular controversy, sometimes being demonized as a supporter of Nazism because he did not make a forthright public proclamation, during the war, against it. However, he did write the 1937 papal encyclical against Nazism, while still a Cardinal—he became pope in 1939. After that there were strong pragmatic reasons for his attitude—it appears, from a more balanced perspective, that Pius XII took a theoretically neutral stance, in order to maintain a position from which he and the Catholic dioceses could protest against specific Nazi proposals, and carry out practical measures to save Jews where possible. This policy was effective and saved hundreds of thousands of lives, a fact that has been acknowledged by Jewish leaders, organisations, and scholars. In 1940 Albert Einstein publicly stated that the churches of Germany were the main force trying to stop Hitler. We also know that Hitler himself did not regard Pius as his friend. Yet, despite these facts, those who wish to smear religion merely repeat the simplistic assertions without resort to the facts.

Third, anti-Semitism on the part of the German churches is a charge often brought, sometimes alongside a similar criticism of Christianity as a whole. In order to understand the element of truth in this, it is necessary to go into specific details.

In terms of the more general charge, the picture is very mixed. There was, of course, always a religious and theological argument with Judaism. Sometimes this went further and cited folklore concerning alleged Jewish anti-Christian practices. This could then be drawn upon to justify persecution. However, this was often tied in with popular resentment over specific issues such as usury, and occasionally it was a response to Jewish antagonism directed at the Christians. At other times, which I would consider the most despicable, the Jews were made into scapegoats and accused of deliberately spreading the plague or causing other misfortunes.

Despite a lot of anti-Judaic rhetoric and despite deeply shameful exceptions, the general attitude of the early church fathers to the Jews was one of criticism on religious grounds, but not of physical attack. The most frequent papal attitude was that the Jews should be protected, a policy carried out by many bishops, abbots, and other clergy, sometimes against the will of the mob. A good example of this policy can be found in the encyclical of Gregory X (1272)*. You may also notice, as has even been pointed out by Jewish writers, that when the Catholic Church is negative about Jews it is equally negative about infidels, heretics, and ungodly princes. This is in line with a vitally important fact, that anti-Judaism was almost entirely focused against the Jewish religion, and occasionally Jewish culture; it did not make any claims about racial characteristics.

Turning to the more specific charge, anti-Judaism is indeed virulently present in the works of Martin Luther, mostly in two works written three years before his death in 1546, by which time he had become embittered

---

* You may not have *www.papalencyclicals.net* in your browser's favourites list, but you can find this document and others using the website's admirable index.

that so few Jews had converted to Lutheranism. These works did contribute to some persecution of Jews in the German states, and were reprinted from time to time, but only for about fifty years. After that they appear to have been largely ignored—they did not become handbooks for anti-Semitism. Johann Andreas Eisenmenger (1654–1704) wrote a pivotal work entitled *Judaism Unmasked* based on scholarly (but highly prejudiced) use of Jewish literature. His work certainly reinforced anti-Judaism but he never mentions Luther. There is a clear intention in his works to make a new case, starting from scratch. Similarly, many Enlightenment writers, including Voltaire, expressed anti-Semitic views yet had little time for Luther.

The evil of anti-Judaism is not to be minimised, and I have no intention of doing so. In particular, Lutheran denominations have all recognised— and renounced—the sad anti-Judaistic elements that marred the closing years of Luther's remarkable life, and Christians today view the worst episodes of the past with great disbelief. However, even while acknowledging the above facts, Luther's influence was much diluted by the time we reach the early twentieth century. Racial theory, on the contrary, was the bright new star still in its ascendancy and contributed hugely to anti-Semitism.

As well as the influence of Galton, racial theory found support in the "scientific racism" of the evolutionist Ernst Haeckel (1834–1919), who influenced many German intellectuals, including Wilhelm Marr (1819–1904). Marr was a left-wing atheist thinker and agitator who founded the German "League of Antisemites" in 1879 and was the first to coin the term "anti-Semitism". Another atheist, Eugen Karl Dühring (1833—1921), wrote in a similar vein, going so far as to state in 1881 that even if all Jews became Christians they would still be a problem because of their *race*. Adolf Wahrmund (1827–1913) claimed in 1887 that the Jews were a nomadic race, living parasitically on settled races.

There were many lesser writers of similar material in the second half of the nineteenth century. The phrase "The Jewish Question" began to circulate in Germany in the 1840s and was used by many of the writers noted above. Theodor Fritsch (1852–1933) published his *Handbook of the Jewish Question* in 1893, which went through forty-nine editions in as many years.

Richard Wagner (1813–83) was the focus of a strong anti-Semitic circle in Bayreuth. His infamous essay *On Jewishness in Music* (full version 1869) was followed up by many other articles and pamphlets. Bernhard Förster was part of the circle, as was Houston Stewart Chamberlain (1855–1927), an Englishman who took German citizenship, married Wagner's daughter Eva, and later joined the emerging Nazi party. Chamberlain's writings were enormously influential in promoting the idea of the Aryan race and its superiority.

The French anthropologist Arthur de Gobineau (1816–82) must also be mentioned. His *Essay on the Inequality of the Human Races* was probably the earliest argument for Aryan supremacy, and warned of the dangers of mixing races. These aspects of his theory influenced Chamberlain and later on Hitler. De Gobineau was not himself anti-Semitic, since the Jews were among the white races, but this aspect of his work was ignored by both Chamberlain and the Nazis. The Bayreuth circle generally promoted his works, with Ludwig Schemann (1852–1938) translating them and setting up a Gobineau society.

On the scientific side, Alfred Ploetz (1860–1940) was particularly important in propagating "racial hygiene" in Germany. He was strongly influenced by Darwin, Haeckel and Galton, taking to greater extremes the views on eugenics that were fashionable in much of German academic life. His views on eliminating the weak were a natural fit with the Nazi party, which he joined in 1937.

Downright propaganda also played its part. *The Protocols of the Elders of Zion* originated in eighteenth-century France, drawing on stories about the Templars, the "Rosy Cross", Freemasonry, and the Bavarian "Illuminati", to name but a few, and gradually becoming more and more anti-Semitic. The Jewish conspiracy, it was claimed, aimed to exacerbate social inequality in order to promote revolution, abolish the free press and promote capitalist multinationals. The book as a whole was published in Russia in 1903 and was widely circulated.

There was, then, a vast body of ideas upon which Nazism could draw. Any belief that could be moulded to the cause was strained to fit. The large number of anti-Semitic writers were endorsed regardless of the falsehoods in their works. The *Protocols* were proclaimed as fact. De Gobineau was twisted into shape, as was Nietzsche, with his sister's help. The line from Darwin through Galton and Haeckel to Ploetz was invaluable. The Bayreuth circle reinforced it all. Luther does have a case to answer, as do those Enlightenment thinkers who were anti-Semitic. By far the greater accusation, however, can be laid at the door of the atheist propagandists, evolutionists, eugenicists, and Wagner acolytes.

Nazis tolerated Christianity out of necessity and expedience. Had they gained the world domination they sought, the (well-documented) plan was then to destroy Christianity completely. They were purely opportunistic in their use of Luther.

Fourth, Baggini and others point to the distinction often made in religion between righteous and unrighteous nations, seeing this as a contributory factor to the holocaust. Yet this claim does not seem entirely relevant, because Nazism also killed people for having biological or mental inadequacies, factors that they patently could not change and which were nothing to do with righteousness, but everything to do with eugenics. In contrast, even the worst of the practices of, say, parts of the medieval church, were to try to bring about change—repentance, conversion to the faith, or liberation of the holy places. Those practices were still utterly deplorable, of course, but radically different from Nazism.

The four factors I have listed would certainly have contributed to *prejudice* against Jews in some quarters; and suspicions of a fifth column or "enemy within" are easy to stir up. Both Bismarck and Kaiser Wilhelm II expressed anti-Semitic sentiments, reflecting the attitudes of those intellectual elements previously mentioned. Even so, German Jews had enjoyed legal equality with other Germans since 1871. Although there was some discrimination against them, they occupied high political positions until the rise of Nazism, many Jews fought in the army, and intermarriage between Jews and non-Jews was frequent. The dramatic leap from prejudice to genocide surely requires an equally dramatic explanation that is not to be found in these counter arguments.

Why did anti-Semitism develop within Nazism in such a uniquely horrific manner? Why did this hatred extend to other supposedly inferior races, who were also slaughtered? Why was it necessary to destroy millions of Polish Catholics? Why did the hatred extend even to those of "pure" race who were judged defective in some way, particularly those suffering from mental illness? Why was medical experimentation on human beings regarded as acceptable? Why was annihilation, even of children, seen as the only solution, when the time-honoured practice of deportation could have met the so-called need?

It seems ingenuous for atheists to highlight the flaws in churches while at the same time down-playing the blatantly obvious exhortations of Nietzsche, the obnoxious views of his sister, the work of the Bayreuth circle and other propagandists, the anti-Semitism of the Enlightenment, and the racism of the developing eugenics movement.

Communism

Baggini is on much weaker ground, as he himself acknowledges, when we consider Communism. Indeed, the atheistic nature of Communism is so well known and so clear, compared to the ambiguities of Nazism, that there is no need to go into great detail.

Marx founded Communism on the Hegelian idea of history, but interpreted the inevitable progress, not in a romantic-militaristic manner, but in economic terms. Instead of the armies of the Reich sweeping down on the non-chosen races with apocalyptic destruction, the workers of the world would unite once and for all to usher in a new age of equality—without God. They were *destined* to be on the winning side. Lenin wasn't too bothered about "collateral damage" as we call it these days, while Stalin and Mao Tse-tung were utterly consistent, accepting such damage as an essential part of the process. These creators of unimaginable grief have not been short of disciples in other parts of the world.

A frequent argument used to be that "proper" Communism has never really been tried, but this claim is beginning to look jaded. This is not to argue that the views of Marx and Engels on class struggle and the functions of capital are wholly wrong. Such ideas have had a huge influence on the development of socialism and social democracy, but whenever the call to forcible re-appropriation of the means and results of production has been taken seriously, the outcome has been massive oppression and deprivation.

The Russian revolutions were hijacked by Lenin and the Bolsheviks with the support of Germany, which hoped (justifiably) to obtain the withdrawal of Russia from the First World War. Thus was opened the door for Stalin, and for the varieties of Marxist-Leninist ideology that subsequently dominated the USSR, China, and their various "client states" across the world. The growth of Communism (including the attempted revolutions in Germany and Italy) was also of great assistance to Hitler and Mussolini in promoting their respective brands of fascism. One would think that, in this turmoil of political activity, "proper" Communism would have taken root somewhere to serve as a reference point as to what could be achieved.

Baggini falls back on the assertion that core atheist values are not Communist at all. Of course they aren't, neither are they fascist, and I would never make that claim. The problem is that once there is a rejection of the core values of monotheistic religions—which, for all their faults, do not normally include genocide—what is there to stop the growth of movements that do include it? I would seek here at least a level playing field; one could equally well point out that killing people is not one of the core values of Christianity, quite the opposite.

It seems to me undeniable that, at the very least, atheism cleared the way for the development of Nazi and Communist thinking and their awful consequences. In addition, I think it is clear that atheists' ethical principles, when severely challenged, are not up to the task of reducing man's inhumanity to man, which, as Burns reminds us, makes countless thousands mourn.

Back to Voltaire

In 1778 the grumpy old *philosophe* uttered his famous last words, "I die worshipping God, helping my friends, not hating my enemies, and detesting superstition." He then recovered and lived for another three months. What a pity that the revolutionaries following hard on his heels were unable to sustain those prematurely-expressed sentiments. The Revolution was followed by the *Reign of Terror*, a phrase with which we are so familiar that the horror of it all is easily forgotten. Things moved very quickly from the deistic anti-clericalism of Voltaire and many others, to the elevation of

Reason as the new God. Since terror was effective in bringing the majority of people into line with authority, it was reasonable to use it—a terrifyingly logical argument.

Of particular note was the attitude of the revolutionaries to the Vendée, the area of the Western Loire south of Nantes. Here took place what is sometimes regarded as the first ever genocide officially ordered by a government. The inhabitants of the region were not keen on the extremism of the Parisian leaders and revolted against them. In response, the revolutionary elite ordered the wholesale destruction of the Vendée population, men, women, and children. For special entertainment many were herded into barges which were then sunk in the Loire. The net result was around 100,000 deaths. Many of those killed posed no threat to the revolution at all. They just happened to be in the wrong place at the wrong time—and with the wrong ideology wielding power against them.

The great problem for atheism, then, is that it tends to be locked into consequentialism—anything else would suggest an external moral arbiter or giver of values. However, whether directly or indirectly, a major consequence of atheism has been immense human suffering, as the power-hungry take it upon themselves to decide what the higher plan—or the higher man—might be. After that, it's just a matter of getting rid of the odd hundred thousand or hundred million people of the wrong race or class who happen to be in the way, and atheists cannot entirely shrug off responsibility here. Blaming the "spirit of the age" as if it sprang from nowhere is false.

Atheism and History

I have already mentioned a certain imprecision in atheists' treatment of history—a subject for which precision is particularly important. When we delve into the past we cannot seek clarification from someone who was there, or from someone who received the testimony of others who were there. This is the realm of history in the sense of motivations, events, and results about which we can only know from written records. Such records have to be collated, analysed, and explained, and it is the role of historical scholarship to do that scientifically on behalf of the rest of us, who lack the necessary patience.

Once the hard work is done, the results can then be translated into layman's terms—increasingly through television. Unfortunately, there is proper history, delivered—sometimes controversially—by people like David Starkey, Simon Schama, Robert Bartlett, Niall Ferguson, and Diarmaid MacCulloch; and there is selective history, delivered by people with an axe to grind who are not historians in any scientific or methodical sense. When the axe being ground is religious, the account can become *hagiography*— "holy history" written from a particular point of view. From atheists it can become just as biased, but in the opposite direction. Interestingly, proper historians with a wide range of personal beliefs generally avoid this, whereas the "new atheist" strategy seems to be simply to accept all anti-religious ideas from whatever source they arise, however distorted or based on popular misconceptions. I have to cite Sam Harris as a leading proponent of this strategy, even though his writings raise crucial points in many ways. Atheist and secularist web sites, however, go many steps further, re-iterating the same opinions and quoting from each other without bothering to tell us the original sources of what they say with such conviction.

It's almost a knee-jerk reaction from atheists at a popular level to protest: "What about the Crusades? What about the Spanish Inquisition? What about Northern Ireland?" The assumption is that simply naming these historical traumas will silence any argument in favour of God. Very well, let's look at these episodes—but let's also try to be historians, however imperfectly. The first step towards doing this is to understand the background and historical context surrounding them. My aim here is not to provide an unlimited justification of the actions of the religious, for this chapter is about atheism. My aim is simply to point out the flaws in the arguments of many atheists.

During the first millennium CE, the Roman Catholic Church had acquired substantial power through its relationship with the rulers of the great patchwork of European states. This dominance was assisted by the fraudulent ninth-century document known as *The Donation of Constantine*, which was not actually proven to be a forgery until the sixteenth century. In this document the emperor Constantine is, in effect, held to have bestowed the Western Roman Empire on the Pope, the medieval equivalent, I suppose, of a decision from the Land Registry.

A good example of how not to deploy legal documents was given by Pope Leo IX. In 1054 he cited the *Donation* to the Patriarch of Constantinople in order to assert his supremacy over the whole Church, East and West. This argument was rejected, and the split between Eastern and Western Christianity was finalised shortly afterwards, with mutual excommunications.

Things generally went better, however, in the West, where the papacy had a strong relationship with Charlemagne from 800 onwards, and with his various successors (memorably Charles the Bald and Charles the Fat—sensitivity was not a priority in those days). This relationship ensured a continued church influence throughout France and the Holy Roman Empire.

This ecclesiastical power is often misunderstood. Even before the adoption of Christianity as the official religion of the Roman Empire in the fourth century, the new faith was a strong force, and became convenient for the empire *because* of that. If there was opportunism it was initiated more by the empire than the Church. With the fifth-century withdrawal of the Romans from the West, "Christendom" was again vulnerable to attack, this time (in Britain) from the Angles, Saxons, and Jutes, followed by the Vikings and ultimately their Norman descendants. *Relatively speaking* the settlement of the first three was peaceful, but the invasions of the Vikings were not, as the monks of Lindisfarne discovered in 793. We all know how it worked out with the Normans.

During these tumultuous years Christianity held its own and gradually became more uniform in adopting Roman ecclesiastical customs. It was common, as with Augustine's approach in 595 to Ethelred, King of Kent, to seek first the conversion of the local ruler—permission would be needed in any case to establish churches and dioceses. Following on from that it would be natural for the ruler and the Church to work in co-operation.

The secret weapon of the Church was the monastery. Augustine and his forty or so colleagues were all Benedictine monks living to a simple pattern of prayer, work, and proclamation of the message. The religious structure at its best contributed much to stability, and this is not to be undervalued. The Venerable Bede of Jarrow, in the early eighth century, was not only producing his exquisite historical and theological work, but also scientific thoughts on astronomy, the relationship of the moon to the tides, and the effect of the earth's spherical (not flat) shape on the length of the day. Further afield the *Lindisfarne Gospels* and the *Book of Kells* show unbelievable sophistication for a period often still derided as the "Dark Ages"—a title increasingly regarded as inappropriate. If there was darkness in this period it was not generated by the Church, but arose from the loss of the stability previously provided by the Romans, together with the lack of access to most of the Greek intellectual tradition that was still available in the continuing eastern empire.

The result of the Church's growth was that by the end of the millennium there was a trans-European network of abbeys, monasteries, cathedrals, and their attendant personnel: abbots, bishops, priests, monks, nuns, and so on. They all wrote in the same language, medieval Latin, so scholarly communication was well-developed throughout Europe. In many respects the monasteries were the first joint-stock companies in history and broadly benefitted the many lay members who were employed. Incidentally, the work of Charlemagne, his clergy and their successors included not only education of the clergy and religious, but also of boys and some girls in the general population. This was provided through the establishment of schools outside the monasteries, and the education given was broad, not limited to religion.

The great weakness of this impressive system was a large degree of centralisation of power in the papacy, not least because degeneracy at the top sometimes led to a run of popes who could not be regarded as good role models. This happened notoriously from 904–964, the so-called "rule of the harlots", and spasmodically after that until the Reformation. The office of pope in many instances became primarily a matter of power and status.

Pax Dei

A crucial factor to bear in mind was the intense violence of medieval society. Constant war between tribes and nations, and local disputes between nobles, had created a large population of knights, who definitely did not fit our usual image of chivalry. Rather, they were prone to murder, rape, and pillage, either on their own initiative or at the command of their nobleman. Anti-religious propagandists, of course, portray the medieval Church as simply part of this general predisposition to conflict.

Yet, as part of the search for peace, a practice was begun in the ninth century whereby local clergy (armed with relics of the saints) would gather nobles and knights to a meeting at which the *Pax Dei* (Peace of God) would be proclaimed. Robbery and violence against defenceless peasants, clergy, women, and children was forbidden on pain of excommunication. Knights engaged in conflict were required to cease fighting on Fridays, Sundays, and Holy days, while merchants and their goods were to be respected. I suspect that these were among the first "rules of war".

The monasteries themselves, of course, generally maintained the principle of non-aggression, supplementing this with hospitality for travellers and care for the sick and destitute. On occasion bishops and clergy provided protection for Jews who were threatened by the mob, along with the general provision of sanctuary for anyone in similar danger.

It's against this rather complex background that we should view the Crusades. These began in 1096 following an appeal from the Byzantine emperor for help against the Turks, who threatened Constantinople. Arab Muslims had already conquered the Eastern Mediterranean and the Iberian Peninsula. Leaving aside for now the religious fervour, this could be seen, at least potentially, as a "just war". There was a degree of idealism for many which also gave those troublesome knights something to do.

Unfortunately this was mixed together with greed and power seeking, epitomised by the Fourth Crusade in 1202–4 which led to the sack of (Christian) Constantinople, partly in revenge for that city's earlier treatment of the Venetians. The Venetians had provided ships for the crusade and therefore had a strong hand to play. It's a moot point whether all the Crusaders put together killed more Muslims or Christians.

However, unwarranted violence was not the universal rule. The Muslim traveller Ibn Jubayr records in the late twelfth century instances around the Mediterranean of peaceful Muslim, Jewish, and Christian co-existence. In the Kingdom of Jerusalem he remarks on the good living conditions enjoyed by Muslims living in Frankish territory. If a line had been drawn with the treaty between Saladin and Richard I at the end of the third crusade, then the whole venture of the Crusades might have been regarded today as muddled, but justified within the world-view of the time.

Dissenting Voices

Another fact often omitted in the atheist account is that not everyone agreed with the Crusades in principle, and there were many dissenting voices. One such protest movement was the *Albigensians* or *Cathars* of southern France. Their members were itinerant, proclaiming an extremely non-orthodox version of Christianity that was pacifistic, devoted to non-material ideals, and severely critical of ecclesiastical authority. They attracted the attention of the early inquisitors who popped in from Rome now and again, and they also had a crusade mounted against them in 1209. This dragged on for about ten years and largely eliminated them.

The *Waldensians* were a similar, but much more orthodox sect founded around 1177 who were persecuted but not quite eliminated. Later absorbed into the growing Reformation, a small number, around 50,000, remain today. Starting in the fourteenth century were the *Lollards* in England, who became part of the English Reformation, and the *Hussites* in Bohemia, who also had a crusade mounted against them, but survive today as the *Moravians* with about a million members.

The Inquisition was intended first and foremost to investigate such aberrations of belief and prevent their spread. During this early period the inquisitors found themselves with more and more to do, the main workload being taken by the Dominicans. If there was confession and repentance that was an end to the matter, and treatment was usually lenient. However, if that was not the case then the use of torture was sanctioned, under certain strict conditions. Burning at the stake was an extreme last resort, not the desired result, but we all know how this was twisted into the extreme behaviour of the Spanish Inquisition, to which we shall return.

In 1171, Henry II had invaded Ireland backed by Pope Adrian IV. Following on from 1066 and all that, various Norman lords had already made preliminary incursions. Adrian indulged in a typical piece of holy horse-trading by supporting Henry provided he ruled for the good of the people, protected the Roman church, and paid an annual tax to Rome. You might think that since the Pope himself gifted Ireland to the English King, then as far as Catholics are concerned that would settle the question. Unfortunately, the fact that Adrian IV (aka Nicholas Breakspear) was English makes it all look rather conspiratorial in retrospect.

Looking at these brief facts it is easy to see where the source of so much trouble lay. The church-state relationship, as we should call it today, meant that the Church gained protection, while the local ruler acquired a strong grass-roots presence in his territory that contributed to social order and administration. It was hardly democratic, but was probably better as a social system than anarchy and constant upheaval, which otherwise could easily have been the post-Roman Empire legacy. However, when forced into a corner, there was always the trump card, that the Church, through the sacraments administered by the historic priesthood, was the means of transmission of God's blessing. Excommunication meant hell and was therefore more to be feared than mere death.

Within the protest movements there was a significant desire to return to the simpler faith of the New Testament. Discontent among the educated also reflected that desire, which eventually bore fruit in the Reformation and in distribution of the Bible in the common languages of the people—fortuitously assisted by Herr Gutenberg's odd idea of sticking metal type to the underside of a wine press platen.

Further Developments

Although there were inquisitions in other countries, the Spanish variety was the most active because of the mixed religious nature of Spanish society following the re-conquest from the Moors, and particularly the size of the Jewish population. It was set up at the request of the Catholic Monarchs Ferdinand II of Aragon and Isabella I of Castile, not at the behest of the Church, although obviously the Church provided the monkpower.

Since the Grand Inquisitor was appointed by the crown, the Spanish Inquisition could easily be used for political purposes, mainly to persecute Jewish converts who were not toeing the line, but then spreading to other functions. Ferdinand and Isabella seem to have possessed a strong streak of religious fanaticism alongside their political aspiration, which was to unite their kingdoms and expel the Muslims from their remaining territory in the south, thus creating, more or less, Spain as we know it today.

Toby Green's brilliant account *Inquisition: the Reign of Fear* makes it very clear that the Spanish Inquisition was part of the wider, complex struggle for power in Iberian politics, both at home and in the new colonies. Surprisingly, he says, "The papacy, with its ancient history and keen appreciation of balances of power, was always a moderating influence on the Spanish Inquisition", and he relates the efforts of pope Sixtus IV to limit its power. It is often the case, when the detail of history is examined, that the true picture turns out to be more complicated than the popular concept of what happened.

The Inquisition was, of course, exported to the Americas. However, much, if not most, of the suffering in Latin America was perpetrated in the pursuit of economic interests through a feudal type of organisation. By 1537 the Pope had decreed *against* the idea that the indigenous peoples were in some way natural slaves and *in favour* of them being humanely treated. Curiously, those colonists who were profiteering suffered sudden hearing loss. As the years went on the Church did seek to improve conditions for the indigenous population. Once again, the facts do not entirely line up with popular understanding.

Meanwhile, Ireland continued as a political football. Key milestones in its subsequent history were the settlement of the planters (colonists) from Elizabeth I's reign onwards; the invasion of William of Orange in 1688 which finally ended Jacobite aspirations at the Battle of the Boyne and the Battle of Aughrim; the rebellion of 1798; the Act of Union in 1801; the Irish famines of the 1840s; the Easter Rising of 1916 and the War of Independence of 1919–21, with partition being formally agreed on its termination. This was followed by civil war from mid-1922 until mid-1923—and that just gets us to the start of the modern period and "the troubles" as we used to call them.

Is this not a classic religious conflict super-sized to cover 800 years or more? No, it isn't. To begin with, Ireland had always been difficult politically, by reason of terrain, physical separation from England, and its equally separate cultural identity. The noted historian Gerald of Wales (c. 1146 to c. 1223) wrote disparagingly of the Irish as primitive and savage people. His bias is obvious to us now, but wasn't then and was influential. Even more difficult was Ireland's long-standing affinity with Spain, which made it a logical staging post for any proposed invasion of England. Those early colonists were adept at changing sides, or threatening to do so, when it suited their land-grabbing ambitions. Religion may provide convenient labels and rallying cries, but straightforward self-aggrandisement was the general motivator.

The same ambiguity carries on down the years. Although William of Orange was Protestant, his expeditionary force was partially financed by a loan from the Pope, Innocent XI, who had an intense dislike of the French Emperor. Both sides in the conflict had in their armies religious minorities that one would expect on the opposing side, because of the tangled political allegiances of Europe. The rebellion of 1798 was led by the *Society of United Irishmen,* which had members from the Anglican, Presbyterian, Methodist, and other "dissenting" churches, who then joined forces with Catholics against the English. The War of Independence was between Catholic and Protestant, but the Civil War was between Catholic factions, tracing a fault line which is still present today in Irish politics.

This is just the merest sampling of the ironies of the "Irish Question", but I think it's enough to indicate that for over 800 years Ireland has been a *political* battlefield, *going back to the time when there were no Protestants at all.* Unfortunately, particularly since partition, it has been all too easy to allocate religious labels to Nationalists and Unionists. This is an example of the process pointed to by Keith Ward in his book *Is Religion Dangerous?* whereby, in many situations, political conflict has happened to coincide with religious distinctions, which have then been wrongly treated as the main *cause* of conflict.

Perspective

I hope you will excuse my rather condensed history, on the grounds that understanding the background to the atheist accusations against religion is crucial. The medieval Church was a mixture of diverse elements: pragmatic co-operation for the good of the Church and also the betterment of the people generally, the growth of scholarship, the flickerings of early science, beneficial stability and restraint on violence. However, that pragmatic co-operation could also lead to compromise and cruelty on the part of those in power, and fanaticism on the part of the rank and file.

With the background of the post-Roman legacy I do not see that for the most part any organisation could have done better in its *general political and cultural role*. The Crusades were not entirely irrational at their outset. The Inquisition in its early forms was not severe in comparison to the "secular arm" and fairer in some respects than the old method of trial by ordeal. Ireland was almost inevitably destined to become a political and cultural battle zone. None of this justifies the terrors that ultimately took place through greed, arrogance and thinly-veiled sadism, assisted by either weak or corrupt popes. And yet this wickedness is all still a long way from the sufferings that have resulted from the propagation of atheism. John Gray's magnificent book, *Black Mass: Apocalyptic Religion and the Death of Utopia,* points out a radical difference between the Christian and atheistic outlooks. He says (p36):

> Medieval Europe was no oasis of peace—it was wracked by almost continuous wars. Yet no one believed violence could perfect humanity. Belief in original sin stood immovably in the way. Millenarians were ready to use force to overthrow the power of the Church but none of them imagined that violence could bring about the Millennium—only God could do that. It was only with the Jacobins that it came to be believed that humanly initiated terror could create a new world.

The religious have sometimes been tragically misguided, particularly over the use of power. Some abuses have arisen from official church teaching, some from undue militarism, others through the misuse of popular piety. Voltaire was right to detest all that. Even so, it wasn't the Christians that set up the guillotines, gas chambers and Gulags, and there were always those who despised the ecclesiastical power struggles and the corruption which they brought.

As Gray points out, theistic religion has always recognised the dark side of human nature. It seems that militant atheists find this difficult to do. Dawkins waxes lyrical about the dark side of absolutism in some religious cultures, something which I also deplore, but it is difficult to reconcile his optimism about what could be achieved if religion could be pushed aside, and the actual reality when that has been done.

Atheists ignore one obvious fact more than any other. I do not believe one can make the case for some kind of equivalence between the actions of part of the mediaeval church and the great purveyors of genocide, but let's suppose, just for a moment, that one could. It would still be the case that the latter acted *after* the much-vaunted Enlightenment had had plenty of time to put its theories into practice.

One result of the recognition of evil (which is writ large in Christian doctrine) is that the Christian Church in the long term has tended to manifest a self-correcting mechanism. We have seen that, even long before Martin Luther, there was an undercurrent in favour of reform and reduction in the power of the Papacy. The flowering of medieval thought with people like Bishop Grossteste, Roger Bacon, and William of Occam (of the razor) in the thirteenth and fourteenth centuries, all within the Franciscan tradition and active in the colleges of Oxford, paralleled in their own ways the efforts of the early reformers. Reform has nearly always been on the agenda of some part of the Christian Church.

The civilisation created in the West by "Christendom" had many faults, but the twentieth century can with some truthfulness be regarded as an atheist experiment that was a disastrous failure. I only had a ticket for the second half, but even so I don't recollect anyone, atheist or otherwise, claiming that the Nazi death camps weren't that bad, that the people in the Gulags somehow deserved to be there, or that the terrible loss of life in the world wars and in more local conflicts was trivial. The indirect effects of it all in the disruption of nations, and the traumatising of their peoples, are also indisputable, for those effects are still with us today.

My complaint here is that Dawkins and others extend the courtesy of "the spirit of the age" argument to the greatest creators of human suffering that ever lived, but not to religion. This is poor historical method, compounded by the habit of many atheists of consistently ignoring the good that religion has done in areas such as education, medicine, social reform, international development, and humanitarianism.

Crisis? What Crisis?

I do not claim that atheists are more wicked than anyone else, nor do I claim that any particular atheists approve of genocide. The great contributions of atheists to science and to our culture cannot be denied, and there is no reason to do so. Nevertheless, there is indeed an elephant in the room—an obvious fact that no one talks about—which is this: atheism *as a belief system* depends on consequentialism, but itself generally has dreadful consequences.

For me the contradiction is summed up in the delightful enigma that is Stephen Fry. While proclaiming from the rooftops his atheism, he also declares openly his homosexuality. Further, his documentary about living with bipolar disorder was rightly acclaimed, and his programme about Wagner (which struggles with Wagner's anti-Semitism, Fry being of Jewish descent on his mother's side) was excellent. Yet it seems that on all three counts Fry would have been eliminated under Nazism, and would hardly have flourished under most communist regimes. The fact is that when atheism really takes hold it does not generate humanistic principles, values which Fry genuinely supports, it produces monstrosities. In accordance with the title of his quiz programme, Fry should surely find this Quite Interesting.

Attacks on religion are a useful distraction for atheists from the elephant in their parlour, but many people make the same connections I have made and see atheism as a cause of problems rather than a solution. Above all, despite the great value of blowing away ecclesiastical cobwebs and opening up hard questions, atheist ideology was a contributor to the greatest suffering ever experienced by the human race at its own hand. It is surely ridiculous to seek to exonerate the great dictators of the twentieth century on the grounds that they weren't actually promoting atheism. I doubt that these subtle distinctions made much difference to the millions who were tortured, poisoned, gassed, and worked to death.

I should like to suggest that atheism ought to square up to one critical fact, namely, that it is not the sole heir of the Enlightenment, as it often seems to think, but simply one response to it. Millions who were fully conscious of Enlightenment insights, and of equal intelligence to the pioneer atheists, chose very different routes. One of these was to embrace gladly the diminution of ecclesiastical institutions and the growth of scientific knowledge, but to reinforce the value of "personal religion".

In order to understand this second response, it will be useful now to look at *Fundamentalism*. Fortunately, in a book concerned with the "new atheists" this is hardly an incongruity, since they discuss it so frequently themselves.

CHAPTER 2

The New "F-word"

In this book we are looking at diverse subjects involving science, history, and religion, with a couple of visits to the *Philosophical Forum* and other excursions thrown in later for good measure. It's a roller coaster, and we continue with a subject that promises a bumpy ride, yet which it is vitally important to understand—fundamentalism. This topic is of great importance to atheists, especially Dawkins, and therefore demands attention. Understanding it can also help us grasp the wider picture of why religions are as they are.

The extreme importance of this subject is not, sadly, reflected in Dawkins' view of things, which makes no attempt to *structure* the various aspects of religion in order to take it seriously. This is his greatest weakness—shared with most other "new atheists". It's the equivalent of rubbishing all evolutionary theory because Lamarck (like most of his scientific contemporaries) believed in the inheritance of acquired physical characteristics.

Any reasonable person would examine the structure of the development of evolutionary theory and show that Lamarckism was an early branch of thought in this field which stimulated further study, but was eventually proven to be wrong in many respects. Yet when it comes to religion, especially fundamentalism, many atheists appear to be ignorant of all distinctions. The critics of religion even imply that there is common ground between Christian fundamentalism and Islamic fundamentalism. The aim of this chapter is to counteract such deficiencies, and the best approach is to pick up another strand of history.

How the West Was Won

I don't recollect a John Wayne movie where the guys in the white hats gather at the end with cries of "Yee haw, we're gonna build us a theological seminary". Nevertheless, that was one of the things that often happened, because religion was a huge concern during the major immigrations to North America during the eighteenth and nineteenth centuries. Many brought with them their religious convictions—producing, in the case of Christians, a large number of sub-divisions, aka denominations. In due course new religions also came into being, including the Mormons, Jehovah's Witnesses, Seventh Day Adventists, Christian Scientists, and so on. Freedom of choice has been the American way for a long time, and not just in hamburgers. That's where the theological seminary enters our story.

With the various waves of settlers came much earnest debate about religion. In the light of the great intellectual upheavals already discussed that should hardly be surprising. What might be surprising, though, is that very little of this debate was about atheism. Most of the argument was about interpretation of the Bible, the same argument that raged in the "old world" during the nineteenth century, relating largely to progressive religious thinking that arose in Germany. We shall look a little more at this later, but for now suffice it to say that, towards the end of the nineteenth century and moving into the twentieth, the conflict led to a crystallising of attitudes. One of the strongest centres of conservatism was the Princeton Theological Seminary in New Jersey. This acted as a focus for conservative views and for the writing of a series of twelve books, between 1910 and 1915, simply called *The Fundamentals*.

These books covered a wide range of subjects—but here's another surprise: very little of the discussion was focussed on evolution. In fact, the foremost of the Princeton scholars, B. B. Warfield, fully accepted the possibility of evolution, believing that God's hand was behind it. If you want to check what *The Fundamentals* really were, straight from the horse's mouth, the text is now largely available on-line. There is *some* negativity concerning Darwinism—one Henry H. Beach mentions the possibility of removing it from education, so we can see here some initial signs of discontent. On the whole, however, the writers of *The Fundamentals* did not regard evolution as a pressing issue.

This should serve as a preliminary indication that a straightforward bundling together of fundamentalism with Creationism is faulty. It's also obvious, even this far into the discussion, that there is no historical connection between the origins of Christian fundamentalism and the origins of that Islamic fundamentalism which is so much at the forefront of our consciousness today.

The sages associated with the Princeton initiative created the basis for fundamentalism as a definable movement within the Christian churches. However, the idea of drawing up a list of fundamentals (and the use of the word) goes back to nineteenth-century argument in the US over the authority of the Bible, and is typified by the *Niagara Bible Conference*, which met roughly each year of the last quarter of that century. Much of the Conference's discussion would harmonise with *The Fundamentals*, but the Conference was also a focus for *dispensationalism* (of which more will be said later), incorporating some views from nineteenth-century English sects.

Often overlooked in the nineteenth-century history of the US is the influence of major evangelists such as Charles Finney (1792–1875) and Dwight L. Moody (1837–99). These were no longer colonial pastors who perhaps garnered a wider fame and influence, but preachers who could attract crowds of thousands in the major American cities as they developed (extending their success to the UK through occasional visits). These evangelists were household names, and their type of evangelism continued apace into the twentieth century with later figures like Billy Sunday and Bob Jones, until radio, the movies and television diminished the attraction of big events.

Within this sector there was probably more alarm in the early 1900s concerning the teaching of evolution than appears to be the case among the Princeton network. Also, although having much in common with the writers of *The Fundamentals,* they do not seem in general to have the same inclination towards protracted discussion. They were much more taken up with the immediate need to get the message across, often mingled with concern over social issues such as prohibition.

The *World Christian Fundamentals Association* was founded in 1919 and became an anti-evolution body, heading up the prosecution at the 1925 Scopes trial, to which I referred in my introduction. There were other such groups as well, but on the whole the issue seemed to die down within a few years after the infamous trial, and the anti-evolution groups more-or-less faded away just as quickly or accepted theistic evolution. There were local disputes from time to time, but very gradually, for a number of reasons, the view prevailed that to ban the teaching of evolution was unconstitutional because such action promoted a religious view. However, the residual creationists regrouped and relaunched themselves in the 1960s, developing "creation science", while theories of intelligent design developed from the mid-1980s onwards.

Those who held to the conservative views expressed in *The Fundamentals* became known, reasonably enough, as *fundamentalists*. Their religious opponents were referred to as *liberals* or *modernists*. Gradually, many conservatives dissociated themselves from the more extreme fundamentalists and became known simply as *evangelicals*, a much older term. Just to confuse the outsider, however, most fundamentalists would probably also call themselves evangelicals, and some of them would class those they disagree with as *neo-evangelicals*. I regret to say that this kind of thing is fairly common, but it's not limited to religion. Think *New Labour* or *Reagan Democrats* for political equivalents of confusing terminology. For even more examples, read some evolutionary theory—there you can have *neo-Darwinists, cladists, punctuationists, saltationists,* and so on, with various overlaps and subdivisions.

As far as the UK is concerned, many evangelicals today are the "spiritual descendants" of the American evangelist Billy Graham. His "crusades" in the 1950s and 1960s were enormously influential, affecting most Christian denominations from Church of England to Methodist and Baptist, all of which already had evangelical elements in varying degrees. Some distinct groups such as the Pentecostals sprang from earlier American revivalism and had already been imported into the UK, encouraging some of the more unusual "gifts of the spirit" such as prophecy and speaking in tongues.

At the other end of the spiritual personality scale are those groups connected with the "reformed" faith, which has its own independent roots in Scotland, Northern Ireland, Eastern Europe, the Netherlands, and Switzerland. These roots go back directly to the sixteenth-century Reformation, the movement through which Protestantism was born. In case you ever need to find your way around this dreadful maze, these groups generally have "reformed" or "presbyterian" in their names.

Just to round off this overview, the so-called "charismatic movement" from about 1970 onwards led many people to value *deeply-felt* enthusiastic faith alongside traditional evangelical doctrine, also—like the earlier Pentecostals—promoting "gifts of the spirit". Over the same period of time others from both charismatic and non-charismatic backgrounds developed significant organisations to respond to social need, particularly in the developing world but also at home.

A Drawer Full of T-shirts

In my introduction I used the phrase, talking of my personal history, "been there, got the T-shirt". I must now confess to having a whole drawer full of T-shirts acquired during my religiously nomadic life. Most places that fundamentalists and evangelicals have trod, I have trodden too, not just as an observer but as a willing participant. Yet in *none* of the many people I have encountered have I found any inclination to violence. On the contrary, many would tend towards pacifism. So what sense does it make to pigeonhole these with Islamic Jihadists? None, as far as I can see, other than to justify prejudice.

Dawkins' method in particular is to put together a raft of different religious groups and smear all of them with the daftness, and even the bloodthirsty criminality, of a few. Having done that he then focuses on Christian fundamentalism and singles out Creationism as the main evil. In fact, there were and are many fundamentalists who follow in the footsteps of Warfield and do not see evolution as an insuperable problem to their faith. Further, I have yet to find the bloodthirstiness with which the *modern* use of the term "fundamentalist" is associated. On the contrary, most of the people I have met within the UK scene appear by all normal criteria to be intelligent, responsible, and contributing members of society.

Indeed, one of the strangest phenomena according to Dawkins' view, which amounts to the belief that all religion is clearly stupid, is that many university towns in this country have one or more churches of evangelical persuasion that are packed to the doors weekly with students, professionals, and even—perish the thought—academics. One or two of these churches could probably create a small university of their own.

Personal Encounters

To give us some useful shorthand terms I should like to refer to three people I met way back in the seventies when I was still a trainee parson. The first was Arthur Blessitt, one of the founders of the "Jesus People" movement in California during the late sixties and into the seventies, who is also thought to have had some influence on the young George W. Bush.

Arthur particularly liked to lead a "Jesus chant" which started "Gimme a J"—you can imagine the rest. His message was, and is, simple—believe in Jesus to receive forgiveness of sins and eternal life with God. The real humdinger, however, was the large wooden cross that he wheeled around in the US, and then in the UK and other countries. I say "wheeled" because it literally had a wheel fixed into a Y-fork at the bottom. As the years went on Arthur wheeled his cross through every nation on earth and now has an entry in the *Guinness Book of Records*. Recently he has made a two-inch cross using wood from the "wheelycross" and plans to have this launched into orbit around the earth. I'm not sure what effect this is meant to have, but I mention it because Arthur Blessitt is a good representative of what I would affectionately call the "daft" element of fundamentalism.

The second fortuitous meeting I had in the early seventies was a small "tea party" with Billy Graham, whom I have already mentioned. He struck me as the very last person that could be described as daft, and has acquired somewhat of an aura as the friend of presidents. (Like Blessitt, he is said to have had an influence on the young George W. Bush.) Despite the throwing of much mud by detractors very little has stuck, and he is often voted one of the most respected men in the US. His hallmark phrase "The Bible says . . ." means he is often still regarded as a fundamentalist; yet many fundamentalists have disowned him over the years for being too co-operative with Roman Catholics, too open to evolution and too tolerant of non-Christian faiths.

Here I merely cite Graham as a prime example of what I shall call the "sensible" element within fundamentalism. His book *Peace with God* is an all-time best seller and an excellent example of the genre, featuring heaven and hell like earlier revivalists but focusing on the positive, redemptive side. In common with his like-minded predecessors, and contemporaries, he puts forward a no-holds barred presentation of atonement, the idea which, according to Dawkins, is simply repulsive. But we'll come to that later.

In the UK the Graham crusades persuaded many of those loosely connected with churches to make a deeper commitment. People were invited to walk to the front of the arena to signify their decision and to receive spiritual counselling. "Your friends will wait, your coaches will wait" became almost a cliché. I did know a man who went forward at one of the Earls Court meetings and emerged to find his coach had gone; however, he still persevered with his new-found faith.

Over the last three decades evangelicalism, including fundamentalism, has carried on in its diverse free-market style. In the US this has led to the development of many independent mega-churches and parallel organisations. However, UK evangelicalism (which was always less fundamentalist) has largely become part of the mainstream Protestant denominations, which I shall call, for brevity, "mainstreamers". A good example of this would be the former Archbishop of Canterbury, George Carey—certainly not a fundamentalist, definitely evangelical in outlook, conservative in some areas such as homosexual priests, progressive in others such as the ordination of women. In other words, maintaining the evangelical core but in *dialogue* with people of various convictions. As far as I know he had no influence on the young George W. Bush, but he was one of my tutors long ago during my Church of England boot camp, so he had an influence on me. I often feel like a consolation prize.

Carey says many of the things that Graham always said, but in more subtle terms—see for example Carey's book *The Gate of Glory*. In particular, there is more stress on God's love reaching out to us and fewer explicit mentions of hell. There is no attempt to *scare* people into faith, and this moderated tone is a highly significant development among evangelicals of a broader outlook. Hell is seen more as C. S. Lewis depicted it in *The Great Divorce*—not so much as a place into which God casts sinners, but a place or perhaps a condition in which people may end up by consistently choosing *of their own volition* to ignore the "light" that is given to them.

Why is all this Important?

These distinctions are important because the Dawkinsian smear tactics work well with those who want to believe his picture of religion but have little experience of it first-hand. He generally speaks of religion as if it should be regarded as a homogeneous mass, whereas there is a clear, verifiable structure to its sub-divisions, and to the sub-divisions of Christian belief. Generally speaking, those fundamentalists with the highest daftness rating live primarily on enthusiasm and not so much on reason, apart from the logic of the basic message. The "sensibles" are less eccentric, less simplistic and more sensitive to other beliefs, but the basic doctrinal formula is never going to change to suit others. The broader style of *evangelicalism*, especially among the mainstreamers, is no longer essentially fundamentalist. It is open to dialogue with those of different views, which can lead to change.

I hope I may be excused one further personal note. As the seventies moved into the eighties, those selfish genes exerted their inexorable will, assisted in a minor way, I like to think, by myself and my wife. Our two children were born, and in due course became proud students at Emmanuel College, Gateshead, the establishment Dawkins singles out as an "educational scandal" because, it has been claimed, one or two of the teachers have taught Creationism rather than evolution.

There are aspects of Emmanuel College that are quite narrow, as shown by the web-published material that Dawkins quotes in *The God Delusion*, and I don't support those views. However, I do know directly and indirectly many ex-students, and I must say that none of them seem to me severely damaged on account of their ordeal. In fact, I am reliably assured that for most students at the College the religious dimension is simply there, to be tolerated, respected, or dismissed. I also believe that most students do not lie awake at night thinking about Creationism *or* evolution.

The result, it seems to me, falls far short of a scandal, and Dawkins is scraping the bottom of the barrel in portraying it as more than that. He also downplays the fact that the Government's schools' inspectorate seems very happy with Emmanuel College.

I cite these stories because Dawkins' language is all broad brush strokes, whereas the reality is more complex. There are many daft elements in fundamentalism and a few in evangelicalism, but we have to pay attention to the structure of it all—then we shall see what the real issue is. *And it isn't Creationism as opposed to evolution*. It's much more important than that.

Middle-age Spread

Many men suffer from middle-age spread. I blame it on things shrinking in the wash or at the dry cleaners. However, middle-age spread has also occurred within the religious movements we have been discussing, and can be seen in two directions. One type is where the daftness takes over and generates extremism. The other is where the moderating process continues, and some become quite broad minded. The balance of these two types, however, is different if we compare the UK to the US.

In the United States I think it could safely be said that on balance the "spread" in the last thirty years has been in an extremist direction. Eventually this will throw up one or two who think it's a good idea to attack abortion clinics, and a larger number who will insult anyone whom they remotely suspect could be involved in anything progressive. An American I know who is a cytologist has been subjected to abuse for going to her workplace, even though the project on which she was working at the time sought to reduce the impact of genetic disorders in children. The types of disgraceful and obsessive denunciations fired at Dawkins and his chums arise from similar sources.

In the UK, such extremism as there is tends to be innocuous, still within the daft dimension of normal human life. I have in mind the wilder forms of worship found in some churches—dancing, raising arms in praise and that sort of thing. It makes sense to those who do it, and, in a democratic society, should not be a cause of dismay. There are some fairly conservative pressure groups which are quite vocal, though always, it has to be said, within the law. However, there is also spread in a more progressive direction; in other words, people who keep many of the evangelical elements, but also take a lively interest in major issues such as world development, the environment and social justice.

This ebb and flow contradicts the Dawkinsian assertion that moderate religion provides a fast-track to the fanatical. It is true that when a new fad catches on there are some who leave more traditional churches in order to drink of the "new wine". However, these trends are often short-lived. In my experience, a good number flow in the opposite direction—moderate religion can "rescue" those involved in the more extreme versions.

The people against whom Dawkins rails most are generally from the extreme American type of church or religious organisation, some of which go beyond mere daftness to fanaticism. However, it's well to remember that Americans, notwithstanding their immense strengths and achievements, have been selling snake oil to each other for hundreds of years. It's part of their culture, and it's not going to stop overnight.

It makes no sense to use a word like "fundamentalism" as a catch-all, because actual fundamentalism has a *structure*. I don't accept the daftness or the fanaticism, and to many Billy Graham's approach was impressive but oversimplified. The broader evangelical movement, probably the strongest Christian force in the UK at present, does appeal to a significant number of people, including some who are not particularly conservative in outlook. These evangelicals reject the daftness and the fanaticism, and the majority would also reject the type of dogmatism that easily transmutes into bigotry. I believe that the same could be said of the US, but there the extreme conservatives are much greater in number. They tend to grab more attention as a result and because of their assertiveness. They are also an easy target for those who want to negate religion in general.

Let's look now in greater detail at some of the less desirable features of fundamentalism, particularly as it has developed in the US. It seems to me that it has fallen into several traps since the Princeton days, reflected to some extent in the UK and in other parts of the world where the "American way" has been influential.

Trap 1: Nominalism
The first source of corruption is the unavoidable *nominalism* to be found in successful movements. They become attractive in their own right, perhaps as friendly welcoming communities, or perhaps as an emotional support in an uncertain world. Some people join for such reasons, but their adherence to the core beliefs can be, to some degree, superficial or selective. It is inevitable therefore that their representation of the movement may not be in line with official beliefs or approved practices. Further, since a widespread

movement is bound to be at the mercy of local leaders, it is also impossible to avoid the occasional rogue trader with a strong personal agenda. Such aberrations, especially if there are sexual or financial overtones, always make excellent headlines.

There is no doubt that some members of fundamentalist churches, at the more extreme end in particular, do get seriously hurt by the practices and opinions of a minority of leaders who do not suffer from a surfeit of common sense. For such victims the rescue organisations that exist to help people leave religions may be a necessary last resort, although they are certainly far more necessary in the world of religious cults. This first type of corruption, then, is to do with the behaviour of individual leaders, and will be found in any large movement—and we should not forget that the fundamentalist element in the US is probably about the size of the entire UK population, possibly even larger. In that context it is surprising that there are not more scandals.

Trap 2: Commercialism
Second, there is the tendency towards commercialism, so that religion becomes a product, promoted by standard marketing methods. You may not have read all of *The Fundamentals* but you have probably guessed, in any case, that these books are hardly sound-bites. Fundamentalist preaching was typically not very concise either; but at least by the second half of the twentieth century a certain formulaic style of presentation had become popular. Instead of twelve printed volumes or a long sermon, the whole matter could be presented in terms like *The Four Spiritual Laws,* a small handy booklet devised in 1965 by an organisation called *Campus Crusade,* which still has a huge and growing presence working among students and other groups. The booklet is a masterpiece of instant communication, easy to pass on, to present to your friends and, indeed, to remember for yourself. The message was also given a makeover, so that instead of starting with the perils of hell—the great classic being the 1741 sermon of Jonathan Edwards, *Sinners in the Hands of an Angry God*—we find that *Law 1* states, "God loves you and offers a wonderful plan for your life." Edwards, in contrast, used to say things like "all you that were never born again, and made new creatures, and raised from being dead in sin . . . are in the hands of an angry God."

The general pattern of *The Four Spiritual Laws* and its countless derivatives is, "Here's the problem, here's the answer, here's what you have to do"— the *call to action,* as my marketing friends would say. This ability to create "transferable concepts", along with a salesman-like style, greatly helped the growth of evangelicalism, including the "ministries" of the so-called televangelists, some of the main causes of Dawkins' ire (and mine at times). However, a sense of proportion is called for. Persuasive presentation is the order of the day in many fields, not just in religion.

Unfortunately, although most of this remains within the bounds of proper religious freedom, it is easy for a commercial mindset to take over. "God's Blessing" almost becomes something that can be bought. I say *almost* because such an idea would be repudiated, I believe sincerely, by the majority of those who seek financial support for their "ministries". Even so, power does corrupt and the resultant scandals cause great disillusionment. Again, though, bearing in mind the size of the fundamentalist movement, it could be a lot worse.

Trap 3: Monomania
Everyone has an inner dialogue. We filter out information that we perceive as irrelevant to us, and fill out the detail of things that seem important. We interpret experience on the basis of the past, and we project our hopes and expectations onto the future. We build mental pictures of how life works. Without this kind of activity we would all become neurotic, suffering from either information overload or terminal boredom.

My third trap for the unwary is concerned with what happens when this process goes wrong in religious people. Some acquire a sense that the everyday world is unreal. However, I do not mean by this the type of major withdrawal that accompanies some kinds of mental illness. Neither do I mean serious delusions that may betoken major paranoid or schizophrenic episodes. Nor do I want to imply that this sense is limited to the religious, because I believe it can also be found in others who have a strong interest in a particular subject combined with an introspective tendency. The absent-minded intellectual might be a non-religious version. The political zealot might be another.

Perhaps what I have in mind is what is sometimes called "religiosity"- it may be that "monomania" is too strong a word. The mundane becomes somewhat unimportant, compared either to great spiritual truths or to the trappings of religion—usually one or the other. If the tendency becomes extreme then, of course, we are on the way to serious obsessional problems, but for the most part it does not. It can, however, produce a mildly dysfunctional, rather escapist outlook.

Trap 4: Utopianism
Sam Harris's vitriolic *Letter to a Christian Nation* rightly sounds the alarm bells concerning the possibility of the more extreme American fundamentalists gaining too much real executive power. I have sympathy with most of what Harris says, yet again a sense of proportion is called for. Certainly many fundamentalists, including some leaders, are biased towards the political right, but other sectors of society have their bias as well. If it were as dramatic as we are sometimes told then the Democrats would never win anything, but they do. Harris focuses mostly on rhetoric and not so much on what religious people actually do. He also studiously ignores the underlying moral issues that genuinely trouble many people and often force them

into the arms of extremists.

There is, though, one area which demands discussion, namely, theories of the "millennium"—the period of a thousand years referred to in the Biblical book of *Revelation* which in recent years has lent itself to utopianism, sometimes with a political bias, and popularised since the 1970s through books by Tim LaHaye, Hal Lindsey, and others. This has been given a higher profile of late through John Gray's *Black Mass: Apocalyptic Religion and the Death of Utopia* to which I referred in the previous chapter. In Gray's view utopianism has caused immense suffering, particularly through Nazism and Communism. The same mistake is being made today by those who believe that democracy imposed on others can bring in a new world of harmoniously co-existing democratic states. He sees such utopianism as having a long history, stretching back through people like the Ranters in seventeenth-century England, the Anabaptists in Reformation Europe, and the medieval monk Joachim of Fiore (1135–1202) in southern Italy. Behind all that is early Christian millennialism.

However, although it is perfectly true that millennialism was the majority Christian view during the first four centuries, it was not held unanimously and was not considered a cornerstone of the faith. Justin Martyr, writing in the second century, makes both these points clear *(Dialogue with Trypho the Jew, ch 80)*. Further, the early church was almost entirely pacifist in outlook. Later dispensationalists like Joachim were regarded as heretical by the mainstream, and in any event did not support armed revolution. Joachim's followers who perpetuated his ideas were mostly among those Franciscans who sought to retain what they saw as the proper poverty and humility of their order—hardly a recipe for violence.

The sixteenth-century European Anabaptists appear at first to offer better evidence for the connection between old and new versions of utopianism, until we get down to the detail. They were not one group, as sometimes portrayed, but a highly-varied assortment. A few Anabaptist groups believed in armed rebellion to establish the true faith, leading to tragic loss of life such as notoriously occurred at Münster; the majority, however, were pacifists, a viewpoint endorsed by the main leaders in the *Schleitheim Confession* of 1527. Their modern descendants in the US (and Canada) are primarily not the "neo-cons" but the Mennonites, Amish, and Hutterites, relatively small *pacifist* groupings. One very small group, the Schwenkfelders, only have a handful of churches remaining, in Pennsylvania, but are credited with introducing saffron into North America, which is difficult to interpret as aggressive.

The Ranters were similarly diverse, and sometimes lawless, but more in the sense of vulgar political protest and individual morality (or lack of it) than in the sense of armed rebellion. Some eventually became Quakers—hardly, one would suppose, a logical resting place for the violent.

The utopianism stemming from some Christian millennialism has sometimes been used as an excuse for violence, but the great majority of its adherents have not followed that path, tending more towards pacifism, experimentation with community living and mutuality, with very little involvement in politics. Gray's linkage of secular movements with extremist Christian ones is not, therefore, as simple as it looks, and is in some ways misleading.

Real issues

I've dwelt on the daftness factors and their negative results because they tend to attract a lot of attention with regard to Christian fundamentalism, especially in the US and on the airwaves of CNN. However, if you could excise these things you would still be left with a bunch of "sensible" fundamentalists and evangelicals worldwide, maybe 70% of those that are there now. Does that not still leave a huge body of people, who should know better, united in their adherence to the main atheist *bête noir*, Creationism?

No, it emphatically doesn't. I freely admit that some groupings are very adept at forming the wagons into a circle to fight off the wicked purveyors of scientific theorising (as they would call it) and they are certainly the noisiest and the most attractive of media attention. However, large numbers of conservative Christians, including evangelicals, accept the view known as theistic evolution, to which I referred earlier. Notable among these is Francis Collins, who was until recently head of the Human Genome Project and therefore presumably knows a thing or two about genetics. The title of his book *The Language of God* (referring to the genetic code) sums up his attitude, which is non-threatening to both science and religion. In many ways, although a century down the line, he is continuing the view of Warfield, whom he quotes. Both Collins and Warfield deny any conflict between evolution and Christianity, and they both believe that Christians should be deeply committed to scientific progress.

Incidentally, this view of the non-conflict between evolution and religion is endorsed by the National Academy of Sciences in the US, in their 1999 pamphlet *Science and Creationism: a view from the National Academy of Sciences*, although naturally the writers are relentlessly critical of Creationism. Anything else would be rather disappointing.

There must, then, be a different common denominator, nothing to do with Creationism, that unites evangelicals, and indeed there is. It is the assertion of a particular view of how one experiences God. It harks back in many respects to times of "revival". The eighteenth-century hymn writer Joseph Hart put it like this:

> Vain is all our best devotion,
> If on false foundations built;

True religion's more than notion,
Something must be known and felt.

Experiencing God in this way shows that we have been *born again*—a phrase taken from the New Testament. This is an individual experience, not requiring a priest or ecclesiastical organisation, only some way in which the message is conveyed to the recipient so that he or she can respond.

Across the broad range of evangelicalism today the emotional dimension is not so much emphasised, and even *The Four Spiritual Laws* counsels against taking too much notice of emotion. Moreover, in many streams of thought the timing of the "born again" experience is left open, and can even be unconscious in the life of a child, or perhaps drawn out over a period of time. Nevertheless, there has to be something, best referred to perhaps as an inner conviction, which brings re-birth to *the individual*. The crucifixion of Jesus is the act of divine love through which the gap between God and mankind is bridged, but this is of no benefit to the *individual* unless he or she believes in it.

This normative evangelical experience fits in well with the classic distinction made by William James in *The Varieties of Religious Experience*, especially lectures 6–10. These lectures were originally delivered at the very start of the twentieth century, and the relevant theme is the distinction between the *once-born* and *twice-born*. The once-born are those who feel the world around them to be essentially good, with each day to be enjoyed in itself. God is the fount of all this goodness. The twice born, on the other hand, tend to see the world as faulty, fallen, a domain of human evil and consequent suffering. Finding God requires that somehow things be *put right*. It's easy to see how this emotional framework would make religious conversion likely, compared to a more sanguine or optimistic outlook.

I would argue that both in theory and in practice the "born again" experience should be judged in its own right and does not necessarily need to be linked to a highly conservative view of the Bible. Keith Ward in *What the Bible Really Teaches: A Challenge to Fundamentalists* is an excellent example of someone who gives a clear testimony to the "born again" experience as a personal reality, yet shows that it is not necessary to link this with a fundamentalist understanding of the Bible. Having recently retired as Regius Professor of Divinity at Oxford, and with a lifetime of achievement in the philosophy of religion, Ward's testimony about the "born again" experience also shows that this is not limited to the ignorant and superstitious, a presupposition that seems to lie behind much atheistic invective.

If we go back to the New Testament the phrase "born again" is rarely used, but on every page there are other words and phrases implying belief, change of direction, a turning to God—in the same way that we may start to take notice of a person that we previously ignored. If we believe in God at all and in the possibility of some kind of relationship with that God, then such a psychological change does not seem to me at all ludicrous. The "born again" shorthand often used by evangelicals may not be exact, but it is not as incomprehensible as sceptics make out.

The other day I was asked for advice about a legal document, which is odd because my knowledge of law could be written on the back of a speeding ticket. I noticed in the document the phrase "for the avoidance of doubt". I'll be using this device occasionally to avoid confusion, and here's my first instance: for the avoidance of doubt, whatever one's reservations about the "born again" experience, no one that I have ever known implied that it involved hearing voices. If you want a parallel to the "born again" experience it's probably for most people a time when "the penny drops"—we see things in a new way. In sophisticated company one might say a new *gestalt* arises. The experience may indeed be emotional—but no voices.

Evangelicals, including fundamentalists, give a uniquely prominent place to the "born again" experience, although inner conviction in general has its place in most types of Christianity—the line should not be too firmly drawn. Possibly the same experience is given a different name and interpretation in different contexts, especially since, as we have seen, there are varied emphases within evangelicalism as to what constitutes the "born again" experience.

Atonement

Evangelicals share with most brands of Christianity the concept of atonement, but it tends to be brought out as a *primary* focus in evangelical teaching and preaching. It is impossible to understand the evangelical mindset without understanding atonement. Along with the idea of individual turning to God it is one of the twin pillars of this type of faith. Unfortunately, Dawkins particularly ridicules the whole concept of atonement as merely one more indication of the villainous nature of the "Abrahamic God", exemplified by the story of Isaac.

Whether historical or allegorical, Abraham intended to sacrifice his son Isaac as a mark of his devotion. Yes, the account says that God told him to do it as the supreme test of faith, and on a first reading the whole idea is obnoxious; but bear in mind that, however dreadful we may find the idea, human sacrifice, including child sacrifice, was often practised in the region. That context is critically important.

It is quite common in this discussion to get sidetracked concerning the date and origins of the Abraham story. It could have been written as late as the sixth century BCE or as early as the tenth century BCE. In either case, it could be using much earlier material, which could relate to an actual historical figure—or could be in the nature of an allegory. In any event, none of this affects the essential message.

According to those who wish to disparage monotheistic religion, the essential message is that God is a child slayer. Personally, I have always seen it as the opposite, with Abraham as somewhat of a tortured soul. In his culture the really devoted follower of a god is prepared to make sacrifices to that god. Since he was probably rich and had no end of animals to spare, what could he do that would be a *real* sacrifice, something that would match the devotion of the followers of other gods? The answer is obvious. The really surprising thing about the story, and therefore its essential message, is the command of God to take the alternative offered. "God will provide" the sacrifice.

In subsequent development human sacrifice is condemned and prohibited, and the prophets claim that in fact no sacrifice is adequate, it's the moral response to God that counts. One of the most striking passages is this: "Shall I give my first-born for my transgression, the fruit of my body for the sin of my soul? He has showed you, O man, what is good; and what does the Lord require of you but to do justice, and to love kindness, and to walk humbly with your God?" (*Micah* Chapter 7)

Monotheism *denounced* the practice of child sacrifice that was all around, it did not institute it, and the story of Abraham has never been taken by any monotheistic faith as implying the contrary.

When we come to the New Testament then of course the atonement theme is developed by a huge leap. However, Christians, even fundamentalists, do not believe that God picked one random person out of the crowd, like some public school headmaster of old, to be made an example. We shall shortly be looking at early *Methodism*, a major leader of which was Charles Wesley. He wrote in one of his many hymns, "Amazing love, how can it be, that thou my God shouldst die for me". Hardly the bloodthirsty or bullying God portrayed by our modern-day atheists, quite the opposite.

Dawkins, in a rare spate of theological concern, asks why God could not just forgive anyway and have done with it. Strangely, some of us numbskull Christians already thought of that. The Scottish theologian P. T. Forsyth (1848–1921) popularised the expression ". . . a cross in the heart of God . . ." implying that atonement is deeply rooted in God's nature, and would have still been so without the literal cross and Good Friday scenario. Going further, some have taken metaphorical views of the cross as being *only* symbolic of a deeper truth about God, but profound nevertheless, because the metaphor speaks also of a deeper truth about ourselves.

There is, then, a breadth of interpretation of atonement, and the wholesale condemnation that Dawkins delivers is not justified. This condemnation arises because atheists (even those who go beyond consequentialism) do not link morality with the existence of a God For atheists, therefore, any concept of atonement, even metaphorical, is inevitably senseless.

Made in America?

Christian fundamentalism is commonly viewed as an American phenomenon, and it should be obvious from the story so far that there is some truth in this view. We have seen that the word was first coined in regard to the Princeton theologians, and the call to maintain the fundamentals of the faith goes back to nineteenth-century revivalism and beyond. In the UK we noted the influence of Billy Graham, earlier evangelists and of some American denominations and movements, influences that are still felt today.

If that were the whole story, Christian fundamentalism would be merely a historical by-way of American history. However, because the fundamentalist outlook did not spring into life from a vacuum, it should be seen as a distinctively American spin on the beliefs quietly held by many during the colonial period. Its roots, therefore, do not lie in the USA but in Europe. It is tied up with our whole culture and is not merely a late addition, as many atheists seem to think.

I must now divert briefly to deal with the assumption made by many that there is a connection of some sort between Christian fundamentalism and Islamic fundamentalism such as led to "9/11".

Wahhabism

The roots of much modern day Islamist terrorism are well documented. At more or less the time that Jonathan Edwards was seeking the conversion of the masses in New England and nurturing the colonial roots of evangelical Christianity, Muhammad ibn Abd-al-Wahhab was founding his fundamentalist Islamic movement in the Arabian peninsular, which eventually became the official faith of the house of Saud and then the Kingdom of Saudi Arabia.

It would be greatly over-simplified to draw a direct line between Wahhabism and modern terrorism, but I think most informed commentators would hold that this austere movement has probably contributed more than any other to the fundamentalist strains of Islam. That austerity stands in the starkest possible contrast to the actual lifestyle of many of the Saudi princes, especially with the massive expansion of that country's oil riches starting in the 1950s. It is quite easy to imagine how such an outlook, combined with the sacrifices in Afghanistan against the godless Communists, would breed discontentment among idealists. It's also easy to see how convenient it would be to blame decadent western influence for this perceived apostasy from the true faith.

To say the least, these are the historical causes and influences that should be investigated. I can't think of anything further removed from that group of conservative, law-abiding Christian scholars assembled at the seminary in Princeton. Wahhabism has a long history of brutal bloodshed. Those leaders who met at Princeton, and earlier at Niagara, may have shared some harsh words at times, but did not engage in mass murder.

Dawkins of course knows about Wahhabism and refers to its obscurantist nature, but still refuses to recognise it as a phenomenon totally separate from Christianity—and from most Muslim thinking for that matter. The fraternity of avowed atheists as a whole appears to ignore the standards of analysis that it wants everyone else to follow. The basic error is to believe that there is some grand movement—perhaps a conspiracy—that can be labelled fundamentalism, which somehow worked its way into Christian and Islamic versions and possibly others as well. There never was such a movement.

The word *fundamentalism* was actually used only of Christian fundamentalism until as late as 1980. At that time it became clear, because of the Iranian hostage crisis, that a new Islamic radicalism was under way following the overthrow of the Shah of Iran. The word was not a good choice, but it suited the media. It is notoriously perilous, however, to build a theory on such a foundation.

To recap: in one sense Christian fundamentalism is an American invention, but it is more accurate to think of it as the Americanisation of one major strand of religion, the evangelical strand, that was taken across to the fledgling new world from the time of the Pilgrim Fathers onwards. In terms of belief, I have said that it rests on two "pillars", the concept of being "born again" and the concept of atonement.

If you have some familiarity with these matters you may be wondering when I will introduce adherence to the Bible as a third pillar. There would be some justification for doing this in relation to certain historical periods, and evangelicals have always denied the validity of any claim to new doctrinal revelation, whether contradictory of, or merely additional to, the Bible. However, this is a boundary rather than a pillar. Within that boundary evangelical interpretation of the Bible varies somewhat, largely depending on which historical period the individual, church or movement happens to latch on to. There is a spectrum from extremely literal to extremely flexible understandings.

The Old World

It is often possible to detect in the work of the "new atheists" a note of genuine bafflement in the face of the simple question: "Why does religion still exist in the developed world, despite the advances of science and technology that have taken place in the last three hundred years?" Religion is like the notorious "bunny boiler" in the film *Fatal Attraction*. Just when you think it's dead, it leaps out of the bath tub like Glenn Close wielding a knife, with no one apparently able to fire the fatal shot.

This resilience is despite the rapid progress of science that formed part of the Enlightenment, starting around the mid-seventeenth century. By the end of that century Sir Isaac Newton was making his indelible mark. It seemed that God was no longer necessary as an explanation of the world we know, and gradually the power of ecclesiastical institutions was eroded.

The new knowledge extended to science, philosophy, mathematics, and eventually technology. Such dazzling progress caused some to move from theism to deism, the belief that God created the universe and its laws but does not intervene in it now. Many of the Church of England clergy moved in this direction, although some were perhaps just too intellectually lazy to resist the trend. Even when not deists, they were generally very much against religious "enthusiasm"—a term which correctly used, in this context, refers to direct experience of God.

The Puritans (known as "dissenters" and later as "nonconformists") had been forced out of the Church of England in 1662 but were still around in the eighteenth century, although not widespread in numbers or influence (except in Scotland). Into the resulting vacuum stepped John Wesley (1703–91), the best-known of the founders of Methodism. He and his brother Charles founded an informal group at Christ Church, Oxford, in 1729, with the aims of Bible study, deepening of their devotional lives, and doing practical good works such as taking food to the poor, visiting hospitals and prisons, and teaching the illiterate to read. Other members of the university attached the name "Holy Club" to the group and devised various other pejorative titles as well. "Methodist" was one of these, mocking their disciplined way of living, but it stuck and became the name of the subsequent movement.

John Wesley was greatly influenced by the Moravians—you may recollect that these were the descendants of the Hussites who survived persecution in Europe. The Moravians had adopted the *pietism*, as it is known, which originated with the German Lutheran Philipp Jakob Spener (1635–1705). Pietism emphasised inner conviction that led on to a simple devotional life and practical holiness. Following an emotional type of "born again" experience Wesley aimed to bring others, wherever they were, into that same experience, and preached in almost every town in the land.

Wesley was a convinced Anglican and had no intention of founding a breakaway group. However, doors were eventually closed by the Church of England—hence the rapid growth of the Methodist meeting houses, in due course to become churches in the Methodist denomination. The stress on individual conviction plus the classlessness of Wesley's approach was too radical for the conservative core of the Church of England. For many of the "respectable", having a Methodist in the family was a huge social stigma, although Wesley became more accepted towards the end of his long life, dying at the age of 87.

John Wesley did not act alone. His brother Charles Wesley and one George Whitefield (another Holy Club member) were equally important leaders. The "Evangelical Revival" that resulted from their work also strongly influenced the dissenters and even the Church of England. Some of the preachers went out to the New World, joining forces with those of colonial stock like the aforementioned Jonathan Edwards. Without the ballast there of an established Church there was no inhibition, and so it carried on through many twists and turns until we get to Billy Graham and Arthur Blessitt.

Incidentally, it is a great mistake to think of those early American preachers as simple-minded—many were involved in the foundation of universities in the colonial period, including Harvard and Yale. Jonathan Edwards was a devoted student of science, fascinated by Newton and the emerging new knowledge. He was also influenced by the writings of the great English philosopher John Locke (1632–1704) whom we shall meet later in the *Philosophical Forum*.

So, we've now pushed back another century or so, and I hope you can see the links between Christian fundamentalism today and the renewal of "personal religion". This religion was in a sense an emotionally fleshed-out version of the beliefs of the sixteenth- and seventeenth-century Protestant reformers, both British and Continental, but the real point of bifurcation is the eighteenth century. Part of the newly-enlightened world wanted to go down the atheist route, but another large part went in the opposite direction into religious enthusiasm and revivalism.

Retrenchment

More traditional Christianity in the West settled down to the long haul. Roman Catholicism re-asserted itself and remained highly conservative until the twentieth century and the growth of more open-minded attitudes. The Church of England after the exclusion of the Methodists gradually became that broad institution that is now its norm, although it still had an evangelical party which communicated to some extent with the dissenters and Methodists. In the nineteenth century the Anglo-Catholic party, starting from the Oxford Movement, re-asserted the validity of Anglicanism as part of the continuing catholic tradition even though not subject to the Pope. As a counter-balance, evangelicals within Anglicanism (as elsewhere) have grown substantially in number over the last fifty years.

For the sake of completeness, the Baptist churches originated from several sources from the Reformation onwards in an attempt to deny the validity of the baptism of infants and strengthen the necessity of personal decision. Other totally independent bodies (for example, the City Missions and the Salvation Army) were founded to meet specific needs of the time, or in some cases to uphold what was perceived as a purer version of the faith.

Gradually, as is the way with these things, Methodism and others who had been influenced by it saw a decline in their fortunes and also suffered from division over various issues—an invariable habit amongst evangelicals. However, until the early twentieth century, there were frequent revivals across the evangelical churches in which large numbers would be added to their congregations. Speaking very roughly, this happened every 25–30 years, the last such event being in 1906, which was the cause of the founding of Pentecostalism in the US.

After 1906 the era of mass movements came to an end in Europe and the US, and the evangelical presence stabilised until the second half of the twentieth century, during which there has been steady evangelical growth in many parts of the world with sudden accelerations in some places. The latest occurrence of this is in China, which on current trajectories could have a Christian "head count" around 20% of the total population within a few years. The largest proportion of this growth is evangelical. This is quite remarkable in view of the expulsion of the missionaries from China during the Mao years, and the many persecutions—including martyrdoms—endured at other times.

The Liberal Challenge

The greatest challenge to this pattern of modest, if sporadic, growth, came neither from atheism nor from the development of evolutionary theory. It came from the tendency of individuals, churches and denominations that weakened in their catholic or evangelical attachment to come under the sway of religious *liberalism*. That's why, if you call in at random on a service held in a Methodist church today, you may not find much that is redolent of Wesley's enthusiasm. If the brand is Presbyterian or Reformed there may not be much that their Reformation founders would recognise. A Church of England service may be neither Catholic nor Evangelical but a rather more bland "middle of the road" affair. Even a Baptist service may not echo much of the evangelicalism that originally invigorated the various types of Baptist gatherings.

Liberalism refers to a broad movement that originated in Germany while Wesley was spreading his message of personal salvation in the English-speaking world. This movement spread through Europe and had a strong influence on Voltaire and Nietzsche, whom we considered in the previous chapter, as well as a general effect on the churches and their leaders. It focussed on *biblical criticism*, a blanket term for analysis of documents and their history. At its extremes, the movement produced many theories of the origins of the Bible and many theories of interpretation, with no particular concern to maintain orthodox views.

As you might guess, the liberal attitude fits in very well with deism, for if God is not involved in our world, despite having given it an initial push, then he is hardly likely to break that self-imposed rule in order to convey infallible truth in the form of a book. The full-blooded liberal aims to treat the Bible just like any other literature, with no special allowances for alleged divine activity. We shall shortly see how important this trend was, once we have wrapped up Fundamentalism.

The Undistributed Middle

I showed earlier that there is no connection at all between Islamic fundamentalism and the Christian movements from which the word "fundamentalist" originated and which are so often the focus of Dawkins' wrath. I hope it is also clear that, while all religion has its eccentricities, the excesses of some American fundamentalism are not definitive of the modern evangelicalism for which Dawkins has so little sympathy. In reality, he's guilty of an elementary logical error. It's a long time since I read any logic, so I had to dig around to remember what this particular error is called. In fact, it's called "the undistributed middle".

Hidden behind the invective of much of *The God Delusion* is a piece of pseudo-reasoning which in effect says, "Some Christians are fundamentalists; some fundamentalists are terrorists; therefore some Christians are terrorists." Or less dramatically (but still not logically), "Some Christians are fundamentalists; some fundamentalists are bigoted; therefore some Christians are bigoted." As it happens, I would agree with the second conclusion, that some Christians are bigoted, but not on the grounds given. In fact, the whole tenor of *The God Delusion* seems to be that *all* Christians are bigoted, which would certainly warrant a "see me" from the logic tutor. In general, extending a fact which applies to *some* as if it applied to *all* is called "illicit process", which is definitely as seedy as it sounds. It's like saying, "Some green trains break down; some green trains are involved in accidents. Therefore all green trains should be replaced by red trains."

As well as the logical problem, of course, we see here the technique of underpinning about which I complained earlier. The existence of bad or harmful religion is only a good foundation for atheism if it can be shown that religion in general is bad or harmful, and that atheism in general produces better results. Since neither of these propositions can be shown to be true, this is a case of underpinning with expanded polystyrene. It just won't take the weight, particularly if we are proposing that atheism is a system of thought that should be adopted by the whole of humanity—which is in fact what the "new atheists" want.

The Prime Question

The different religious groupings that we've discussed so far attempted to provide answers to a major question that arose from the ferment of the seventeenth and eighteenth centuries: how, if at all, can we know God? Unfortunately, this is tangled up with the question of how, if at all, we can know *anything*. In other words, the problem of *epistemology*, as philosophers would call it. This is the prime question for today, not the artificial problems raised by setting evolution against Creationism. It is an issue that affects all of our futures and warrants proper discussion rather than a barrage of name-calling based on gross confusion.

As the Enlightenment took hold, some gave a very simple answer to the question of how we know things. They answered that we should rely solely on reason, with the raw material for our reasoning processes provided by observation rather than any claim to revelation. Others did not accept this exclusivity, claiming that the spiritual truths of Christianity, although not *against* reason, could be discovered in the Bible and validated inwardly. These were two opposite reactions to the Enlightenment.

To be more accurate, the Enlightenment was not so much a starting point but a staging-post for both fundamentalism and atheism. A staging-post lies between two points, which makes sense once we realise that the Enlightenment followed on from the Reformation, which in parts of Europe destroyed the monolithic authority of Roman Catholicism and made thinking a less risky pursuit. Protestantism, contrary to popular perceptions, did not initially support total freedom of religious thinking—people were still denounced as heretics, but they were no longer sent to chat to an inquisitor. That sort of thing died out until "staff performance appraisals" became popular in the 1990s.

A Longer View

Taking a very long and generalised view, those Protestant churches and denominations that eschewed the "born-again" faith (generally in favour of liberalism) were destined to slow decline, which accelerated as the twentieth century progressed. Even those among the long-standing Methodist, Baptist, Presbyterian and Reformed bodies who took the liberal route were part of that decline. The Church of England had its periods of resurgence, and it also had a social role which slowed the shrinkage, but this did not last forever, although I think there are fewer "C of E" carpet warehouses, design studios, and curry houses than nonconformist ones. I refer, of course, to the re-use of church buildings, not new religions.

It must have seemed, particularly as the post-Second World War babyboomers took over the reins, that all the atheists had to do was wait. So what went wrong? Why do we find Dawkins, more than two centuries after the full blast of the Enlightenment, making a kind of "Custer's Last Stand" against the circling forces of religion?

Well, I have referred previously to the crisis of atheism, the problem that, by its own benchmark of consequentialism, it does not measure up very well. For many the dismissal of moral absolutes is a far more profound matter than mere atheistic belief. If one goes back to the Scopes trial in 1925 and the controversy surrounding it, there was actually more concern about the perceived attack on morality than anything else. These were times of great social disorder, and there was a growing view that Darwinism had encouraged various ills of society as well as the aggression of the First World War—Vernon Kellogg's work became well known.

We have seen that many fundamentalists of this period had no problem with evolution. Even those who did, including those who took part in the Scopes trial, were of the "old earth" type, not Creationists as we understand the term today. However, the perception that Darwinism destroyed morality was a major driver towards the conservative cause. Consequentialism may not have been a word on everybody's lips, and the horrors of the Second World War had not yet unfolded, but enough had become clear to make adherence to a faith seem *more* important, not less.

Atheism has never explained how it can tackle moral questions better than a general humanitarianism, which could stand equally well alongside humanism, agnosticism, or many beliefs within the religious spectrum. The situation in the evangelical world was the exact opposite.

Now, if we add in the question of epistemology, we can see that atheism was actually doubly weak. Atheists generally assume that scientific observation and reason are the *only* true sources of knowledge, and we shall examine the philosophy behind this assumption in due course. For now, it is enough to remark that many people over the last three centuries have simply not held to this point of view, even when science is given full credit for its efficacy within its own sphere.

Atheism shares in the great weakness of the Enlightenment, which is that it did not really resolve the huge question of epistemology. What kind of enlightenment is that? Suppose you were to ask a medieval monk why he believed in mythical creatures, which were thought to be half animal and half human, living in distant lands. He would probably just say that everyone knows these things exist, and we would be somewhat amused at such naivety. Now ask a secular child of the Enlightenment why scientific observation and reason are taken as the *only* true sources of knowledge and his answer will probably be fairly similar. It's just the way it is. Yet once this answer is given, we have not just one but two elephants in the atheist parlour, and things are getting crowded. We must hope they are not a breeding pair.

To be fair, the various Christian groupings did not solve the problem of epistemology either, but it was less important for them to do so in a hurry. Evangelicals simply fell back on their interpretations of the Bible, and of course Catholics did the same but with the addition of traditional dogma—and there was great strength for both in the fact of having something on which to fall back. In such a situation long-term reconstruction is possible; and whatever the other influences involved, post-Enlightenment religion had one huge advantage over post-Enlightenment atheism. Its roots were very long and well-nourished.

These roots encompassed not only Christian belief in the narrow sense in which we often understand it today, but whole areas of science and philosophy. The connections with science are particularly important—and will give heart to religiously apathetic readers. Through exploring these connections we shall discover a third key response to the Enlightenment, alongside those of the evangelicals and the atheists.

CHAPTER 3

The Appliance of Science

On the basis of my account so far the atheists and evangelicals might have appeared to have it all their own way as the results of the Enlightenment unfolded, but such a picture would be incomplete. Catholicism remained, of course, a huge force, and carried on regardless—it always does. Within Protestantism it was very different. I have already mentioned some of the numerous smaller groups that arose from the "radical reformation"—people like the Mennonites, Amish, Hutterites, and Schwenkfelders, all of whom found religious freedom in the New World. We have also noted the Moravians, who trace their history back to pre-reformation Bohemia.

In Britain there was a similar but more eccentric profusion of sectarian bodies, with, to our ears, rather odd names—for example: Diggers, Levellers, Seekers, Ranters, and—my favourite—Muggletonians. The European movements mentioned above retained mainly orthodox Christian beliefs, but these slightly later sects did not, and some added to their beliefs a degree of political activism. None had a great deal of long-term influence—but as their movements faded some members joined the Quakers, who, on the contrary, were highly influential.

George Fox (1624–91) along with others had founded Quakerism in the mid-seventeenth century, based on broadly orthodox beliefs supplemented with a commitment to pacifism and simplicity of life and worship. Unlike other nonconformists, however, revelation was almost entirely inward, and the Bible was not therefore a boundary to belief in the same way that it was for the more conservative. There was no need for theologians, sacraments, religious organisations, and specialised religious leaders. The simple attentiveness of the believing heart was sufficient.

Doctrine was therefore of lesser importance for Quakers, and almost from the beginning the movement began to diversify and very often to simplify. In 1681 William Penn (1644–1718) established Pennsylvania as a Quaker colony—it was to be a place of religious freedom, and brotherhood was sought between all who believed in one God. This principle won him the later admiration of Voltaire.

The Growth of Deism

Science as it developed during the Enlightenment almost inevitably encouraged deism. As the seventeenth century progressed this relatively new religious trend began to be established as a movement. Thomas Hobbes

(1588–1679), Lord Herbert of Cherbury (1583–1648), Charles Blount (1654–93), Matthew Tindal (1657–1733), and John Toland (1670–1722) are key names—this was a very British affair, but its effects spread rapidly into mainland Europe and to America. The key theme is that religion is a simple, natural, and rational belief in one God, who created the universe and then left it to operate according to natural law, which he also created. Reason became the key to understanding the purposes of God.

That might sound alien to the Christian beliefs of the time; however, the value of reason had long been recognised by great scholars such as Augustine and Anselm, and was further entrenched in the Reformation. In particular, it is right at the foundation of Anglicanism in the works of theologian Richard Hooker (1554–1600). That way of thinking used to be called "latitudinarian"—still a useful word for heavyweight crossword enthusiasts, but for the rest of us perhaps "tolerant" would suffice. Unfortunately, when separated from Hooker's zeal, it is obvious that this principle could result in apathy. We have seen how Methodism challenged this in practical and devotional terms, but the intellectual battle with deism had already been lost within the Church of England. Once the Puritans were out of the way and those irritating little sects put in their place, there was nothing to stop the clergy and educated laity following the deistic route if they wished to do so, and many did.

Similarly, there was nothing to stop many of the Quakers—and others for that matter—de-emphasising traditional Christian doctrine in pursuit of a wider purpose such as social action, philanthropy, political reform, or community cohesion. The deistic trend, in fact, can be traced back to the early days of the Reformation in the first half of the sixteenth century, when *Socinianism* (named after Italian Lelio Sozzini) and the early precursors of *Unitarianism* both moved away from the orthodox view of God, although initially they did still believe in a certain degree of divine intervention through the miraculous. As early as 1564 a French writer, Pierre Viret, used the word "deism" to describe a new Italian heresy, with Sozzini or his fellow thinkers clearly in his sights.

It is quite wrong to suppose, then, that deism was a result of the Enlightenment. Rather, it was one set of beliefs arising from the Reformation that became influential in its own right, although officially rebutted by mainstream Protestants. Unofficially, it was the kind of belief towards which Christians could lean, with suitable discretion as necessary, if they ceased to believe in traditional views of God, the Bible, or the miraculous. The Enlightenment atheists, on the other hand, were atheists because of their materialism—by definition, the material universe is the only reality there is, so there *cannot* be any God at all. This way of thinking was frequently despised by deists, notably by Voltaire, and by Unitarians like Newton. Unitarians did not entirely rule out revelation in the Bible, but were very similar to deists in their view of God.

Deism as a movement declined at the end of the eighteenth century, but its beliefs continued to be influential within the more traditional religious denominations, producing a comfort zone for disenchanted Christians— they were not forced to declare themselves atheists or to place themselves outside the religious fold. This is, of course, greatly simplified, but it perhaps prevented atheism from drawing in disillusioned Christians and becoming a movement.

Bring On the Theologians

The tacit acceptance of a degree of deism within some of the Protestant churches allowed a crucially important debate to take place between theologians. For atheists, of course, the whole thing is a damp squib. Indeed, one could be excused for thinking, on the basis of *The God Delusion*, that theologians are the ultimate scumbags of modern life, pursuing futile arguments about a non-subject. Many others would at least be puzzled as to the purpose of theology.

The very word "theology" has acquired bad connotations—if a dispute or discussion is becoming very detailed we accuse one or more parties of being "a mite theological". We now need to see to what extent this attitude is justified, first leaping back once again over the Reformation traumas to the calm of the medieval monastery, where we seek the answer to a rather important question. We'll return to deism later.

Can We Prove God's Existence?

The usual starting point in reviewing this question is St Anselm of Canterbury (1033–1109). He was first to formulate the "ontological argument" for the existence of God. It goes like this. "I can conceive of God as the greatest possible being. If such a being did not exist, he would not be the greatest possible being. Therefore if I can conceive of the greatest possible being he must exist."

Are you puzzled by this? I am, and always have been. As Dawkins rightly points out, it seems like a word game. Criticism of Anselm's views began more or less immediately, as soon as the ink was dry on his parchment, and the final nail in the coffin is usually put quite simply as "existence is not an attribute". In a sense Anselm does not help his own cause, restating the argument in various different ways as if he is still wrestling with it himself. Some have concluded that he did not intend to prove the existence of God at all. Others consider his discourses to be an extended meditation rather than a formal proof.

Yet the genius that was Bertrand Russell believed in the ontological argument for a time, so obviously it is not total nonsense. Even after his "unconversion" Russell continued to admit that the argument was difficult to refute. Other philosophers, notably Charles Hartshorne, Alvin Plantinga and Norman Malcolm, have also developed and supported the argument, as did the mathematician Kurt Gödel. Unfortunately, their arguments mostly depend on modal logic, which for most of us is akin to solving Rubik's cube in the dark, so I suppose one must accept the wisdom of greater minds and conclude that the argument *could* be valid in some way. Dawkins prefers the easier path of crude disparagement.

So, that's one slab of mediaeval theology dealt with. St Thomas Aquinas (1225–1274) focused on God as the ultimate cause. Matter exists, so it must have been brought into being by something, a first cause. Things move, so there must be a prime mover that set everything in motion. Unfortunately, a large number of people look at all this sceptically and ask "Why? Perhaps existence and movement are just there, and don't need a first cause or a prime mover" (which, for our purposes, are approximately the same thing.)

Unjustifiably, the question "who made God?" is often quoted as a knockdown argument against a first cause. The question is unjustified because Aquinas was not trying to explain where God came from. He just is, and the existence of causation points to that fact. He is *sui generis*, unique and uncaused. Even if we did want to raise the question of the causation or non-causation of God, that doesn't invalidate the question of the causation or non-causation of everything else. The two matters are separate.

This question of causation has become somewhat fashionable due to the concept of the singularity. Most of us probably came across that term via Stephen Hawking, with reference to the "Big Bang". I accept of course that Hawking is not presenting a religious viewpoint, but I still find it hard to see how scientific critics can complain too much about a first cause when they seem to be stuck with something very similar, at the Big Bang, themselves.

Design

That's another few hundred volumes of scholastic discussion dealt with; but we must now slow down a little, because Aquinas focused also on the subject of design, and today this argument is generally considered more relevant than the previous two. Basically, it starts from the simple idea that there is obvious design in the universe, so there must be a designer. This view was famously expounded by the English cleric William Paley (1743–1805) using the illustration of finding a watch. Seeing the design involved, one naturally concludes that there is a watchmaker. Likewise, when we see the obvious design of the natural world around us, we conclude that there is a designer of the universe. Of course the sceptic, (for whom Dawkins' *Blind*

Watchmaker is iconic), pipes up again and points out that perhaps the sense of design is illusory, more in our own perception than in the reality itself. If you're thinking, "Aha, it's that epistemology thing again", then you're quite right.

Paley attempted to plug the Church of England back into the much older medieval tradition of which Aquinas was a part. His arguments are not entirely original, some of them being found in the writings of the pioneer naturalist John Ray (1628–1705), who was also a clergyman and one of the first members of the Royal Society. There was already a developing Church of England tradition of "natural theology" as it's called—theology that does not rely on any alleged special revelation such as the Bible—which suited those of a deistic tendency. Some had also used the watchmaker illustration before Paley, but in his case the whole was truly greater than the sum of the parts.

Three Unlikely Bestsellers

Most people today who have heard of Paley only know of his 1802 work, *Natural Theology; or, Evidences of the Existence and Attributes of the Deity*, often referred to simply as *Evidences*, in which the watchmaker illustration occurs. Most of us have only a vague idea of him as a person—a typical image is probably that of a clergyman running around the meadow wielding a butterfly net, a cross between Alan Bennett and Jane Austen characters. In fact, many of the clergy from Ray's time onwards were true experts in their fields, became Fellows of the Royal Society or other academic bodies, and built massive collections of plants, rocks, insects, and animals according to their interests. Some of their collections were eventually acquired by the major museums of natural history.

Paley was certainly a member of the establishment, but he was also a child of the Enlightenment, well known for his radical views on property ownership, abolition of slavery, ethics, taxation, and women's rights. His writings on politics and philosophy were mandatory reading in the universities and were sometimes quoted in Parliament and Congress. Naturally he also studied and wrote on theology, of which the *Evidences* was his last work. It is an impressive and lucid presentation containing an incredible amount of detail, far beyond that of a "gifted amateur". Apart from its main purpose it was used later by jurists to illustrate sound legal argument, and even Dawkins admits its brilliance in many ways, even though he disagrees with its conclusions.

Unlikely as such a thing might seem to us today, the *Evidences* was a bestseller throughout the Victorian era. Charles Darwin was greatly impressed by Paley's writings, not only by his religious viewpoint but also by his attention to detail concerning the adaptation of living organisms to their environments. Somewhat intriguingly, Darwin also drew on the work of his renowned contemporary, the American botanist Asa Gray (1810–88). Although Gray was an evangelical Christian he supported Darwin's views in the US. His work *Darwiniana* maintains the validity of evolution while at the same time reconciling it with much of Paley's thinking.

It is legitimate to regard Paley and those who supported his views as part of a third key response to the Enlightenment, a response that I have called "the appliance of science". This response reached back to the medieval, and with good reason: within the horizons of their day, medieval thinkers were also scientific. Although mostly monks, they were not obscurantists who spent all their time praying and keeping bees. Even as early as the Venerable Bede there was an interest in the natural world. Alcuin of York (c. 735–804) was interested in mathematical puzzles, the Marcus du Sautoy of his day, and was one of the scholars summoned by Charlemagne to establish schools throughout his empire.

A significant handicap was that only fragments of Greek culture had survived in the Latin-speaking West. Most of the original Greek documents were lost during the early centuries CE, many being destroyed by violence or by fires in the library at Alexandria. It's tempting to think that someone was after the insurance money, but actually fire was an everyday peril in cities of the time.

However, the old knowledge was preserved in the Byzantine world, and many of the classics were also translated into Syriac by Syriac Christians. With the rise of Islam they were also translated into Arabic and contributed to the foundation of Islamic intellectual culture, which took off in extraordinary fashion in centres like Baghdad. As the first millennium came to a close this knowledge was beginning to filter back into the West. As an example, Gerbert of Aurillac, who became Pope Sylvester II in 999 (having avoided the rule of the harlots), was greatly interested in mathematics and the Islamic developments in astronomy, which he encountered in Spain.

From the twelfth century onwards there was a steady flow of translation from Greek and Arabic into Latin, notable early figures being William of Conches (c. 1090 -1154) and Adelard of Bath (1080–1122). In England their work gradually focused on Oxford, where the proto-university was in the process of formation. By the thirteenth century there we had the Franciscans Bishop Grossteste (1170–1253) and Friar Roger Bacon (1214–92) who both did extraordinary work on astronomy, optics, and mathematics. Slightly later another Franciscan friar, William of Occam (1288–1348), marked a turning point in the development of scientific method. All these medieval monks and clerics—and many others—were part of the European network that I outlined briefly in Chapter 1.

Incidentally, I make no claim of exclusivity. Muslim scholarship had the likes of Avicenna (980–1037), Averroes (1126–98) and many others less well known in the West, while Jewish scholarship was exemplified by

Moses Maimonides (1135–1204) and those who followed in his footsteps. All three monotheistic faiths co-operated in the translation work in Spain, notably in Toledo, and the route from Toledo to the rest of Europe was well trodden, including the road that led to Oxford.

A fascinating account of the medieval contribution to science can be found in *God's Philosophers: How the Medieval World Laid the Foundations of Modern Science* by James Hannam. His work chimes in with the famous comment by the late Robert Jastrow, who held high office in NASA and other institutions. Although an agnostic, he had a strong sense of the limitations of science, and I can't resist his conclusion from *God And The Astronomers*: "For the scientist who has lived by his faith in the power of reason, the story ends like a bad dream. He has scaled the mountain of ignorance; he is about to conquer the highest peak; as he pulls himself over the final rock, he is greeted by a band of theologians who have been sitting there for centuries."

The argument about design or teleology (which strictly refers to purpose, but purpose and design amount to pretty much the same thing in this context) has indeed carried on for centuries. Paley's bestseller brought it forward into the modern era. Dawkins' works aim to knock it on the head once and for all, using two arguments. The first is that evolution adequately explains the apparent purpose or design of living things without recourse to a designer. Just because we see the astonishing functionality of living cells, organs and organisms we should not take Paley's view, but Darwin's. Whether Dawkins has succeeded in his ambition we shall judge later.

Dawkins supplements this line with a second argument relating to the *Anthropic Principle*. The weak version of this principle (we'll partake of the strong stuff later) basically states that how we see things in the universe is dependent upon our situation as observers. John Barrow in *New Theories of Everything* says that the Weak Anthropic Principle is "the recognition that our own existence requires certain necessary conditions to be met regarding the past and present structure of the visible universe". We need to be careful, he continues, not to draw conclusions as if we were taking a purely objective view. We may *feel* that all those aeons during which the universe and the earth developed in such a way as to support life, with evolution completing the job, were all geared to creating us. But if the result had been different, we would not be here making that observation. There is, therefore, a certain inevitability about our perception of design. It's all in the mind.

Design and Creation

It may well have occurred to you that even if natural theology is taken to have proven its point, it doesn't prove all that much. Paley was used to a large extent by evangelicals and catholics to support scientifically what they already believed. That's very different from using his work (and that of his predecessors back to the Reformation) to justify a reinvention of Christianity in the form of deism. After all, it is well known that almost all cultures have creation myths, so why should science not be regarded as demolishing all of them, including that of Genesis?

Well, the diversity of these myths is huge, involving various gods and goddesses, giant primordial creatures like spiders, turtles, fish, frogs and serpents, and sometimes a demiurge (a kind of assistant God responsible for creation); while the process of creation can involve vomiting, copulation or masturbation, and a variety of other activities. The Genesis creation story, by contrast, exhibits a simple grandeur: in the beginning, God created the heavens and the earth. There is a six-day sequence of creation culminating in the creation of man and woman. God rests on the seventh day.

In other words, if one accepts that Genesis is to some extent allegorical, it is not in full-blooded contradiction to the idea of development that was gaining ground in Paley's time and before. The same kind of reconciliation was still possible later when Darwin entered into public consciousness, as we saw when looking at the early fundamentalists and the role of Asa Gray.

There is also in the Old Testament an element of independence of the creation from God. Although he is a performer of occasional miracles on behalf of his people, he is also in one sense distant. This is part of the meaning of the word "holy". This relative independence is not glossed over, and there is plenty of questioning in, for example, the books of Job, Ecclesiastes, and the Psalms, as to why God does not intervene to set things right. The problem of suffering may have come to the forefront since the Enlightenment, but it was certainly not invented then.

This independence leaves the way open for understanding the created order in its own right—this is the basis on which those medieval theologians dealt with "natural philosophy" as they called it; we call it science. In the New Testament, John's gospel takes this further. It's as if John goes out of his way to stop the reader in his or her tracks by starting off with "In the beginning was the Word, and the Word was with God, and the Word was God." No shepherds, wise men or manger here, this is the cosmic view of things. Creation took place through the Word, yet that same Word dwelt in Jesus Christ. "Word" is the conventional translation of the Greek "logos" but that translation misses out the very strong overtones of *reason* and *logic* contained in the original. One could almost say, "In the beginning was reason."

Now, returning to our historical theme and edging towards the science, just a few months after publication of the *Origin of Species* a compilation called *Essays and Reviews* was published by seven liberal Anglican academics, mostly from Oxford. It may seem incredible today, but this volume greatly outsold the *Origin* for many years. This is my second surprise bestseller.

The subject of revelation was at the heart of the *Essays*. In essence, the Bible was to be studied scientifically, just like any other book—prophecy or any other type of miracle is impossible. The public response to such frankness was vehement on all sides, liberal and traditionalist. It probably took some of the pressure off Darwin, for the threat from liberalism was immediate and radical compared to that from evolutionary theory.

The issues debated in *Essays and Reviews* had actually been on the go for a century, particularly in Germany. Although the *Essays* are not entirely supportive of the *Evidences*, it must have seemed to many that Paley's natural theology combined with liberalism could be a lifeline. Why? Because neither of them needed a historically accurate, let alone inspired, Bible. Now of course the evangelicals (of all denominations) would have no truck with this, but the deists and those who tended in that direction did.

Although liberalism appeared totally heretical to many, it was in fact reaching back to ancient roots in its own way. St Augustine in the fifth century argued that interpretation of Genesis should not be literal, *and should not contradict facts known by observation or reason*. Augustine's principles were carried forward into the medieval church, where we have seen that theology became a synthesis of ideas claimed to be revealed in the Bible with other ideas drawn from observation and reason. Those medieval theologians, including the odd pope, had no trouble in believing that the earth was a sphere and that the light of the moon was reflected light originating from the sun, even though the Bible might indicate otherwise if taken literally. The *Essays* also brought forward the idea of progressive revelation, in other words, the idea that the Old Testament starts from a limited understanding of God which unfolds gradually up to the final revelation in Christ. This idea was not new either, but the *Essays* used it, in many people's eyes, simply to devalue revelation altogether.

Despite the furore, liberal ideas eventually even influenced the evangelicals and Roman Catholics. Notwithstanding the diehard fundamentalists, most evangelicals today reject any idea that the Bible was somehow dictated directly by God to the writers. Even conservative Christian theologians do not claim that the Bible was written by someone in a trance in order to convey the precise words delivered by God; in general there is full recognition of human agency at work.

Dawkins claims that the gospels are just like *The Da Vinci Code,* except that one is ancient fiction while the other is modern fiction. Yet it is a matter of historical, proven fact accepted for centuries that the gospels *did not* originate in the mind of one person, a kind of Dan Brown prototype, who then went and persuaded his mates that God had spoken to him. Perhaps Dawkins is confusing the New Testament with the *Book of Mormon*, which *was* allegedly delivered to Joseph Smith in this direct way, 1,800 years later.

Restoration

Just one more piece of Victorian liberal religious thinking requires our attention at present, focussing on the idea of *restoration*. There is an intriguing word (I believe the longest Greek word in the Bible) in Paul's Letter to the Ephesians Chapter 1 verse 10. The word is *anakephalaiosasthai*. The nearest equivalent verb in English is *recapitulate* but that doesn't seem to make much sense. Adding in the rest of the verse, however, translations generally read that God's purpose is to restore everything with Christ as the head. St Athanasius of Alexandria (c. 295–373) in his masterpiece *On the Incarnation of the Word* (Chapter 14) puts it in a wonderfully quaint way:

> You know what happens when a portrait that has been painted on a panel becomes obliterated through external stains. The artist does not throw away the panel, but the subject of the portrait has to come and sit for it again, and then the likeness is re-drawn on the same material. Even so was it with the All-holy Son of God. He, the Image of the Father, came and dwelt in our midst, in order that He might renew mankind made after Himself . . . This also explains His saying to the Jews: "Except a man be born anew . . ." He was not referring to a man's natural birth from his mother, as they thought, but to the re-birth and re-creation of the soul in the Image of God.

Athanasius points us toward the word *restoration*—the human race can be restored to its former glory. But we need to be careful. This is not a human-centred moral re-armament, but a statement about the "Cosmic Christ" if you like, as illustrated by the famous Salvador Dali painting *Christ of St John of the Cross* in which the crucified figure straddles the world.

We can see here a belief in the real activity of God in the world, but with a broader outlook than that put across by the evangelicals. This difference of outlook was taken up by radical Anglo-Catholics with the publication of a volume entitled *Lux Mundi* ("Light of the World") in 1889. Like the earlier *Essays and Reviews* this was a compilation created by Anglican clerics, and again was a bestseller—number three on my select list.

The writers of *Lux Mundi* accept evolution, welcome the progress of science, and acknowledge the human process behind the writing of the Bible; so they were liberals in those respects. However, they stress the presence of Christ in the world and are more orthodox than the writers of *Essays and Reviews*—they are somewhat anti-deist. They were also more adventurous for their time, addressing issues such as the truth to be found in non-Christian faiths, and the relationship between Christianity and politics. This was a partially liberal reworking of orthodox Christianity that pulled the remote deistic God back into his own universe.

I described the rejuvenation of natural theology by Paley and the liberalism of *Essays and Reviews* as a lifeline for institutional religion. Balance this with *Lux Mundi* and the resultant mix—part liberal, part orthodox—might seem like a fully-functioning lifeboat for the Church of England and possibly for others. There would be an element of truth in that, but unfortunately it all appeared increasingly irrelevant in the turmoil of the early twentieth century. In terms of church allegiance, the lifeboat came to the rescue, but not enough people got on board.

One problem was that none of these new ways of thinking were easy to popularise. The message of atheism is simple by its very nature. The message of the evangelical is more complex but can be honed down to a few key points like the *Four Spiritual Laws*. The message of these new approaches was, and is, so varied and often abstract that it is hard to know where to start.

It seems odd to us today that the *Evidences, Essays and Reviews* and *Lux Mundi* should have been so popular in the nineteenth century. The reason for the popularity of these works was that churches still had strong memberships, but an increasing number of the Victorian middle-class were acutely aware of the issues that were being raised by science.

The Age of Science

This growing awareness highlights a more substantial reason for the failure of the ecclesiastical lifeboat, namely, that the age of science had begun in earnest. In view of my book title, I should perhaps explain that I see the age of science as beginning around the mid-nineteenth century. The Royal Society had been formed in 1662 but had very mixed fortunes until the 1830s. The Royal Institution was formed in 1800 and the British Association for the Advancement of Science in 1831. In 1840 William Whewell (1794–1866) suggested the term "scientist" for a practitioner of science, instead of terms like "natural philosopher". Whewell, a clergyman and influential Cambridge don, did impressive work in several scientific fields, reinforced Francis Bacon's scientific method, consolidated the history and philosophy of science, wrote on natural theology, and taught Charles Darwin. In general, the first half of the century saw unprecedented scientific progress. Science as a dominant cultural force really took off, and has continued as such until the present.

This third reaction to the Enlightenment was an attempt to get back to some of the ancient roots of faith and graft onto them a number of reinterpretations which did not rely on the rather specific understanding of personal commitment held to by evangelicals. Neither did they require a narrow view of the Bible. The pace of the development of science gave it enormous momentum. Established religion was left in a position of catch-up.

An Extended Footnote: C. S. Lewis

Although we have been looking at the nineteenth century and earlier, sometimes much earlier, one later development to note on the religious front is the work of C. S. Lewis. Amidst all the Victorian controversies there were many theologians and others who simply carried on trying to figure out the meaning of the Biblical text and interpret it for their own times, without going to extremes. Lewis is a culmination of that process as it carried on into the twentieth century. It is hard to think of an appropriate label for this—terms like "neo-orthodoxy" and "neo-conservatism" were long ago stolen for other ideas. The best I can come up with is "core orthodoxy".

If Anglicans were in the habit of creating saints, there would certainly be a St Clive. He was born in 1898 in Belfast, fought in the trenches of the First World War, studied at Oxford (gaining three first-class degrees) and then taught as a Fellow of Magdalen College for most of his life. He died on the same day as President John F. Kennedy in 1963. He is well-known in general for *The Chronicles of Narnia* and his science fiction works, but in religious circles he is also revered for his writings in support of the Christian faith.

Lewis moved from convinced atheism to monotheism in 1929, then to Christianity in 1931. Among his many religious books probably the most influential has been *Mere Christianity*. The purpose of this book was to make available an account of the core Christian faith which would cut through secondary controversies and enable people simply to understand the main message. He is orthodox concerning the nature of God, the moral law, the revelation and atonement that God has given in Christ, and the need for faith. His belief system was non-partisan.

Lewis was not alone in his approach, but is best known in the English-speaking world because of his standing both as an academic and as a writer. His belief in open discussion with atheists—and taking their views seriously—chimes in well with our modern democratic outlook. His writings are understandable to the non-specialist, unlike those of many twentieth-century professional theologians. Finally, as a world expert in the field of literary criticism, he was able to mock with authority the excesses of the *avant-garde* type of liberalism.

One of Lewis' important contributions was to promote an argument for the existence of God, known as the *moral argument*. I mention it here because it will enable us to summarise the whole business of whether we can prove the existence of God.

Immanuel Kant (1724–1804) is usually cited as the originator of the moral argument, but it corresponds to a very natural assumption that many have made both before and after his work. In Kant's view, there are moral facts just as there are empirical facts. Nearly everyone agrees that murder is wrong just as they agree that the sun rises in the morning. That sense of obligation—in this case, not to murder—is not rational without also believing in a God who created a moral order.

With the advent of Darwin it was not difficult to create an evolutionary view of morality. Maybe a tribe or other grouping of primitive people are more likely to survive if they don't kill each other, steal from each other, and have sex with the neighbour's partner, creating major jealousy issues. So the tribes that happen either to garner the highest number of morality genes or to establish the most moral social traditions are the most likely to survive.

Well, that seems simple enough until we consider how it would happen in reality. Although there may be survival advantages to a fully-fledged moral law, it seems unlikely that such a law would arise *fully formed*. It would be fragmentary, starting with a few individuals. Those individuals or groups would actually be at a distinct *disadvantage* in the quest for survival, and therefore would die out. In a game where only one side plays by the rules the outcome is fairly predictable—notwithstanding Dawkins' claim to the contrary which I shall examine shortly.

In other words, a moral code only works if it is held by everyone in a social group, and if competing social groups have higher level rules that are followed. Without the first we have injustice within communities, and without the second we have warfare between them. If there is a universal morality, and if it could not arise as such through a gradual evolutionary process, we are likely to conclude that it must have been implanted in human nature by God.

Altruism

In support of this argument Lewis shows, especially in *Mere Christianity* and *The Abolition of Man,* that the moral law is practically universal and very similar in form across otherwise diverse cultures, indicating a universal knowledge. A key feature of this is altruism, which extends into many situations where it is difficult to see any advantage to the individual. On a trivial level, why should I let someone (whom I shall probably never meet again) into the traffic queue when I've been standing there for ten minutes myself? On the ultimate level of life and death, why did Oskar Schindler—not a religious man—risk his life on a daily basis in order to save others to whom technically he owed nothing? Dawkins' arguments here miss the point, particularly in his presentation in *The Genius of Charles Darwin,* where he tries before the cameras to explain and validate liberal values without recourse to God.

There may indeed be evolutionary advantage to practicing altruism which results in other people helping me at times. This could obviously aid survival more than the members of the herd or tribe acting indifferently to each other, and this would apply even more within kinship groupings. However, if the human urge to altruism were merely an instinct, genetically determined like that of, say, ants or termites, it seems odd that we so often act in contradictory ways. Sometimes we feel the urge to altruism but ignore it, leaving a sense of what we *should* have done. This is a much more complicated feature of us than is often acknowledged, and I believe that Lewis was right to focus on it.

I would not wish to claim here that Dawkins' pivotal claims concerning altruism, which lie at the heart of *The Selfish Gene,* are entirely false. They rest on strong game theory and statistical foundations, particularly the ingenius work of W. D. Hamilton (1936–2000) who specialised in developing a theory of altruism. That theory is based on a difficult mathematical proof, so one has to accept on trust that it explains how the social behaviour of ants and termites evolved. Yet we do not observe ants or termites wracked with indecision on a particular course of action. They just get on with whatever they are programmed to do. The word "altruism" is being used here in a rather different way from its more common meaning of voluntary self-sacrifice.

Further, although Dawkins elegantly shows that behaving unselfishly will eventually pay dividends—the "nice guys" do come out on top—there is a lot wrapped up in that word *eventually*. Complete victory for the altruistic may take hundreds of generations. The implication is that, from the time that the altruistic trait appears, the "nice" members of the population will need to be largely shielded from the "nasty" members around them. This could happen through geographical isolation or just the natural tendency for organisms not to move away from their place of origins very quickly. Although I would not go to the stake on this point, it seems to me rather like special pleading. Even if such convenient localisation occurred, it would surely make the group concerned more vulnerable to the weaknesses normally associated with in-breeding. Not being versed in either game theory or advanced statistics my doubts remain, but with a slight sense that I could be wrong. However, as far as altruism in human beings is concerned, involving moral convictions, conscience, decision, and sometimes guilt, I am sure that Lewis' argument is the stronger.

In Summary

Taking the opportunity to summarise and simplify, there are basically four classic arguments for the existence of God:

- Our concept of a supreme being demands that such a being exists.
- Everything has a cause, so there must be a first cause of everything.
- Design is present in the universe, so there must be a designer.
- The shared morality of human beings across cultures indicates a lawgiver.

If you like exotic words, these are known as the ontological, cosmological, teleological, and moral arguments, but the terminology is optional.

These arguments have been presented in various ways over the last two thousand years. I have illustrated this with just a few fragments—after all, there are large libraries covering such matters. I hope it conveys some idea, though, of how this stream of post-enlightenment debate developed. With all its diversity, the common thread is the acknowledgement of science and the attempt to apply it to faith.

Dawkins' treatment in *The God Delusion* of arguments for God's existence is not extensive; further, less than a quarter of his chapter on the subject deals with these main arguments. The rest deals with trivia and with "arguments" that have never been regarded as pivotal. Moreover, he seems to be totally unaware of the theological debates on which I have touched in this chapter, preferring a crude portrayal of fundamentalism as if that were the only version of Christianity to exist since evolution came on the scene.

Darwin is now almost at the front of the queue. However, there is just one more response to the Enlightenment that needs to be briefly taken into account. My next chapter contains nothing about atheism, fundamentalism, or theological shenanigans, but is just as important in its own right. It concerns the subject of the irrational.

CHAPTER 4

Daftness and Beyond

For most people reason has to be thrown out of the window at times, in favour of activities or beliefs that seem incomprehensible to outsiders. I should initially like to survey some examples, not for novelty value but to provide some insight into the irrationality involved in being human. After that I will put the whole subject into the context of our culture and its development since the Enlightenment.

First of all, what about those people that pile everything into the car on Friday night and set off to re-enact seventeenth-century battles *yet again?* Members of *The Sealed Knot* and the *Civil War Society* that I have known appear to be well-balanced individuals, so why do they put significant amounts of time and money into re-enacting battles that took place hundreds of years ago?

Here's another quaint and rather English activity: *Morris Dancing*. A group of grown men dancing and waving handkerchiefs or sticks according to a formula known only to them, and wearing outfits that frankly could not have been designed to look more silly. Why do it?

For another example: I live in the north-east of England near Hadrian's Wall. From time to time, at venues along the wall, a group of men in full, highly authentic costume, meet together to demonstrate Roman military tactics. I particularly like the marching where the commander calls *Sin, Dex, Sin, Dex* and so on. The demonstration of shield usage is particularly impressive, but keep clear when the siege catapult is fired, just in case.

Surely these are just interesting hobbies? Well, of course they are, although the dedication exhibited by some appears to be at least quasi-religious; but it doesn't stop there. Over the last few years I've had the privilege of attending graduation ceremonies at Newcastle University. Why do they have that solemn procession with the convocation mace, the quaint language and the "hooding"? Why does that professor's gown have the go-faster stripes but the others don't? Why does the other chap on the platform have a silver tassel on his mortarboard—does that rank higher than scarlet? If redbrick land maintains these traditions it must be even more elaborate in places like Oxford that are much older. Or did I watch too many episodes of *Inspector Morse?*

For the sake of brevity, I shall put all these folk under the general heading of "re-enactors". A university convocation in ritualistic mode is re-enacting even though that is not explicitly stated, and so are the Morris dancers. It doesn't really matter, by the way, if what is done corresponds only loosely to the historical reality, it's the sense of participation in history that appears to be important. Incidentally, no slur is intended on those who take part in these activities—there is no doubt that when not acting daft these people are first-class professors, accountants, brain surgeons, and bricklayers.

There are many other examples of re-enactment strewn throughout our national life. Daftness really takes off, however, when you look at what people believe.

The *Most Haunted* Approach

I arrived at my office building recently to overhear a conversation between two other tenants. One was relating to the other that she had been at some kind of fortune-telling meeting the night before, but the medium hadn't turned up because her car broke down. I, of course, jumped in with both feet. "Unforeseen circumstances, eh?" I should have known better. Let's just say I had to tread warily for a very long time.

This interest in the occult has been cashed in on by the television series *Most Haunted*, which is broadcast in the UK primarily on the *Living* channel. (Was the irony intended?) On a good night, knocking sounds may be heard in response to questions, a table may lift during a séance, or an object may move inexplicably. On the live spectaculars, which run for several nights, there is always a large viewer response via e-mails and text messages. Sometimes there are psychic drawings.

Those who produce programmes of this type—and there are many others—often refer to themselves as investigating paranormal phenomena, and some are true to that aspiration, employing a relatively scientific methodology. The majority, however, fall back on traditional views of spirits and other presences subsisting in a parallel, unseen (i.e. occult) world.

David Icke Syndrome

I happened some time ago to be in Bristol with time to kill, so I popped into a bookshop for a look around the Alternative Everything section, something I do from time to time. There I browsed through a book by David Icke, former Coventry and Hereford goalkeeper, BBC sports commentator, and environmentalist, and now a widely-acclaimed guru. This particular book started off promisingly with a lot of interesting thoughts on royal families and heads of state, delineating how they are all connected, then going into conspiracy theory mode on the control of world power. A bit tenuous at points, I thought, but worth pursuing. However, on turning a few more pages I discovered the reason for all this.

Apparently these rulers are in some way descended from a lizard race that came to the earth thousands of years ago and interbred with humans.

These, and many other claims, are a kind of secret wisdom now revealed through Icke's meticulous research. In his view there always seems to be something going on behind the scenes, and his job is to help us all to see what it is. For people like Icke the challenge is not so much to contact a parallel world like that of the occultist, but to understand the things we know with a deeper insight, somewhat like the Greek *gnosis* of old.

My experience in Bristol was a bit of a Damascus Road for me (or, more correctly, a bit of an M5, but that doesn't quite resonate). Suddenly daftness was everywhere. Aliens, cosmic force fields, crop circles, corporate astrology—and so on. The list seems endless. Like David Icke, most of these folk appear to be perfectly sincere, and when not pursuing their particular belief do not seem daft at all, although there are exceptions. Our local *Waterstones* has gradually cleared out much of its computer section and expanded the Alternative Everything shelves. It's as easy to get a volume on psychospiritual quilt breeding as it is to get something on, say, *Photoshop*. There is certainly no let-up in the proliferation of alternative beliefs.

Alien Abduction

All this seems very strange in a time of increasing scientific understanding and educational attainment. We should note also various overlaps. Some "alternative" beliefs overlap with popular psychology and with business practice, which could affect attitudes to valid work in areas such as motivational psychology. Others may veer towards the closed-off world of the cults. Yet others seem to form a wide base for an essentially human need, a theme perceptively explored by Bryan Appleyard in *Aliens: Why they are here*.

The most intriguing phenomenon examined by Appleyard is the claim to have been abducted by aliens, a particularly frequent claim in the USA and a development of the earlier trend of claims to having been in contact with alien beings. In fact, polls suggest that millions of Americans claim to have had the abduction experience. Whatever the exact number this is clearly a common occurrence, and one can even buy insurance against it—presumably covering the costs of treatment for any physical harm, psychotherapy, loss of income and so on.

It sounds bizarre, yet the fact is that most of those claiming this experience would not be classed as mentally unstable by normal clinical criteria, unless of course a claim to abduction is taken by definition as a sign of such instability. The problem with making such a definition is that, logically, one would have to deliver a similar verdict on many more people who claim to have seen UFOs, say they have communicated with departed spirits, or lay claim to out of the body experiences or psychic knowledge. Add in ghosts, premonitions, and other common phenomena and you will pretty soon be classifying most of humanity as mad.

There is, of course, no scientifically repeatable evidence to verify the claims of "abductees" (or of the earlier "contactees"). It is objectively true, however, that a large number of people have experienced something extremely vivid to them, which they describe in similar terms to each other. While it is difficult to imagine, therefore, that every day a large number of alien spaceships manage to land, do their abducting and leave without detection, some supporters claim that the phenomenon is real but takes place in a psychic dimension not accessible to those outside the experience. Sceptics, of course, regard the whole thing as purely psychological, a modern expression of a mythology stretching back through goblins, the "old hag", witches, hauntings and numerous other elements of folklore. The fact that common features are shared between stories can be explained by the imagery propagated by the media, or by theories of a collective unconscious.

Cults and Charisma

For my final example, I turn to religious cults. Recently, as part of our extravagant *Easyjet* lifestyle, my wife and I were walking through Prague on our way from the old town to Wenceslas Square. Suddenly, dancing around the corner from a cross street, came the mother of all *Hare Krishna* bands— very high volume on account of a backpack PA system, which seemed a bit against the spirit of the thing—and including two women in sari-like outfits with small cymbals. With immaculate performance skills they assembled into two lines facing each other and went into a kind of line-dance. At this point my wife, being of Methodist stock, dragged me away to something more important like shopping.

Unfortunately, the secretive world of cults is not merely an entertainment phenomenon. ISKCON, the movement behind the street chanters, is relatively open compared to most, yet even there it's possible to see something which is common to extreme religious movements. I can only call it the "glazed but happy" look—a rather fixed expression of joy, coupled with a kind of not seeming to be quite there. I have noticed this type of thing since the cults really took off in the seventies, at which time the "moonies" were the best known and probably the most aggressive. Incidentally, older movements such as the Mormons and Jehovah's Witnesses used to be called cults by the more mainstream religions, but that is now inappropriate. They do not have the same overwhelmingly manipulative approach.

The Broader Picture

I have touched on five categories of irrationality: re-enactment, the occult, secret knowledge, alien abduction, and religious cults. There are various ways in which these can be graded or arranged into a rough spectrum.

The re-enactors know, initially at least, why they are doing what they are doing—inasmuch as it goes beyond simply having a good time, they are seeking to preserve something that they feel is important. Many of those who do not belong to their groups can at least understand what they are about, and may take an interest in what they do. Cults, on the other hand, generally have their own distinctive and all-encompassing world view, to the point where the majority of people have to make a great "leap of faith" to become involved with them. Some propagate their own cosmology and anthropology, while for others it's more to do with accepting a peculiar version of Christianity or another mainstream religion (Hinduism in the case of ISKCON). The need for this intellectual jump accounts for the almost universal accusations of coercion that are made against cults, accusations that are largely justified.

Re-enactors and cultists, then, stand at the extreme ends of a spectrum stretching from voluntary support of a *personal* cause or interest, to coerced support of a *group* cause or interest. The other differentiating feature that perhaps separates out those between the two extremes is the claimed evidence for their beliefs. Those who enthuse about the occult will claim that there is observable proof of their parallel world, while sceptics question this. Others, such as Icke, view the facts of this world with their own interpretation or gnosis. The abductee speaks of a personal experience so intense that it validates itself, at least to those who experience it. Note, however, that this is not a spectrum of rationality. This is an absolutely crucial point, and worth underlining.

If you asked the committed re-enactor to explain his cause, he would certainly be able to give a reasonable first-level explanation of what he does. For example, the academic would say something about affirming the historic place of education in our culture. He might continue to a second level—that historic place exists because of the perceived value of education down the ages. But why is education valuable? A third-level explanation might be offered, but eventually the reason is simply that the academic believes in education, and so do many others. The cultist merely leaves out the preliminary stages and jumps straight to the conclusion: "I believe in trapezoidal yeng-samdara beta transformation, and so do many others." It's not a question of *whether* the irrational will rear its head, but *when*.

There is much more that could be said on this subject, but for now I'm simply pointing out an element of our humanity, the urge to daftness. Reason alone is seldom sufficient for us humans. There are those, of course, who deliberately seek inexplicable experiences, and play into the hands of charlatans of one sort or another. The James Randi and Derren Brown schools of debunking are at their best in pointing out the susceptibilies of those actively seeking something out of the ordinary, who are probably the most vulnerable to psychological suggestion.

Two more brief points before putting all of this into context. First, followers of mainstream religion are not immune from the irrationality dealt with in this chapter. However, I have explicitly acknowledged the daftness to be found in fundamentalism, and implicitly acknowledged the same tendency when it has occurred down the centuries in Christianity. I mentioned, for example, the popular fanaticism that contributed to the Crusades, elements of anti-Judaism, and the activities of some of the splinter groups created during the Reformation. Mainstreamers are never totally separated from the surrounding culture and can easily absorb the daftness most on offer at any one time. The difference is that the sense of continuity and universality of a major faith tends either to defuse radical new movements or absorb them in a way that, in time, mitigates their worst features.

Second, there is one category that I have excluded from discussion in this chapter, namely, unsought strange experiences, of which the most common are the "mute ghost" (sometimes called a "place memory" or "residual"), short-term premonitions, thought-transference and mild poltergeist phenomena. Among these the ghost is probably the best attested, with a recent UK survey by the think tank *Theos* finding that 40% of those asked believe in ghosts, 15% because of personal experience. From now on I shall simply call these "paranormal experiences" and we shall look at them more fully later, but one major question calls for immediate attention.

Whatever Happened to the Enlightenment?

We have seen up to now three reactions to the Enlightenment. First there was atheism, derived mainly from European materialism. Second, we looked at evangelicalism and its origins in the mainstream Reformation. Third, there was the attempt to return to and re-state deeply rooted "big ideas", especially those of natural theology. This often involved a scientific reworking of traditional beliefs, sometimes with a deistic slant. We can now add a fourth strand, for it seems clear that while the Enlightenment cultural leadership proclaimed the age of reason, they also engaged in a dramatic leap into unreason.

No sooner had the Reformation settled down and the Enlightenment got under way than the reformed and enlightened obviously became bored. Jacob Boehme (1575–1624) was a German shoemaker inspired by personal visions. He was a Lutheran but also studied esoteric beliefs, both medieval and ancient. Although heretical, he was influential on succeeding generations, sowing seeds that were taken up by others. Avowed followers were known as Behmenists, but most of his influence was through his writings rather than any type of organisation.

Emanuel Swedenborg (1688–1772) was a prolific, and highly respected, Swedish philosopher and scientist—the first to propose the nebular theory of the formation of the solar system. However, in the mid-eighteenth century he turned to mysticism and theology, producing his own version of Christianity and claiming to communicate with angels and spirits. (Newton's proclivities in this direction are well known, but without the claim to direct communication, as far as I know.) I confess to not having read Swedenborg myself, but apparently his work, even after his revelatory experience, is pretty coherent, not what you would expect from madness but simply the work of someone seeing things from an unusual point of view.

The *Bavarian Illuminati* were founded in 1776 by Adam Weishaupt, with the purpose of creating a new world order free of monarchies and ecclesiastical authorities. By this time secret societies were quite the fashion, with the Rosicrucians and Freemasons making great progress from around 1600 onwards, so Weishaupt was building on this model, and also making use of insights from his Jesuit education. The potential for conspiracy theory is obvious, and such an accusation was first made as early as 1798—long before David Icke or Dan Brown. The movement itself had been outlawed as seditious in Bavaria in 1784.

These esoteric movements influenced many individuals. Although they are very different from each other, and have various divisions within themselves, there are certain significant common features. First, they are most often deistic and unitarian, denying the necessity of Christian doctrines such as the trinity. Second, they tend to believe in the potential for human moral improvement rather than in the Christian perspective of original sin. Third, they generally believe in the existence of occult knowledge. Fourth, the key members of these movements are frequently highly intellectual people, often within the scientific sphere. Fifth, such movements unapologetically appeal to the irrational side of human nature—gaining knowledge through direct revelation, communicating with spirits, or performing rituals that link with some kind of cosmic *gnosis*. Sixth, they are often eclectic, drawing together several western and eastern traditions, ancient and more recent.

The Victorian Drawing Room

The eclectic tendency is most clearly seen in *Theosophy*, founded by Mme Helena Blavatsky (1831–91) and two colleagues in 1875, but this remained a small movement, although influential. *Spiritualism*, on the other hand, became a major growth industry from the mid-nineteenth century onwards, because of its popular and simple aspiration to contact the departed through mediums. In Victorian middle-class England, when not engaged with the latest piece of heavyweight theology such as *Essays and Reviews* or *Lux Mundi*, it was fairly routine to attend a seance or try out the craze of mesmerism, named after Franz Mesmer but now generally known as hypnotism. The aim of the hypnotic trance was not to provide entertainment or therapy, but to contact spirits.

Much that claimed to be paranormal was, of course, fakery. Even so spiritualism in various forms grew, and won the support of many of the good and great, famously including William Crookes, Lord Rayleigh, Alfred Russel Wallace, William James, and Sir Arthur Conan Doyle. The tragedy of the First World War is generally held to have further facilitated the growth of mediumship. The movement continues to the present day, both informally, as the Spiritualist Church, and as other associations.

Spiritualist elements can be found aplenty in the "New Age" movement, but that movement also includes a vast range of other ideas of a psychic, religious, and astrological nature. The term "New Age" is an umbrella for much that developed during the second half of the twentieth century and even includes some so-called alternative therapies that are gaining *guarded* medical acceptance. The dawning of *the Age of Aquarius* may have created a unified cosmic consciousness, but it certainly did not create a unified set of earthly beliefs.

This is all at a popular level, of course, although again it has to be said that many adherents of these movements were and are highly intelligent. There has also developed a strong tradition of scientific investigation, exemplified by the *Society for Psychical Research*. The SPR was founded in 1882 and has had many dignified presidents, including three Nobel Prize winners and many other academics. Although dealing with the irrational, organisations like the SPR have clearly moved away from daftness to scientific investigation. However, the academic respectability bestowed by such investigation is sometimes misused by others. The well-known interest of Carl Jung in spirituality, psychic phenomena, and even UFOs is vulnerable to similar misuse.

Putting all this in very broad terms, it does seem that alongside the growth of Enlightenment knowledge there is a parallel interest, even among the knowledgeable, in those areas that we normally term irrational. As time went on alchemy worked its way out of relevancy with the development of chemistry. Likewise, astronomy displaced astrology and mathematics displaced numerology. Nevertheless, the non-existent God of the atheist and the rather remote God of the deist seemed to leave a gap, which for many was filled by the esoteric.

In some of its elements our modern irrationality overlaps with that broad movement known as *romanticism*, which is sometimes linked to the idea that there was a counter-enlightenment movement in the late eighteenth and nineteenth centuries. There are certainly connections—attempts to get away from mere rationality to mythology, intuition, aesthetics, emotion, and mystery, for example—but endless classification gives us little increase in understanding of why cultural movements occur. I have not created a further category for romanticism because it seems to me to cut across many others. Thus one can have romanticised religion such as the later Victorian Gothic Anglican style, or romanticised atheism, as is often found in non-religious funeral ceremonies, or romanticised science, as found in the presentation of much popular science.

The Stage is Set

The post-enlightenment period has not witnessed the emergence of a powerful rational consensus concerning the great issues of life and death, of meaning and morality. The removal of ecclesiastical authority did not resolve such questions, it merely ensured that the proposed answers became increasingly diverse. Behind the diversity lies our old friend epistemology, for the question of *how we know things* is prior to the particular question of how we might know religious truth and ultimately how we might know God. Some claim that observation and reason are the basis of all knowledge. Some believe in revelation. Some lay claim to direct inspiration. Some devise their own mixture of beliefs.

These issues were all in play, and somewhat gridlocked, when *The Origin of Species* came onto the scene. In fact, we could call this the "Post-Enlightenment Gridlock", or "PEG" for those who like acronyms. Punmeisters can reflect on how much of our subsequent history hung on that peg.

The issues involved did not, of course, merely provide material for drawing room discussion, but influenced (and were influenced by) the huge social and political movements of the time. Such forces were always in the background, and sometimes the foreground. The struggle against a generally conservative establishment attitude, in the name of progress, is a recurring theme. The sheer momentum of science, which I outlined in Chapter 3, is another.

The brilliant and revolutionary work of Charles Darwin, then, did not take place in a vacuum—and neither did the ensuing controversies. The stage had been set for a potentially fruitless debate by over two hundred years of discussion about conservative Christianity, deism, atheism, science, esoteric ideas, natural religion, liberal Christianity, and progressive thinking. That is why we are still arguing with such fervour today.

CHAPTER 5

Mr Charles Darwin had the Gall to Ask

If you are not a fan of the late-lamented band *REM* then the meaning of the title of this chapter will be a mystery. If you are a fan it will still be a mystery even though you recognise *Man on the Moon*—the band's lyrics are not noted for clarity—but they do throw out some interesting questions at times. What exactly *did* Mr Charles Darwin ask?

Simply put, Darwin asked where the diversity in the living world came from. However, he did not start from a blank slate. Some sixty years or so before the publication of the *Origin of Species* his grandfather, Erasmus Darwin, together with the Frenchman Jean-Baptiste Lamarck and other lesser lights, were quite sure that complex organisms developed from simpler ones. Such ideas had been suggested by philosophers as long ago as the first century BCE, but without scientific evidence to support them. Early progress in fields such as comparative anatomy and palaeontology, from the sixteenth century onwards, began to give support to the general notion of development, adding credibility to early views.

Vestiges of the Natural History of Creation, written anonymously in 1844 by the Scottish writer and publisher Robert Chambers, extended the evolutionary principle to the physical world. The book became extremely well known, and "guess the author" was a popular pastime among the Victorian intelligentsia, at least on days when they weren't beefing up on theology or contacting spirits. The general idea of evolution, then, was already in the air, being espoused by "progressives"—radicals, freethinkers, liberal Christians, and atheists. It was not viewed so sympathetically by the more conservative scientists and Christians—they were the parties that complained about Mr Charles Darwin's gall.

Mr Charles Darwin's second question was more specific. Given that "transmutation of species" occurred, how did it come about? How did development occur in succeeding generations of a living organism to the point where eventually a new species had arisen? Yet Darwin's answer—natural selection through variation and the survival of the fittest—was not unique to him. Alfred Russel Wallace (1823–1913) worked on a theory similar to that of Darwin and is regarded by many as the rightful co-founder of "Darwinism". Darwin's vast wealth of evidence and clarity of expression, however, gave him the higher profile. In addition, Darwin was much more the right sort of chap. Wallace continued to hold religious beliefs, and held that some kind of Spirit must have intervened in the creation of life, consciousness, and the human spirit. He also adopted spiritualism and was given to supporting populist political theories rather too openly. None of this helped his cause as far as the scientific establishment was concerned, although Darwin recognised his expertise and lobbied successfully to obtain for him a government pension, which I find rather moving.

Surprisingly, though, the concept of natural selection did not predominate. Even many of Darwin's friends found it odd, including his normally staunch defender T. H. Huxley. By the early 1900s, although it was accepted that Darwin had offered brilliant and incontrovertible evidence for evolution as a process, natural selection was almost dead on its feet. Wallace and the German biologist August Weismann (1834–1914) were practically alone in still maintaining its validity.

Social Science

The main importance of evolution after the publication of *Origin* was philosophical as much as scientific. The general idea of evolution boosted the liberal tendency within Christianity as expressed in *Essays and Reviews*, but "survival of the fittest" also added weight, as we saw in Chapter 1, to the arguments (often misrepresented) of Marx, Nietzsche, and the eugenics movement. In addition Darwin's son Leonard was a leading light in that movement well into the twentieth century, and we previously noted the similar influence of his half-cousin Francis Galton. Selective compulsory sterilisation was accepted in many countries (but not in Britain) until after the Second World War. Today, of course, such precepts are regarded as gross violations of human rights. Wallace, incidentally, did not support eugenics.

From 1900 onwards the work of the monk Gregor Mendel (1822–1884) on inheritance was rediscovered. This allowed the development of a statistically rigorous genetic basis for variation, eventually leading by the middle of the century to the synthesis that we now regard as the scientific understanding of evolution.

We have seen that those who did not accept the atheistic response to the Enlightenment had a huge reserve of "big ideas"—theological ideas—on which to draw. Some took these in a fundamentalist way, some in a more liberal way. Others delved into the esoteric, with its eclectic mix of longstanding traditions. Atheism, by comparison, was a relative newcomer to the belief industry and therefore eagerly rolled out the red carpet for Darwinism.

Dawkins stands honourably within this Victorian tradition. Yet, despite his eminence in his own field, an eminence that is abundantly clear in his purely scientific writings, he puts forward a poor argument regarding the non-existence of God. As I remarked earlier, he seeks to underpin his atheism with anything he can, and now it's the turn of science, his strongest card.

The Scope of Science

Many schemes can be drawn up showing science and religion occupying different "domains" or "magisteria". Dawkins discusses these with a view to claiming that religion should not be exempt from the attention of rigorous science. I absolutely agree. However, if we are going to open up religious claims in this way it seems only right to establish what science can and cannot prove, especially in the area of the existence and activity of any alleged God.

Science proceeds by hypothesis, observation and experiment, and it will be helpful at this point to look at three landmark examples.

Einstein's *General Theory of Relativity* predicted the deflection of light rays by the mass of the sun. In 1919 Sir Arthur Eddington travelled to the island of Principe off the west coast of Africa in order to observe the solar eclipse, and brought back evidence showing that Einstein was correct, as well as giving the islanders a claim to fame which is still celebrated and proclaimed by their tourism board.

Returning to the Victorians for a moment, it was generally believed that light needed a medium (termed the *luminiferous ether*) through which it could be transmitted. This was disproved by the famous Michelson-Morley experiment of 1887, which aimed to measure the "drag" on light waves when a light source was moved relative to the supposed ether. No drag was detected, disproving the theory of the ether. Pretty good for an experiment that was, strictly speaking, a failure.

Even earlier, we had the *phlogiston theory,* broadly accepted in the eighteenth century. This was an explanation of what occurs when a substance burns. It's obvious that something drastic happens because the resulting substance is very different from what was there before. Wood is nothing like ash. The received explanation was that during combustion a substance called *phlogiston* was lost. Along with the experimentation of others, Lavoisier showed that in fact oxygen was gained during combustion, before losing his head in the French Revolution. He was later exonerated of all crimes, but that didn't help him very much in a practical sense.

In all three cases the key factor was observation. On the basis of such observation, either of the natural order or of circumstances deliberately produced in an experiment, reasoned conclusions are drawn. That's the essence of the scientific method. We uncover scientific facts by looking, testing, and thinking, not by meditating, perusing a holy book, or reading the entrails of dead animals. Obviously, then, the pressing question for both the atheist and the theist is, "What proposed observation could prove the existence of God?"

I am not alone in confessing that I cannot think of such an experiment. If the light beam deviation mentioned above had been noticed before Einstein, I doubt that anyone would have declared it a proof of the existence of

God. No, other observation posts would be set up for similar events and the repeatability found would lead to a modification of scientific understanding, not to the invocation of a *deus ex machina*. Even if such a modification were not immediately available it would be assumed that the paradox would be resolved—some day.

My Career in Science: the Early Years

Shortly after my arrival at that august local institution *The Grammar School for Boys, Gateshead* our student teacher managed to explode a glass hydrogen generator. As we came out from under the benches, looking for glass embedded in each other's faces, the head of chemistry came in and instructed the said student teacher on how to avoid doing that again. A bit late, but at least an important conviction was planted, namely, that chemistry was certainly more entertaining than Latin.

More seriously, a genuine milestone for me occurred in biology, dissecting a dogfish. Seeing how everything fitted together was one of those genuine "a-ha" moments, where it all made sense. Some things seem to have a quality of revelation about them, and I still remember it clearly. Fortunately, my "study buddy" in this exercise was equally fascinated and we carried out other dissections at home—his father was a part-time chiropodist, so we were able to get our hands on cheap scalpels.

Finally, there was sixth-form physics with Mr Hawkins, unsurprisingly known as "Jack", under whose supervision I recollect performing an experiment to determine Planck's constant, the ratio of the energy of a photon (E) to its frequency (ν). I don't remember the details, but the experiment involved coloured glass filters, a light, a photoelectric cell and a galvanometer. Even though I seem to remember the margin of error was at least 50%, the idea of being able to show that $E=h\nu$ was quite something. I already knew about $E=mc^2$ and so could have moved on to reconcile quantum mechanics and relativity, but the school's facilities did not extend to a particle accelerator. The disillusionment was so great that I eventually turned to theology, but the scientific yearning never completely died.

The Wilderness Period

Following my move into theology I became an armchair scientist, an interested observer of goings on, but generally occupied with other matters. However, all was not lost. The coffee table acquired more and more learned volumes over the years. *Brief History of Time, Blind Watchmaker, Fermat's Last Theorem* and so on. But my interest was just that—interest.

Even having acquired the ambition to become a theologian I never thought that scientific experimentation could *in principle* prove the existence of God, and that fact was never a source of sleepless nights. This might seem complacent, but was based on a fairly sound argument. If science cannot prove the existence of God, then that means that science cannot *disprove* the existence of God either. It's obvious that any experiment that can prove the non-existence of God must also be able to prove his existence. Otherwise, when the result "no God" came back every time, how would we know whether this were a true conclusion or just a feature of the experiment? The same demand is made in all science. On any other basis the three landmark experiments referred to above would not have been landmarks at all, merely interesting curiosities.

Yet those who claim that science disproves the existence of God never seem to tell us what experimental evidence would prove his existence. I strongly believe that truth is indivisible and that there is no room for obscurantism, but Dawkins seems to want a one-way bet. He wants to make a *scientific* claim about the non-existence of God. He rubbishes the idea of science and religion as "non-overlapping magisteria" (NOMA), a term aptly coined by Stephen Jay Gould, the eminent American palaeontologist, reflecting a frequently held view among the more conciliatory members of both the science and theology communities. We have already seen that Dawkins regards such views from the scientific side as equivalent to appeasement, an altogether shameful thing.

Almost is Not Enough

Because of the above reasoning it is hardly surprising that the title of the fourth chapter of *The God Delusion* is, "Why there almost certainly is no God". Even though not surprising, it's rather disappointing in view of the hype given to the book. Is this the best that scientific atheism can do? *Almost?*

The key illustration (attributed to astronomer Fred Hoyle) is that of the hurricane and the scrap yard. One day a hurricane sweeps through the scrap yard and when the dust settles, *voila!* Purely by chance a Boeing 747 has been assembled from the bits and pieces lying around. It doesn't take much knowledge of statistics to see how unlikely this is. We should be thankful for this illustration, for without it I should have had to expound at length on my personal encounter with the dogfish, which would not be so easy on the imagination. I can still smell the formaldehyde all these years later.

Dawkins famously argues in *The Blind Watchmaker* that in the case of inanimate objects such as pieces of metal the chance assembling of the Boeing 747 is indeed so unlikely as to be termed, in normal parlance, impossible. However, evolution is not like that, because it is guided by the process of natural selection, which does not apply to aircraft, only to living matter.

At this point I need to make a full and frank admission. My coffee table, as well as hosting books by the good guys already mentioned, has also been home to Michael Behe's book, *Darwin's Black Box*. I'm not a biochemist, but with my substantial background in science already outlined I found this no problem. In fact, Behe explains himself so well that a wide audience could understand his case. The problem he highlights is that some parts of organisms, particularly at the level of cell biochemistry, exhibit what he calls *irreducible complexity*, which in his view implies intelligent design, at least in some stages of evolution. Irreducible complexity means that a useful mechanism cannot be reduced to something simpler without losing its usefulness. It's hard to see how something irreducibly complex could evolve by small simple steps, because there would be no advantage, to the organism concerned, in any one such step in isolation.

It is this process whereby thousands of small steps may be taken to produce (apparently designed) complexity that is at the very heart of Dawkins arguments on the biological front. His view is unquestionably elegant, and in *Climbing Mount Improbable* he explains it with a stunning poetic grandeur and beautiful illustrations. So it's hardly surprising that the thought of irreducible complexity really gets him annoyed. Unfortunately, before answering Behe's arguments for the benefit of the wider reading public who invested emotionally and financially in *The God Delusion*, he spends considerable time on the following: eulogising Douglas Adams (a great writer and personality but not a scientist), attacking the "God of the Gaps" approach to theology (which is not widely followed in the mainstream church or theological world) and knocking down the Creationist assertions of a book published by the *Watchtower Bible and Tract Society* (aka Jehovah's Witnesses). This all amounts to about a third of this pivotal chapter.

This does seem an insult. Those of us who have some contact with the world of marketing can perhaps see a little more clearly than most what's happening here: associate the brand (atheism) with someone generally admired (Douglas Adams); imply that anyone who does not value the brand practices underhand activities ("God of the Gaps" thinking); associate rival brands with an organisation that is not widely admired (Jehovah's Witnesses); and broadly group together all opponents under one over-generalised smear word ("Creationist"). In case we haven't got the message, Dawkins adds a snide little footnote that "Intelligent design has been unkindly described as Creationism in a cheap tuxedo." So what?

An Unsatisfactory Answer

Shooting the messenger doesn't disprove the message. It's intriguing to note that Victor Stenger in *God: the Failed Hypothesis* (p56) is similarly irrational, claiming that the problems raised by Behe had all been addressed by H. J. Muller, the renowned geneticist, in 1939. Is he really implying that knowledge of cell biochemistry has made no progress since then? I somehow think that much of the evidence cited by Behe has arisen much more recently than that, and could hardly have been answered in 1939 except through some kind of psychic channelling. Stenger then goes on to point out that Behe is a biochemist, not an evolutionary biologist. Well, Stenger himself is neither, though undoubtedly a significant physicist. What's his point?

Dawkins likewise chooses to attack Behe in a very personal way. When he addresses Behe's argument about the bacterial flagellar motor, for example, he does so in a somewhat condescending manner. The flagellum is a filament, projecting from the bacterial cell membrane, that rotates and acts as a propeller. The flagellar motor drives the flagellum, and the biochemical mechanism involved is very complex. Dawkins points out that certain elements of the motor's mechanism can be found in other bacterial biochemical mechanisms. "Commandeering existing mechanisms is an obvious way" to develop new ones. Which seems fine until you ask *how* exactly this happened.

Who did the commandeering? John Lennox points out an interesting feature that occurs in Dawkins' writings, namely, the tendency to personalise processes that are claimed to be impersonal. Since he uses crucial phrases like "selfish gene" and "blind watchmaker" which he explains, the impression is given that this is merely a harmless way of speaking, even when the meaning is *not* explained. Lennox calls this a "sleight of mind" and his criticism seems to be valid here. The implicit question, "obvious *to whom?*" is just left hanging.

The process we are discussing here is known as *exaptation*, and there are certainly many examples of it happening. Yet when it comes to intricate mechanisms such as we are discussing, Lennox's criticism carries some weight. How did a little piece of biochemical engineering that originally (for example) hauled a molecule of toxic protein through the bacterial cell wall come to be tugging on molecules on the motor "armature" so that, as part of a much more complex and co-ordinated mechanism, it effects a turning motion? What could have been the small in-between steps, and, most important, what would have been the enhanced survival value of each of these small steps? Remember, each step has to be advantageous for survival, facilitating reproduction, or at least not disadvantageous, for the change to persist. (The question of neutral changes is dealt with in more detail later, so I beg the patience of those who are aware of that issue).

These seem to me like reasonable questions, not grounds for a dismissive attitude. However, most of us have little concept of the bacterial flagellar motor and they don't sell them in Halfords, so I think it's easier to talk about the evolution of the eye—an *incredibly* intricate imaging device, as we all know. Paley, Darwin, and Dawkins all spend time on this, so I'm standing on the shoulders of giants.

The complexity of the eye seems to demand a designer—this is Paley's whole point, of course. However, the neo-Darwinist view is that there were thousands of small steps that each occurred one after the other, through random genetic mutation, and some persisted. Why? Because they offered some kind of advantage in the struggle for survival. In *The Blind Watchmaker* Dawkins is quite happy to allow us to imagine 100,000 steps, more if necessary. In *River Out of Eden* we are told that the necessary steps would take less than half a million years. This was the result of computer modelling carried out by two Swedish scientists, Dan Nilsson and Susanne Pelger. *Climbing Mount Improbable* is more specific (in its treatment of the same model) at 364,000 years in order to accomplish the 1,829 steps required by the computer-generated model.

I ought perhaps to say, before jumping in at the deep end on this, that I have a love-hate relationship with intelligent design. I don't buy into it in the sense that God steps in from time to time to modify, against the laws of nature, the course of evolution. The obvious question attached to such an idea is this: if God tinkers in the natural order of things, why does he not tinker a bit more and simply sort out, at a stroke, the persistent problems that we see in our world?

However, that is a theological question, not a scientific one. My other reason (apart from fear of wearing a cheap tuxedo) for not jumping right into the intelligent design camp is scientific. I believe that the issues raised under the heading of irreducible complexity are utterly real, but also that intelligent design supporters perhaps do not try hard enough to resolve those questions before drawing their conclusions.

The discussion that forms my next chapter in some ways seems like a throwback to the half-century or so following Mr Charles Darwin's original questioning. The reason for this is simple: the "Post-Enlightenment Gridlock" of which I have spoken was not, and is not, resolved. Like the arguments in a troubled marriage, the same issues are discussed repeatedly, in the hope that the ever-beckoning divorce can somehow be avoided. My excuse for going round the loop yet again is that there just might be a resolution that would save the situation by breaking out in a new direction—if only for the sake of the children.

CHAPTER 6

The Evolutionary Enigma

Discussion on the eye usually starts from the idea that through random mutation and natural selection a creature evolved with a few cells that were sensitive to light. I always imagine this as being similar to having one's eyes shut but being able to detect light and dark. In a dangerous predatory environment this would appear to offer a distinct advantage to survival, compared to not having any light sensitivity at all. It seems so obvious—but bear with me, please, while we carry out a little thought experiment on this "obvious" scenario.

Meet Protoworm

Imagine a creature such as, for example, a predecessor of the earthworm, maybe with a couple of clumps of nerve cells or *ganglia* at one end, a primitive forerunner of the human brain. This proto-brain has very little processing power. It's definitely the ZX80 of the brain world. In case you weren't there or didn't care, the ZX80 was an early home computer, launched in 1980 by Sir Clive Sinclair.

Our hypothetical worm comes along millions of years later than the time when the earth looked like a mass of congealed lentil soup, so there is actually some dirt for our primitive worm to burrow around in and emerge from. Unfortunately, when it does emerge, there is the primeval equivalent of the Early Bird waiting for lunch to arrive. Early Bird may of course not be a bird, but you get my drift.

Of what advantage is it to our newly adaptive worm that when it does emerge it can detect light and dark? The fact that a number of synapses in the primitive brain fire just before it gets eaten doesn't seem to offer much advantage—even supposing that the chain of mutations bringing about the sensitivity to light had also caused the formation of some primitive optic nerve. How would the ZX80 brain determine that an impulse from this nerve didn't just mean the skin was being touched by soil or vegetation, like it used to in all previous generations, but now has a newfangled meaning to do with something called "light"?

A further problem is that Protoworm would have to possess not only the light-sensing cells and some kind of primitive optic nerve, but also a link to motor activity that would move it out of harm's way. There are only two ways that this could happen. The first would be a reflex—a direct connection between the light stimulus and the "flight response" as we should

85

call it nowadays. Therefore, we would now need to add to our list a third requirement, namely an automatic muscular, pneumatic, or hydraulic action of some sort that would fling Protoworm out of the way of Early Bird. The second way in which the escape could happen would be some kind of understanding of the danger at hand, some sort of consciousness, however primitive.

The difficulty with the reflex idea is that the information conveyed by primitive light sensing is likely to be highly ambiguous. Does a sudden decrease in light intensity mean that the predator is moving towards or away from Protoworm? It would depend on the position of the sun and the predator. Here's another problem. If Early Bird is moving away, then a reflex jump might just attract his attention and cause the very fate that supposedly this primitive eye is said to help avoid. And how does Protoworm "know" in which direction to jump (assuming that there are options in this)? It might jump towards the predator instead of away from it.

Consciousness

Having wracked my ganglia over the matter, it seems to me that no kind of automatic response can really help very much. We have to impute to lowly creatures like Protoworm and thousands of others some kind of primitive consciousness, which is of course a highly dangerous thought likely to be influenced by our natural anthropomorphic tendencies. In fact, walking around with my eyes shut imagining what may or may not be there (and how dangerous it might be) is an extremely bad parallel—I have a human brain with all the other senses to help, including proprioception (the sense of one's own body position); and this is all backed up by a lifetime of learning about my environment and the likely hazards therein. Nevertheless, even while taking into account the dangers of anthropomorphism, it does seem that some kind of consciousness—though extremely rudimentary to be sure—is essential if the primitive eye is to offer survival advantages.

Immediately, of course, one can undermine this proposal by supposing that the main predator, as far as our worm friend is concerned, is not agile, but only marginally faster than a thoroughbred slug. A sophisticated response would not be required, almost anything would do. That's a fair comment, to which I would reply, "How likely is it that such a creature would cause a sufficiently rapid change in light intensity (rapid enough, say, not to be just a cloud passing over) to be detected by a primitive light detector such as we are supposing to have mutated into being?" Even if this charge fails, the problem of *interpretation* of the stimulus remains. Protoworm is still just as likely to move closer to Protoslug than further away. It is also quite likely to attract Protoslug's attention, which otherwise was directed elsewhere.

My purpose here is simply to point out that even an apparently simple piece of adaptive behaviour can actually be quite complex. This fact seems indisputable, but is frequently omitted in presentations of the process of evolution. However, having established that fact, I can now admit to the omissions in the story so far.

To start the ball rolling, it could be objected that Protoworm's light-sensing abilities originated millions of years earlier in its ancestors. Originally, the simple light-sensing ability could have been extremely valuable to Protoworm in preventing it from *accidentally* surfacing and making itself available to predators. Alternatively, we might suppose that Protoworm originally occupied an aquatic environment. We might devise a different scenario in which avoiding shade was always beneficial—maybe that was one way of ensuring a good supply of nutrition from phytoplankton, which have to inhabit the sunlit upper layer of the oceans.

It is an easy trap to fall into, when considering complexity, to assume that the context we see in the present has always been that way. In fact, we could go even further. The simple light-sensitive patch did not come into existence in one generation—light sensitivity goes right back to monocellular creatures like *euglena*, which has such a patch or "photoreceptor" to assist in maximising its light input. This is a Good Thing because it photosynthesises like plants, even though it can also absorb food like an animal. This is simply adapting to survive, with no designer needed.

Such a counter claim certainly carries much weight, but—as you might have guessed—this argument also has some difficulties contained in it. First, if we allow ourselves unbridled speculation, the same tactics could be used against *any* claim of irreducible complexity. It will surely always be possible to construct a complex hypothetical chain of events showing what could have happened, which seems to devalue the argument. As I remarked in my previous chapter, it is essential for any claim meriting the epithet "scientific" to be disprovable.

A second, and more substantive problem, is that we are still left with an area of paradox. If we take the discussion back to the single-celled *euglena*, or even some precursor of which we can now know nothing, there must have been a point at which the photosensitivity appeared—but so what? It must have been able to generate a positive movement towards the light in order to produce any benefit. The problem of my Protoworm illustration may be greatly diminished, but it is not completely eliminated.

Third, we might note that discussion about light sensitive spots or patches is usually deceptive, as if such things were easy to create. They aren't. Light sensitivity requires a sequence of many complex reactions. How could that evolve in small jumps, each of them being advantageous *on its own*?

Fourth, the photosensitive spot in *euglena* is a tiny organelle, part of one cell, whereas the sensitive area found in multicellular animals comprises a huge number of more complex cells, each with different functions but acting together as a *system*. The implication of this is profound.

Systems

I apologise if my illustration initially seems childish, but I believe it brings out a vital point in the current discussion. For my photosensitive worm I cannot see that the extremely primitive eye alone conveys any benefit without some kind of consciousness, however rudimentary. Thinking back to possible antecedents, the level of consciousness required may be little more than a simple stimulus-response loop, barely meriting the name at all. Nevertheless, in parallel with increases in light sensitivity and then image formation, there must have been a growth in consciousness, even though we might wish to use a different term for it in its earliest stages.

It is hard to see the usefulness of even a complex eye like ours that can see in colour, with incredible focusing and correctional mechanisms, if that organ did not have the back-up of our highly-developed optic nerve, visual cortex and general brain power. These are all necessary for us to interpret images, meanings and indeed possible actions to be taken as a result of what is seen. In other words, the whole is greater than the sum of the parts—which is what we mean by a system. Each part needs the others, and as we track backwards in time down the evolutionary tree I do not see where the systemic nature of life suddenly stops. It doesn't.

Returning to the Boeing 747 allegory, the reason it works so well is that we all know that a modern airliner is one massive interconnected system. If our imaginary hurricane blew through the scrap yard, and we found that even the basic structure of the 747 were there, we should regard this event as so extremely unlikely that words like "miracle" would spring to mind—even when we found a few insignificant errors. Maybe one connection in an onboard computer is missing, one engine has an impeller blade a centimetre too short, and two very small software modules do not have the latest upgrades. Still a miracle perhaps, but you wouldn't fly in it, even with the excellent emergency instructions given by the cabin crew before each flight. You know in your heart of hearts that even a minor fault can have catastrophic knock-on effects, because everything in the aircraft is part of a system.

The problem gets worse when we reflect that the Boeing 747 alone (even with minor faults remedied) is utterly useless. It also needs fuel, a runway, trained pilots, stewards, radar, and ice for the bar. This is what we might call the operating environment, or in the case of the natural world, the ecosystem. It's not much use if Protoworm escapes Early Bird or Protoslug a few times only to perish due to the soil acidity being intolerable, or due to a lack of suitable food.

We must avoid over-simplification, and we must avoid unwarranted assumptions about the development of irreducibly complex mechanisms. Yet even if we trim away all such assumptions there is still a residual element of irreducible complexity, and when we consider the development of systems in which the parts are dependent upon each other there is likely to be much more.

I do not think we should rush from these observations to an assertion of intelligent design. On the other hand, although Dawkins' exposition of natural selection is ingenious, there are still valid questions left unanswered, and he seems to know that. In *The God Delusion* he has to fall back on the argument that, however unlikely a cosmic or evolutionary development might be, an intelligent designer must be more complicated. It gives the distinct impression of a poor argument when its chief advocate has to keep a "Plan B" in reserve. In this case, the impression is justified.

Creator or Created?

When engaged in religious polemic Dawkins does not seem keen to overburden the reader with detail, because he has in his mind one infallible safety net if his argument seems weak. It is that, however unlikely his theory might be in the eyes of theists, the theory of a God is more unlikely, because it requires that famous hurricane to blow through the scrapyard and create an ultimate 747 called God. However complex and unlikely the universe, any hypothetical creator must be more complex and therefore more unlikely.

In my introduction I referred to Terry Eagleton's comment that Dawkins and his allies "invariably come up with vulgar caricatures of religious faith that would make a first-year theology student wince". Dawkins' idea of the ultimate 747 is a supreme example of this tendency. No theologian I've come across, living or dead, believed that God had to be assembled from a kit of parts. The whole point about God in all three major monotheistic religions is that he is uncreated and eternal. The implication that for God to exist he would have to be assembled in some way is nonsense, and to stake his existence on the likelihood of that happening is also nonsense. Even if Dawkins does not intend his remarks to be taken that literally, to talk about the complexity of God as having a bearing on whether or not he could exist is simply a massive distraction from the issue of complexity in the universe.

There are issues such as those raised by Behe which still need to be convincingly addressed. I believe that the whole question of consciousness is crucial. In my worm illustration one could argue that the *system* of which the photosensitive cells are part must include consciousness of some sort for there to be any advantage to Protoworm at all. A mere reflex twitch won't fill the bill, or stop Early Bird from filling his bill.

The neuroscientist Susan Greenfield argues that consciousness should be seen as a continuum, rather than as something that is either completely absent or present. In *The Private Life of the Brain* she suggests a sliding-scale from, say, octopuses to Van Gogh. Perhaps my scale would be from Protoworm to Picasso, but in any event I find her argument convincing, not just because of the dexterity with which she makes her case, but because of the clear need for such a level of consciousness—the ZX80 level if you like—within the development of the systems that make up organisms, with increasing complexity as we move along the evolutionary timeline.

More from the Black Box

I was thinking, a little while ago, that it was ten years or so since the publication of Behe's *Black Box,* and that perhaps he'd given up the struggle, when those kind people at Amazon informed me of the publication of his latest book. Entitled *The Edge of Evolution* it takes the argument a stage further by looking for advantageous mutation in very rapidly multiplying organisms such as malaria and the HIV virus. It's all very ingenious, including the maths, but not too hard to follow.

Above all, and for me this is critical, Behe's argument is based on actual evidence, not merely on hypothesis. This is refreshing, because it doesn't rely on what might have happened in a hypothetical world, it relies on what is biologically possible and scientifically observed in the real world. The upshot is that in real life the likelihood of advantageous mutations is simply too small to account entirely for evolutionary development in the strict neo-Darwinian, Dawkinsian form. A key word here is *advantageous.* The harsh reality is that almost all mutations that have any effect at all are severely *disadvantageous,* leading in humans to the 2,000 or so genetic disorders that occur infrequently, but regularly, in our species.

Some of Behe's further treatment of the bacterial flagellar motor, by the way, is astonishing. Not only do we have to account for the complexity of the motor itself, but also the machinery, equivalent to a modest industrial plant, that is needed to maintain it. It's as if the hurricane blew through the scrap yard and accidentally created a 747 *assembly plant,* complete with design department, metal fabrication, precision engineering works, electronics facilities, testing, quality assurance, personnel section, and works canteen. In other words, an exceedingly complex system.

A Test of Faith

I have said that I do not make the automatic step from irreducible complexity to intelligent design. However, my faith in the theory of natural selection in the *narrow* way presented by Dawkins also breaks down at this point. I can see and appreciate the elegance of it all, but can't help remembering that the old billiard-ball model of the atom seemed elegant until I heard about quantum mechanics and "Jack" Hawkins led us through the Planck's Constant experiment. I use the word *faith* deliberately, so perhaps I should give a concise statement of the terrible heresy to which I am tempted. It is this: a change that is small enough to occur through one random mutation will generally be too small to confer significant survival advantage. A mutation would need to be accompanied by other mutations such that, for example, the visual *system* was improved. Yes, it's a subjective thing, but that's the nature of the Dawkinsian argument. I desperately need some numbers.

The elegance of hardcore neo-Darwinism is illustrated in *Climbing Mount Improbable, River Out of Eden*, and *The Blind Watchmaker* by use of computer programs that draw patterns and allow selection of variants, thus allowing for rapid simulation of thousands of generations, millions if necessary. The eye study by Nilsson and Pelger is often claimed as the most advanced because each generation is assessed for optical efficiency using recognised optical formulae. However, there are some features of the study that are often overlooked.

First of all, we are given the impression that Nilsson and Pelger devised a few parameters, put them into a computer, and lo! behold, the machine drew a succession of images leading up to the human eye—a computer-driven simulation of evolution in action. This impression has often been fostered by drawings and animations showing how it *must* have happened. Yet any half-competent designer or animator can produce these, or alternatively show that the eyeball is actually a dodecahedron. Nilsson and Pelger's original and creditable work is in fact a number of equations which show what would happen if a more-or-less flat light-sensitive patch randomly altered in flatness due to genetic variation. It is not a simulation, and the authors have since stated that it is not; but the impression persists like an urban myth.

Second, the assessments of optical effectiveness may be objective, but that's not the same as added survival value, which is the crucial thing. This is what my homely tale of Protoworm is meant to express. When light sensitivity first appears then obviously optical effectiveness rises from zero to a smidge, but it's hard to see the value of that in real-life situations. Even in the extensive treatment of the *Mount Improbable* version of eye development, additional survival value is simply taken for granted. Further, the Nilsson and Pelger model is concerned only with spatial resolution, one aspect of effectiveness, so even that assessment is somewhat limited.

Third, there is intentionally nothing in this model about how the photosensitive cell itself first developed, yet it's at that level that Behe's work seems critical. In fact, just to get to one such cell requires significant modification of a normal cell, involving the development of many precise sequences of chemical reactions. The more one delves into this, the more complex it becomes. As Nilsson and Pelger themselves put it, "we avoid the more inaccessible problem of photoreceptor cell evolution". Somewhat of an understatement.

Fourth, the diagram of one human retinal cell given in *Mount Improbable* has ninety-one pigmented membranous layers for trapping light, but we are assured that just one layer would be enough to enhance survival value. Given that humans have over 150 million retinal cells per eye, each cell being ninety-one times better than the hypothetical original photocell, that seems like a big assumption. Even if Protoworm had, say, a thousand or two retinal cells plus optic nerve(s), the resultant eye would only be about a millionth as sensitive as a human eye. I am not convinced that such a poor relation of an eye would be useful in any way, even if we leave out the problems of interpretation.

Fifth, there is nothing here about the necessary neurological development already discussed. The aforementioned diagram of the retinal cell just has a little stump to the left of the page labelled "connecting wire". I wouldn't have minded more space being given to that diagram, and some indication of how this "wire" developed in parallel with the eye, especially since it is actually about 1.2 million wires. These wires are rather thin. In case you're wondering, incidentally, how 1.2 million wires can handle the messages from 150 million retinal cells, there is some pre-processing of the data within the retina itself—another detail somehow omitted from the computer models.

Sixth, the model only runs to the formation of a fish eye with a lens. Apparatus for focussing the lens, the creation and control of the iris, precise movement of the eye as a whole, stereoscopic vision, and all the image processing that goes along with such refinements, is absent. As these features develop, of course, the brainpower requirement gets much bigger and the generational time gradually gets longer. These features plus the questions involved in getting to the first photocell are merely lumped together as "other details" with no attempt to estimate the number of generations needed to produce them.

The totality of human vision, analysis, and response is probably one of the most complex systems to be found in the entire universe. It involves a huge amount of computing power that interpolates and extrapolates using remembered experience, particularly from the early years of life when the brain is still establishing its neuronal connections. Even working at the exceedingly popular level at which most of us can get some sense of the subject, it's obvious I think that my quibbles about systems and consciousness are entirely reasonable; and every time new facts are added they seem to confirm that assessment. For example, the eye has a complex non-visual function in adjusting our "body clocks". In effect, the Nilsson and Pelger model needs to be extended so as to include the development of this second system in parallel with the purely visual one, but without the two systems interfering with one another—which raises an even more troublesome spectre.

Interlocking Systems

The word "system" by itself only begins to express the complexity that we are discussing. The optical and neurological elements needed to develop in step with each other, as we have seen, but the hardware for all this needs oxygenation by the circulatory system and nutritional provision laid on by the digestive system. Dozens of systems had to develop in parallel, with many cross links or synchronicities. Similar complex developments had to take place in the biochemistry of the myriad of different types of cell found in higher organisms. The complex ecosystem of which we are now aware had to maintain atmospheric and climatic balances for billions of years, and indeed that same ecosystem is now recognised as having substantially influenced the geological history of the earth. The development of life, then, is the development of a "metasystem" comprising a multitude of interlocking systems. A narrow focus on one or a few genes, with limited functions, mutating and then being selected or not selected, simply does not relate to this level of complexity.

At this point the pure neo-Darwinist has to fall back on the assertion that any explanatory difficulties can be resolved simply by recognising the amount of time available for the whole process to take place—four-and-a-half billion years or so. For the first four billion of these years the earth itself was settling down, continents were moving around, the atmosphere was gradually becoming oxygenated, and bacterial life was developing, leading up to the simplest single and multi-cellular organisms. The rest of evolution—the part we normally associate with the word—took place in about the last 500 million years or so. That's still a long time, but, as we have seen, when we are discussing the development of dozens of interlocking systems it's not the sheer length of time that is important, it's the synchronising of the various systems to each other.

Let's take the Nilsson and Pelger model once again, and extend it from the fish eye to the human eye. Given the increasing generational time and the complexity involved, we would surely need to increase the manufacturing schedule for the human eye to a couple of million years. Let's assume that around 500 million years ago a lucky protozoan ended up with some light-sensitive bacteria built into it. Hey, there's still time for 250 attempts to get to the full human eye! How much time do you want?

Unfortunately, this simple narrative fails. Early attempts at eye development would be doomed, since they would peak before there was enough brainpower available to manage the fully developed eye. Later attempts would not succeed because everything is now much more fixed—that last little adjustment to the optic nerve simply can't happen, the whole thing's now just too specialised in structure. No doubt the computer modeller could add a sub-routine to his programme showing how the main retinal artery and vein came to dive into the optic nerve just behind the eyeball in order to get through into the enclosed retina. Making this happen in real life, however, without interfering with the development of optic nerve functionality, would be a much greater challenge.

Obviously, the only way out of this predicament is for the eye to evolve in parallel with the brain, so that they match each other's functionality, especially since the human eye is an outcrop of the brain. From that point of view, eye development is going to have to take 500 million years whether we like it or not, and important synchronicities are going to be needed. For example, the part of the brain that controls eye movements will have to be up and running to give those newly developed primitive eye muscles a survival advantage. It would also help if the brain had developed the capability to compensate for eye movement, otherwise the lucky owner of the first (slightly) moveable eyes will be unable to distinguish between moving its eyes to the left and the visual field moving to the right. Such confusion would be an extreme *disadvantage* in the struggle for survival.

The Real World

The fact is that genes and the creatures that embody them don't dwell in a protected computer world. What *could have* happened and what *actually* happened are two different things—and I still want those numbers. At least Behe's work moves in that direction. Now there's a thought—why not try to create an experiment in the real biological world that would demonstrate the formation of the famous light-sensitive patch? With our skills today to make genetic modifications, would it not be possible to try out a *huge* number of different variations on a *huge* number of some kind of fast-breeding species and see whether any physical sign of such a mutation appeared and subsequently assisted survival? At least then we could stop arguing about it.

My bold suggestion originates, incidentally, with "Darwin's bulldog" himself, T. H. Huxley. As I mentioned in my introduction to this section, he would not accept natural selection until some observation of a new *species* being produced, possibly by artificial selection, could be brought forward. Even by Dawkins' standards I'm in good company—and Huxley's ghost is still waiting.

Supercharging Evolution

The moral of my Protoworm story is that the strict neo-Darwinian view is not sufficient. It depends too heavily on the immediate survival value of just one very small change at a time, and it does not recognise the need for parallel development of the various parts of a complex network of interlocking systems. This is not, however, merely my opinion, which can never be more than that of the interested onlooker. There are professional voices to be heard.

Lynn Margulis has spent a distinguished career studying the development of the simplest life forms, including the formation of new species by the process of *symbiogenesis*. This is an extension of *symbiosis*, the process by which two separate species rely on each other (for example, cows and the microbes in their stomachs); in symbiogenesis a fusion takes place, so that one of the partners suddenly acquires a huge number of genes from the other. If the resulting organism is viable and has some survival advantage then it may be the foundation of a new species, and is likely to herald a huge step forward. Read all about it in *Acquiring Genomes: A Theory of the Origins of Species* by Margulis and Dorion Sagan. Needless to say, Margulis' opinion of exclusively neo-Darwinist thinking is low, and her criticisms scathing.

Co-evolution is a widely-recognised concept that, in a very broad sense, includes symbiogenesis, but also extends to other situations where two organisms depend on each other and therefore to some extent have to evolve together, sometimes forcing the pace for one or the other. This can happen in the context of symbiosis, parasitism, predator-prey relationships, and in more general situations of mutual dependency.

Carl Woese, among other formidable achievements, drew particular attention to the lateral transfer of genes. This is now generally considered important in the early evolution of single-celled organisms, but also to a lesser degree at higher levels of the "tree of life". It's as if the said tree had mysterious creepers connecting its branches and twigs from time to time. Viruses may have a particularly important role in this type of transfer.

Eldredge and Gould's theory of punctuated equilibrium attributes importance to geographical isolation of small groups of a species, particularly under harsh conditions, which would increase the rapidity of the evolutionary process at certain times. An excellent account of the Dawkins-Gould argument (sometimes heated) can be found in *Dawkins v Gould: Survival of the Fittest* by Kim Sterelny. The debate is still carried on (but from Gould's side by his supporters since his death in 2002).

Spandrels are the triangular spaces found in buildings lying between an arch, the horizontal beam or dome that it supports, and the pillars on either side. Such a space is a by-product of the three members surrounding it, but can be used for a secondary purpose, usually decorative. Similarly, the term *spandrel* is used in evolutionary biology to designate an accidental by-product of other developments, which later becomes useful in its own right. The idea was introduced by Stephen J. Gould and Richard Lewontin in 1979, generating enormous controversy but not, as far as I am aware, producing a huge catalogue of proven examples. I suspect that it may be very difficult to prove that a certain phenomenon is a spandrel rather than a straightforward adaptation in its own right. Nevertheless, the concept is useful because by-products of evolutionary change must arise, and it seems inherently likely that some of these will prove valuable later.

Richard Goldschmidt produced his theory of "hopeful monsters" in 1940, claiming that major jumps or *macromutations* could occur, which normally would be fatal but on rare occasions would survive and possibly even form the basis of a new species. This idea was instantly rejected by almost everyone else, but certain elements of it have been restored to credibility by some, including Gould. Sudden changes in several genes at once can occur, due to a knock-on effect of one gene on others, or due to imperfect copying of a chromosome.

Freak hybridisation is a theory in which two individuals of different species mate, sometimes in an unlikely combination, to form a hybrid. We are familiar with the mule and the zeedonk as examples of hybrids, but even close hybrids like these are infertile. It is possible, however, that this is not always the case, and if the new hybrid is more adapted to its environment than were its predecessors it could in principle displace them. As more and more plant and animal genomes are mapped, there is increasing evidence for this kind of cross-breeding. Michael Rose comments: "The tree of life is being politely buried. What's less accepted is that our whole fundamental view of biology needs to change." *(Guardian, 29th January 2009)*

Gene duplication can provide a "spare" copy of a gene, which has the advantage that this copy can ultimately mutate to have a different function without disrupting the original version. On the other hand, many such duplications are extremely detrimental.

Mass extinctions, of which there have been several on a global scale, are generally recognised as another significant factor in the pace of evolution. Such events might seem to be always negative—and they certainly are not life-enhancing experiences for the individual dinosaur or other organism that happens to be crushed, frozen, suffocated, drowned, or starved. From the evolutionary point of view, however, catastrophes eventually make room for further development—they can get evolution out of a rut. Less global events would have a similar effect but on a smaller scale.

Neutrality has two aspects. First, *neutral traits* are those (such as eye colour in humans) which offer no advantage or disadvantage to survival and are therefore simply inherited according to the influence of one or more genes. However, a change in the environment may make a neutral trait advantageous or disadvantageous, so neutral traits could play a role in future selection. Second, *Motoo Kimura* developed during the 1970s the *neutral theory of molecular evolution,* which holds that the majority of changes to DNA are neutral, producing different versions of genes that can gradually drift through a population. These variations are termed neutral because there is no change in the expression (i.e. the effect) of the gene. Some have extended this definition to include versions that are only slightly deleterious. There is much debate about the whole subject, but from the point of view of supercharging evolution, neutrality could allow a step-by-step build-up to an advantageous—and potentially dramatic—change. Each individual step no longer needs to provide *immediate* advantage.

Epigenetics is a complex story which starts from the fact that the number of human genes is surprisingly small, around 23,000. These genes are not all that different from those of our common ancestor chimpanzees—the difference is only around 2.5%. But the expression of these genes differs radically between the two species. Some contributory factors are the effects of control genes, of differences in the way that the DNA itself is packaged and chemically modified, and of information passed around by special small RNA modules. In addition, some environmental factors during embryo development, and even after birth, can cause differences of expression. Most intriguingly, some of these effects appear to be inherited for a small number of generations, even though the genetic code is not changed. These effects could therefore affect survival, if they occurred at critical moments, and in so doing might affect the course of evolution.

Convergence raises the question of whether there are higher laws involved in evolution. From the field of evolutionary developmental biology, Armand Leroi points out that science is about more than telling a story, it is meant to be predictive. (See Leroi's BBC documentary *What Darwin Didn't Know*). Higher evolutionary laws, as yet undiscovered, would give this quality to evolutionary theory. Leroi gives an example of convergence in the *Cichlid* family of fish in the African lakes—although many species have developed in separate lakes for millions of years, some of them are so similar they can only be distinguished by DNA analysis. More familiar examples of convergence are found in the evolution of the wing and—of course—of the eye. Cephalopods like the octopus have a camera eye of similar complexity to that found in mammals but their most recent common ancestor only had a photosensitive spot. There are hundreds of other examples. Simon Conway Morris, the apostle of convergence, carries this further, applying the idea to areas like intelligence and music.

Such hypotheses and theories—and there are no doubt others known to experts or waiting to be discovered—have the potential to speed up the overall progress of evolution. They come close, in their own ways, to matching up with Darwin's original outlook, in which evolution was multifactorial rather than governed only by natural selection, even though that might have been the greatest influence.

My purpose here is not to explore every byway of evolutionary theory, but simply to point out that Dawkins' is not the only show in town. At the very least, his picture—even according to many of his fellow-scientists—is over-simplified. Once a broader view of evolution is allowed some credibility, the whole process becomes much more obviously subject to chance. Variation and natural selection viewed in isolation may be simple, elegant and non-random, but the context in which the process takes place is none of these things. In addition, this over simplification does nothing to address the systemic aspect of evolution.

In normal circumstances simplification may be regarded as a necessary peril, almost impossible to avoid when explaining difficult concepts in a popular format. Dawkins, however, uses the claimed simplicity and elegance of his view to bolster his argument for the non-existence of God: You think you need a God to account for the natural world? Nonsense—here's what happened, and it's so simple that anyone with any sense can see it! Yet many scientists with a pretty large amount of sense, and no religious axes to grind, disagree with him in various ways.

If we give proper weight to the systemic nature of evolution and the random factors involved, I think it is obvious that we need a new metaphor. Fortunately, I have one up my sleeve. I doubt it will catch on like the "blind watchmaker"—but there's no harm in trying.

CHAPTER 7

The Blind Project Manager

My Protoworm illustration might be described as a naive approach to the issues of complexity and design so I would like now to delve deeper by asking the question, "How would a project manager run evolution?"

Project management is a set of techniques used in projects as diverse as building a motorway to launching a new brand of vitamin supplement. Amidst the inevitable paperwork is the vital step of drawing a diagram that shows all of the tasks that have to be undertaken to accomplish the project—steps like "buy ten miles of crash barrier" or "research advertising schedules". The purpose of the paperwork is to show that everyone agreed about everything. One useful spin-off from this is that no individual is to blame if things go horribly wrong.

Needless to say, things can go horribly wrong, and the most frequent cause of horrible wrongness is that the planners didn't spot all of the *dependencies* involved in the job. Crash barriers arrive but the posts that should hold them up are not yet available, or the advertising happens before *SuperMightyVitPlus* has hit the supermarket shelves.

Let's suppose you are in charge of a motorway contract. You start by organising the groundwork, including drains, cable conduits, and the right amount of concrete per mile, carrying on to posts, crash barriers, lighting, signboards, and the occasional bridge. Your assistant, who is just learning the ropes, sorts out the service areas. All is well. The goal is reached.

However, evolution is not held to be goal directed. So, as a better illustration, let's suppose another job comes up and you go back to the proverbial drawing board. You open your briefing document on day one. Alarmingly, it informs you that a stretch of motorway is to be built starting from Eastbourne and ending somewhere else—as yet unknown. Fortunately, an endless supply of raw materials is available, including prefabricated concrete slabs, not to mention posts, crash barriers, lighting, and so on, all to be delivered randomly by levitron power. Teams of robot construction workers are available, programmed to carry out all necessary tasks. All you have to do is signal the commencement of work and then use the "abort" tool on your project software when necessary. You can supervise progress via satellite borne cameras. It all sounds easy enough, so you click the start button.

After day one you have accomplished the following: the countryside around Eastbourne is randomly littered with pieces of crash barrier, support posts and signage. Two fast food outlets have been demolished by robot bulldozers. Three concrete slabs have been dropped into the sea. One is in a field two miles from the town, but with no underlying groundwork apart from a flat and very startled cow. You have spent the whole day aborting all these locations.

All aborted sites are cleared by robot recyclers, but these are now required so often that they are getting in the way of everything else. After a year or so, one concrete slab lands on top of a bulldozed patch, but there are no drains. After fourteen years, finally, one viable section complete with barriers, drains and conduits, has come into existence. With great glee you mark this as an exemplar, and the *Reprofix 2* robots move in to copy it. Within 48 hours there are twenty sections waiting to be transported to their final locations.

Unfortunately, everyone knows that the *Reprofix 2* did not feature the ability to lift and move completed objects—it had not yet developed that function. After a further ninety-three years (your descendants have taken over the contract) with the advent of the *Reprofix 47* this problem is overcome. After many more years of randomly shuffling large pieces of concrete a three-mile stretch finally gets lined up—purely by chance—ending at a charming village green to the west of the town. Members of the local cricket club get fed up with traffic driving across the wicket, but the problem is resolved eighteen months later when the whole area falls into the sea due to coastal erosion.

Ridiculous? Of course, because we know that this method would not be employed in any serious construction project. The chances of anything useful being produced by this technique, let alone linking up with other similar projects to produce, say, a national motorway network, are extremely small. The main reason is that there are so many dependencies involved. Everything has to happen in the correct order, and the logistics need to be impeccable. Similarly, we may look at the development of the human eye and calculate that it could just about happen by chance, assisted by natural selection, in a couple of million years; but parallel development of the brain and its many complex support systems, in tandem with the eye, is a lot more to ask.

In order for us to be here today, a whole spectrum of developments at all levels—parts of cells, the cell, the organ, the organism, and the population—had to edge forward in parallel. The work of a project manager seems to be required much more than the skill of a watchmaker. Without such an overarching control the development of the whole system of systems seems extremely improbable, to the point of being impossible.

There is, of course, a humdinger of an objection to my argument, but before launching into that some clarification of my illustration will help, for this will also clarify the objection. Obviously, pressing the "abort" button happens when some new modification of an organism is simply not viable and it dies without reproducing. The role of the robot recyclers is fulfilled by the microbes that bring about the decay of dead organic matter. The raw materials are the products of evolution up to the current time.

The major objection that might be raised is that I have smuggled in a hidden purpose, because although I said that the project manager does not know where the proposed motorway is to terminate, at least he knows that a motorway is to be built. However, this is not a fatal objection—because it is not necessary for the project manager to know what the final product might turn out to be. All he has to be able to do is to spot when two items among his raw materials fit together in some way, and that is the kind of decision that could be covered by rules. In fact, it is possible that the whole illustration could be honed down so that every activity in my scenario became rule based. For example, the robot recyclers might have a maximum size or weight of object that they could work with. That means that if two or more objects in some way clung together they might be too big for recycling and would survive. Just as neo-Darwinism envisages four basic rules requiring variation in the genotype, expression in the phenotype, selection of the best adapted, and reproduction, there could be other rules that assisted evolution in a wider sense than simply the cell, organ, or organism.

In responding to this objection it may now seem that I have made exactly the same point as Dawkins, except that while he eliminates the watchmaker I have eliminated the project manager. My new metaphor seems to be reduced merely to another illustration of the same idea, that whatever the complexity involved, evolution can safely be regarded as an automatic process. Whereas Dawkins' model needs four rules, mine will need more, but that is hardly a radical departure, and to invoke God as an explanation at this point is premature. That is why I value the concept of irreducible complexity, but do not automatically follow through to intelligent design.

My new metaphor is radical in giving due weight to the systemic aspect of things—the wider set of rules that it proposes could cover developments from the sub-cellular level right up to the global. Further, the chaotic nature of my model compared to the simple elegance of neo-Darwinism seems to correspond well with the broader picture suggested by the various "supercharging" factors previously outlined. As a bonus, it is more open-ended and possibly can generate new ideas. Here's one I prepared earlier.

A Genetic Filing Cabinet

While musing on the project manager approach, it occurred to me that there is one way in which the whole process could be improved. My thought is this: a project manager saddled with the random method of motorway construction would immediately set up holding areas, so that anything surviving the march of the robot recyclers (i.e. having two or more parts fitting together) is stored for possible future use. However, all this clutter would take up a lot of space and would eventually need to be cleared away. Suppose, though, that the instructions followed in putting the failed items together *are* preserved, even though the materials themselves are not. Now and again, by chance, these instructions get fed back into the whole process, so that they have a second opportunity to prove their worth. Such a mechanism in the genetic environment could accelerate the evolutionary process by retaining a record of partial successes and re-using that information from time to time.

Where would we find such a mechanism? Well, that rather badly-named "junk DNA" comes to mind. Over 90% of our DNA falls into this category, and it's a puzzle as to what much of it does. Perhaps one of the things it does is to act as a genetic filing cabinet containing piles of crumpled up plans, which get dusted down now and again and tried out in new situations. Most of these efforts would still, of course, be doomed to failure, but when a success occurred it could be a leap forward, because some useful echoes from the past have now been built in.

My concept, by the way, is more dynamic than *front loading*, the theory that some or all of the information needed for the progress of evolution was built into the DNA from the start. (Incidentally, I use the term "front loading" only in the descriptive sense, without necessarily implying that the information was placed there directly by God). In my proposed scenario faint memories of partial success would come and go, and many of them would be lost through accidental mutation, which is the classic problem with front loading as a theory. Some faint memories would survive long enough to pass on the message. This would be a delayed positive feedback loop, and the message would be, "This partly worked, try it again in a different context". This kind of mechanism appears to make complex exaptation more likely, and for an encore provides perhaps one rationale for convergence. If there is a genetic filing cabinet, whether in the "junk DNA" or elsewhere, then it is surely possible that this is the source of the similarities that occur between otherwise highly divergent organisms. There need not be some kind of intangible cosmic pattern book.

My thought could, of course, be entirely wrong, or already well-known to experts in the field, but pursuing such notions seems more worthwhile than creating hypothetical explanations stretching back millions or billions of years. Such hypotheses are non-provable. More importantly, they cannot be falsified, so they are hardly part of a scientific case.

The genetic filing cabinet does not need a divine filing clerk. It could, in principle, be automated like the other processes governing project management, although how exactly this might work would depend on what the substrate of the filing cabinet would be—which part of the cell, organ, or organism acts as the repository for the information. My suggestion concerning DNA is only a possibility, there could be many others.

There is one more detail to consider concerning the process of evolution before drawing the discussion of this chapter to a conclusion. Having suggested a competitor to one iconic phrase in the dictionary of evolution,

I find myself on a roll. So here's another—one might as well be hung for a sheep as a lamb.

The Helpless Gene

The concept of the gene and its functioning is beautiful in relation to data transfer. Unfortunately, this phenomenal piece of work is constructed from a DNA chemistry set that allows the necessary transfer with great elegance, but is in other respects rather fragile. DNA is constantly open to damage simply through the normal wear and tear of cell metabolism and division, but also from external factors such as X-ray, gamma ray or UV radiation, toxins, and viruses. Genes should be described not as selfish, but as helpless.

The helpless gene is only kept intact by a constant maintenance programme which repairs DNA damage—thousands of times a day in any one cell—by a special set of complex procedures (yet another necessary parallel system). Without this all cells would quickly cease to function. If the repair process cannot keep up, or the damage is too severe, then we may get a mutation. If the cell in question is a sperm or ovum (or is in the sperm or ovum production line) then the results will be passed on to the next generation. Mutations are described as random because their causes—and the efficiency of the maintenance programme—are unpredictable.

The error checking done at the sub-microscopic level of our DNA is phenomenal, just as good as that carried out by computer communication protocols. The repair mechanisms are infinitely better, since computers, routers and so on cannot repair themselves—a source of great comfort to the IT support industry. Without this maintenance work in the cell all genetic information would be short lived.

The genes that control the maintenance programme are highly conserved—that is to say, very old—which is what we should expect, since they are clearly essential from the beginning of cellular life. That fact leads to a paradox, since it is difficult to see how the maintenance programme could have evolved without the protection of the maintenance programme itself. Talking of paradoxes, even though it is possible that the evolutionary process could be automatic, it clearly could not have started automatically, for it requires some initial genotype and phenotype on which to work. This is a dual chicken and egg situation, because the evolutionary process and the repair process need each other. There is an irreducible complexity of the cell which is very difficult to escape, and we shall discuss this further in the next chapter.

Paley and Probability

Paley (and Darwin for that matter) could not have foreseen the need for the systemic approach which I have invoked as regards Protoworm, development of the eye, and so on. The need for such an approach has only become apparent relatively recently, as we have gained more understanding across many fields. I like to think that if such knowledge had been available to Paley then he would have created something like my project manager illustration. Perhaps his would have involved the developing organisation of the industrial revolution—canals, early steam power, import and export, shipping and, of course, those dark satanic mills.

I am sure Paley would have followed this route because he would have realised how much it strengthened his case. If one is impressed with the intricate mechanisms redolent of a small mechanical device such as a watch, how much more impressive it would be to reflect on a whole army of such devices working together in co-operation. I am not sure, though, that Paley would have agreed that the activity of the project manager could be coded into rules, since initially this seems to go against his argument, even though ultimately, as I shall show, it does not.

Fault Tolerance

Given that we only have one example of evolution as a sequence of events, how much departure from that sequence could there have been, while still allowing intelligent life to emerge? For example, would it have mattered if one particular catastrophe had only eliminated half of the then-existing species instead of, say, 95%? How "fault tolerant", as an engineer would say, was the process of evolution? If evolution was highly fault tolerant, then clearly that would increase the probability of it producing intelligent human life. If it was not very fault tolerant, then the amount of luck needed is correspondingly higher.

To illustrate the question further, there probably was a moment when an amoeba divided as usual but the cells failed to separate, forming a colony in which the cells could eventually specialise and become a primitive multicellular organism. How important was it for that to happen when it did—could a million years either way have made any difference? If it had not happened, would multicellular organisms have developed by some other route such as symbiosis? Again, if that parallel development necessary for human vision as we now know it had faltered and left us with eyes of a similar nature to those of fishes, would our brain development have suffered likewise, removing the potential for the arrival of *homo sapiens*?

I agree with the atheist that the fecundity of evolution, once started, would probably have guaranteed a profusion of living organisms of some sort. However, with the more rounded picture of all the probable factors involved (as distinct from the strict neo-Darwinist view) I think it is difficult to see how the tightly knit, exceedingly complex, system needed for human intelligence could have developed without a very large amount of luck.

In order to quantify the amount of luck required, bring to mind the "tree of life" as it has been drawn, with ever-increasing detail, since Darwin himself. Some say it should be more like a bush, others that it should be more severely modified, but for the current exercise it is probably near enough. There are various versions, with differences in detail, but as a rough model let's say there are about forty forks or "nodes" between amoebae (we shall look later at even more primitive life forms) and hominids. On this long journey hundreds of other major groups of animals were produced, of which at least half became extinct. I am using the general word "groups", by the way, to avoid discussion which is irrelevant to our model. Taxonomists would use terms such as *phylum, class, order,* and *genus* for different levels in the tree, but that does not affect my argument.

Accepting the scientifically-established facts, it seems there were at least forty opportunities for the line between amoebae and hominids to die out—not necessarily right at the nodes as indicated in the various tree diagrams, but certainly before the next node came along. The probability (on average) of making it from one node to the next can reasonably be taken as around 50% because, as already noted, we know that at least half the groups of animals that evolved did become extinct. It could well be that this figure is too low, because it is likely that many other groups that became extinct have disappeared from trace entirely.

You may be puzzled here because it is commonly accepted that 99% of species that ever existed became extinct, whereas I am only talking about a figure of 50%. The reason for the difference is that I am talking about groups of related species, not individual ones. Many individual species even within the *surviving* groups also became extinct, accounting for the higher figure.

The task now is to estimate the chances of beating these odds of 50% all forty times. Fortunately, that's easy—it's the same as the chance of tossing an unbiased coin forty times and showing heads each time. Since we are talking round numbers here, we can just say that the chance of doing that is less than one in a trillion. That is to say, 1 in 1,000,000,000,000, or 1 in 10^{12}. (For the non-mathematical, the "12" is the number of times the "10" is multiplied by itself, which is the same as the number of zeros in the long way of writing the number.)

Dawkins' view of complexity recognises the bare statistics of this kind of argument, but then claims that there is another side to the matter. Once natural selection is involved, a sequence of slightly improbable events becomes more improbable than one of those events, but not devastatingly so. (*God Delusion* p. 147 f.) However, my figures in the last paragraph are based on a sequence of events in which natural selection *does* take place. I have never before seen statistics used in the way Dawkins uses them. It seems that no matter how many steps we may imagine and however unlikely they may be, natural selection will always come to the rescue. We may need a million steps with only 0.001% likelihood for each one, but that would still be no problem. I find such a panacea unconvincing.

A much stronger objection to the simple statistical approach is that, even if the line of descent had been broken, it is possible that some other group would have stepped into the breach. For example, the marsupials might have evolved a super-kangaroo. Put the break somewhere else and we might have had a super-crow, a super-dolphin or a super-octopus. By "super" I mean capable of evolving intelligence in the way that the hominids were able to. Incidentally, when I speak of evolving, progressing or developing, that is intended only chronologically, not as any kind of arrogance or "species fascism".

The objection is very reasonable—in fact, I think it is the only substantial counter argument to my picture of the hazardous nature of the tree of life. However, although we rightly regard many species apart from our own as sentient creatures (which should, therefore, be treated with proper respect and humaneness) they simply have not been the platform for transition to human-like intelligence that was provided by our hominid ancestors. There isn't even a close competitor, not even among the other 5,000 or so species of mammal, from the tiniest shrew to the massive blue whale, to be found outside the hominids. The counter argument would have considerable weight if we could point to some close competitors, but we can't.

It is important to note that the progress of the line to the hominids did not prevent the kangaroo, crow, dolphin or octopus developing to their own full potentials. Hominids scarcely competed with any of them for resources or for a particular ecological niche—this is not a race in which there could only have been one winner. The same would apply to the many thousands of other non-hominid species, and it is important to remember that significant new directions in evolution did not halt continued development of those other species. When the vertebrates arrived the invertebrates did not call a halt and settle for what they were at that time. Likewise, when the mammals arrived on the scene, fish and amphibians continued to flourish and develop—and so on.

It's all very well, then, to speculate as to what could have happened in terms of alternative precursors to intelligent life. The fact is, it didn't. Those who know a lot about the kangaroo, crow, dolphin, and octopus would be able to show us many reasons as to why it couldn't possibly happen. No doubt there was some tolerance—the *exact* path of evolution that happened was not essential in all details—but as far as we can see the broad path that evolution followed to the hominids was essential. Nothing outside that path worked very well as far as intelligence or its precursors go. Making a preliminary estimate of the chance (without any designer) of getting from amoeba to the hominids at one in a trillion is not unreasonable.

Stephen J. Gould puts the matter succinctly when he says, "Humans arose . . . as a fortuitous and contingent outcome of thousands of linked events, any one of which could have occurred differently and sent history on an alternative pathway that would not have led to consciousness." (*The Evolution of Life on Earth*, Scientific American, October, 1994). Even with the blind watchmaker and the blind project manager working together a lot of reworking was called for. The helplessness of the gene is part of this, and other facts in support of Gould's view will become clear in the next chapter.

Returning briefly to the history books: when Darwin died in 1882 he left behind a world with no knowledge of genetics, quantum mechanics, relativity, or cosmology. Gregor Mendel had died two years earlier with his foundational work on genetics completely unrecognised for another two decades. Max Planck was still climbing the academic ladder, Albert Einstein was at junior school and Edwin Hubble, who laid the foundations of cosmology, was still seven years away from being born. Understanding DNA had to wait another 70 years, and the technology essential to modern research even longer.

We now need to move to the bigger picture that has resulted from the work of these pioneers and many others. Above all, without the minor adjunct of the solar system and the rest of the universe, the whole subject of evolution would be somewhat hypothetical. Before moving on to that bigger picture, however, I would like to insert one thought in order to draw at least a dotted line under the evolution debate, for the time being.

I have made a distinction between irreducible complexity and intelligent design, because I do not believe that the second necessarily follows on from the first. Yet irreducible complexity does indicate design, even though we might argue that no deity was involved in its production. In particular, we might want to avoid the idea of God setting up the laws of nature and then tinkering with them if things aren't going quite to plan. I propose therefore that a useful expression would be *implicit design,* which avoids the tinkering imagery, and leaves open the possibility that the process of evolution could be subject both to design *and* the outworking of the laws of nature. Using more neutral language of this sort might be a small step towards breaking the "Post-Enlightenment Gridlock".

CHAPTER 8

The Golden Grain

The argument from evolution made by Dawkins aims once and for all to replace the divine watchmaker with the blind one. While the divine horologist was traditionally regarded as infinitely clever, his blind counterpart has an IQ of zero—but perhaps makes up for it with the proverbial luck of the Irish.

This leads us seamlessly to the subject of Richard Boyle (1566–1643), first Earl of Cork, one of those English colonists who featured earlier in my lightning history of conflict in Ireland. In the midst of a tumultuous life the Earl somehow found time to father fifteen children, of which the fourteenth was Robert Boyle (1627–1691), "father of modern chemistry" and a founding member of the Royal Society. All who value science should be thankful for the Earl's stamina, and sympathetic to Lady Boyle, in equal measure.

Less well-known than Robert was his older brother, Roger, who became the first Earl of Orrery. He was primarily a poet, writer and dramatist, but his grandson Charles, who became the fourth Earl, was elected a fellow of the Royal Society in 1706. Around that time George Graham, a renowned clockmaker and also a fellow, designed a mechanical model of the solar system, with the sun, planets and moon represented by globes, which were linked together by a central clock-like mechanism at the base. The fourth Earl commissioned a version of this device, which became known as an *orrery* in his honour.

Among his many brilliant achievements, Sir Isaac Newton had shown how the universe ran like clockwork because of the fixed and all-pervading laws of gravitation and motion, completing the work of Nicolaus Copernicus, Tycho Brahe, Johannes Kepler, and Galileo Galilei. These key figures of the Renaissance and Enlightenment, and many others—aristocrats, priests, gentleman scientists, members of the new middle-class, and the occasional "local-lad-made-good" (like Newton) put together the foundations of modern science. The orrery vividly illustrated this and became an almost magical teaching aid for those who couldn't begin to grasp Newton's *Principia* but still wanted to understand the new "natural philosophy". It would be true to say, I think, that to a great extent the medium was the message. That message was clear: we now understand how the universe works because it can be explained by a few simple laws.

These laws were, of course, held to be created by God, and I think it's obvious how the new insights made deism a much more attractive belief than previously, for in the mechanical universe there was no need for a day-to-day God keeping things in their place, or, for that matter, listening to prayers or bringing into being sacred literature.

The mechanistic universe of the orrery was treated as gospel until the early twentieth century, when the twin attacks of quantum mechanics and relativity showed that Newtonian principles could not cope with the very small and the very large. Just as important, however, was the development of cosmology as a specific area of study linked to astronomy and physics. Together, this research has created a picture of the structure of the universe on both large and small scales far removed from the simple mechanical one. The aspect of this research most relevant to our discussion in this chapter is the concept of "fine tuning", which is our next subject.

The Goldilocks Planet

"Fine tuning" in general refers to a system in which various values each have to lie within a highly specific range for the system to function properly. Consider that most valuable of gadgets, the pop-up toaster. If the spring that causes the popping-up were too strong, either we would not be able to load the toaster with our crusty wholemeal, or else on completion our toast would fly off into orbit. If the time clock is set too low we end up with warm bread, too high and we have a feast of charcoal. Therefore these two values must each fall within a fairly narrow range. Let's say there are ten possible springs that could be installed in this toaster at the factory, of which three will work properly; and let's also say that the timer will execute any whole number of seconds between one and a hundred, of which generally speaking something in the range of 40 to 60 seconds will produce bearable results.

A sloppy manufacturer has left all sorts of springs lying around, which are duly installed. Your chances of getting a suitable spring are therefore 3 in 10, or 30%. The first user is not a "morning type"—possibly a student—so the timer is more or less set by random fumbling. The chance of this working out is roughly 20%, since there are around twenty acceptable settings out of a possible hundred. Therefore the probability of satisfactory toastage at the first use is only 20% of 30%, which is 6%. This toaster is not finely tuned, so disaster is likely. However, the tuning could be improved by better quality control so that the springs installed were always within 10% of the optimum value, which is near enough for everyday use. A thermocouple could measure the surface temperature of the bread and adjust the timing to within 10% of perfection—again, near enough. Breakfast bliss ensues as a routine experience, all other things being equal, because our toaster is now fine-tuned to produce an acceptable slice of toast.

The obvious question now follows: if the universe were a giant toaster, how many physical values would have to be set precisely in order to ensure acceptable results, and how accurately would this need to be done?

A good treatment of this question can be found in *The Goldilocks Enigma: Why is the Universe Just Right for Life?* by Paul Davies. The four most fundamental physical values are the strengths of gravity, electromagnetism, the strong nuclear force, and the weak nuclear force. However, physicists derive other constants from these, and vary over which are most crucial for the formation of the universe as we know it. Dawkins focuses on the six fundamental constants described by the Astronomer Royal, Martin Rees, which are partly related to the above four but also include, for example, some of the ratios between them. It's difficult without a fair knowledge of physics really to get to grips with this, but for our purposes we don't need to know everything. The concept of six values that have to be set pretty tightly to make the universe that we know is enough for now.

These physical values are crucial in themselves, but they also determine the laws of chemistry, including organic chemistry. Organic chemistry is essentially the chemistry of carbon, because all life that we know is carbon-based—it depends on the unique ability of carbon to bond with itself and thus form the huge molecules that are necessary for life processes. Yet the way in which carbon forms within stars is extremely improbable, as was famously pointed out by Fred Hoyle. In turn, the substantial presence of carbon in the universe is necessary for the large-scale production of oxygen. The generation of the whole periodic table of elements within stars in different ways is fascinating, much more interesting than suggested by the faded charts found in school chemistry labs everywhere. Nearly all those elements were important for life as it developed on earth.

We have then a viable universe, which initially at least seems like a huge stroke of luck if there is no divine guidance. Yet even with a viable universe, life as we know it could not have got under way without a further set of happy circumstances, which, fortunately, are easier to understand than fundamental constants. The nature of our universe is such that, even when we have the right constants to stop everything falling apart completely and to provide useful chemistry, there are numerous crucial variables that apply to any planet, variables such as gravitational pull, atmosphere, temperature range, and so on. In our case everything seems to be arranged for our benefit. In particular, our planet's distance from the sun is such that we are neither too cold nor too hot for life to exist. Our planet exists in a "Goldilocks zone" in the solar system—not too hot, not too cold, just right.

Of course, there are bound to be other Goldilocks zones in the universe that might offer hospitality to creatures like us, but living in such a zone is just the first step. We are like fussy hotel guests who check in and then immediately complain that the plumbing makes a noise, the lift is too slow, the bed is too hard, and the guests upstairs are too noisy. In our cosmic hotel we needed the right amount of iron and the right convection currents in the earth's core to create a magnetic field that would protect us from nasty radiation, and a moon just the right size to stabilize our axis. The production of that moon required us to collide with another planet the size of Mars (there were some spare planets wandering about in those days) and live to tell the tale. We then needed water to be flown in by meteorites like a kind of cosmic room service, otherwise we shouldn't have much water at all; but we have enough to support life, and to work with the whole vast mechanism of plate tectonics, which in turn is part of the system that regulates our atmosphere. That's just the crudest assessment of a few of the cataclysmic events needed to make an evolution-ready earth—even *after* the basic physical laws were in place and *after* we settled into our Goldilocks zone.

From there, even with the right sort of universe and a suitable planet, we have only sketchy ideas as to how life started. Dawkins admits this without a struggle, and also allows that it is difficult to explain the formation of the eukaryotic cell (i.e. a cell with a nucleus and mitochondria, unlike bacterial cells). So altogether we have a chain of tricky things that had to happen before *homo sapiens* could even start to evolve. Towards the end of that evolutionary process, more-or-less in the blink of an eye, we made a further huge—and mysterious—step forward to human consciousness, including our use of language, leading to the cultures that we know today.

I think it is useful to make a comprehensive, if provisional, list—the executive summary if you like. Here is what had to happen for us to get to where we are:

- Formation of a universe at the Big Bang with the six "magic numbers" correctly set.
- Formation of one planet set in a Goldilocks zone and with very specific needs fulfilled.
- The inception of life on that planet, including a cell able to replicate itself.
- The development of the eukaryotic cell.
- The evolution of the "tree of life"—a complex network of interconnected systems.
- The development of human consciousness and cultures

You could call each of these events a singularity in the sense in which the word was used before it was hijacked by physics, software companies and miscellaneous gurus; in other words, to refer to a unique event with an extremely low probability. Perhaps, however, an alternative is now needed, to avoid confusion. My choice is "megafluke".

The question, of course, is whether this fortuitous series of megaflukes was probable, improbable or impossible (i.e. requiring the actions of God). The general scientific answer seems to be improbable—in fact, immensely improbable, if we consider simply the universe that we know and observe in the normal course of scientific endeavour.

Undaunted, Dawkins points out that there are at least a billion billion planets in the universe. He allows that the inception of life may be extremely improbable, maybe as low as one in a billion. But that still implies a billion planets in the universe on which life got started. What's the problem?

The Spark of Life

The problem is that, apart from the initial assumption of a billion billion planets, Dawkins' other numerical estimates are either non-existent or hopelessly optimistic, starting with the question of how life began.

In order to consider how the initial spark of life could have happened we'll assume that the "RNA world" hypothesis (that a replicable version of RNA came into existence prior to DNA) is the best of the bunch, even though it is only a hypothesis and there are many acknowledged problems contained in it.

Towards the end of my last chapter we examined the probability of life evolving from amoebae to hominids. To press back before this—the story from inorganic molecules to the amoeba—our obvious next job is to work out how likely it is that on our potentially life-friendly planet some primitive precursor of RNA (let's call it XNA for fun) could form, without any help from either a designer or a pre-existent design.

In case you are not familiar with RNA, it's basically a much shorter, much simpler, single-stranded version of DNA with various functions in the formation of proteins and in DNA duplication. It comes in thirty or so different types that perform specific tasks in cells, all of which are complicated. What we are looking for in XNA is a much earlier version, a kind of "RNA lite" as some might say, that is stable, has a key enabling role in primitive cell metabolism (the basic chemistry of life), and somehow replicates itself.

We'll start with a ridiculously easy test case. Suppose that there are four types of molecule that have to link together, in the correct order, into a chain 100 molecules long, to form a macromolecule—a mere bagatelle as these things go. The most obvious *Statistics for Dummies* question is, "How many possible combinations are there?"

Since each of the hundred positions can be occupied by one of four types of molecule then obviously there are 4^{100} alternatives (i.e. 4 multiplied by itself 100 times), which comes out at over a million, billion, billion, billion, billion, billion, billion, or 10^{60}. If you prefer, it's one followed by sixty zeros.

There are, of course, many other features of this process that we don't understand. Perhaps there are several different versions of XNA that would work—maybe as many as a hundred; but there may be other factors that would reduce the chances of success by a similar proportion. Who knows? We are only making a stab in the dark—but it's a reasonable stab in the dark.

On the other hand, 100 bits of data is not much, even with four options per bit instead of the usual two found in computers. It could well be—indeed, I should think it highly likely—that 100 bits is so little that it could never work as part of an information transfer system detailed enough to get life going. The first sentence of this paragraph contains 100 characters (excluding spaces, if you must count them). It doesn't seem a lot. It might function as a *tweet*, but surely not much else. Life is definitely an information-hungry enterprise, the human genome containing around 3 billion bits of information, while even simple bacteria can contain several million.

We may well have to vary our figure of 100 bits, but it's a start. Pressing on in hope, we can say that even if every available atom were thrown together for a billion years the generation of a replicator such as our hypothetical XNA might happen—or it might not. Bearing in mind that RNA is not all that stable its cousin XNA might well form many times and fall apart again without ever being able to do anything useful. In any case, there never was a time when every available atom was thrown together in the manner suggested. Life probably had to get started with a few billion atoms located in a very specific environment that could temporarily act as a chemistry lab. Looking at the situation *from a purely statistical point of view*, then, the formation of our XNA molecule is extremely unlikely.

This raises a further point—another chicken and egg situation. Even if a workable XNA molecule happened, there would have to be some kind of metabolism—perhaps a few of the core cyclical reactions that lie at the heart of cell biochemistry as we know it today—already going on, so that our XNA hopeful could prove its worth in improving metabolism. That metabolism would itself be vulnerable to the chemical maelstrom going on all around, at least until some kind of control mechanism became established by the new XNA phenomenon. In other words, XNA, metabolism and control are all essential.

Fred Hoyle spent much time considering the likelihood of such a primitive cell arising by chance and settled for a probability of 1 in $10^{40,000}$ on account of the enormous number of enzymes needed to organise even a simple cell. As Hoyle was wont to put it, this figure showed that, even if the whole universe were made up of primordial soup, the probability of life arising purely by chance would have been infinitesimally small. Others have come up with even larger numbers (i.e. smaller chances). If they are correct then I think it's obvious that Dawkins' billion life-friendly planets, which at first sounds generous, is actually somewhat mean. It's a bit like the chap—we all know one—that fumbles with his wallet on entering the pub, but somehow never gets to the bar in time to pay.

I am aware that there are several possible objections to my claim of cosmic meanness. It could be that Dawkins is being overly conservative, and that in fact there are as many as a billion billion life-friendly planets. Another objection might be that the number of life-friendly planets is less important than the number of separate opportunities for life to arise on each one, which could be enormous. Moreover, if the universe were infinite, how could we limit the likely number of life-friendly planets at all? These are all good points, and I will be touching on them shortly. In the meantime, it is probably best to look at the strongest argument against Hoyle's pessimistic view.

A robust rejoinder to Hoyle would be that if we were discussing a purely random process then of course the whole thing would be terribly unlikely, and our apparently generous universe would indeed be revealed as a cheapskate. We are not, however, talking about such a process. On the primordial earth there would certainly have been much random chemistry going on, and if we are waiting for that random chemistry to produce all the enzymes for a simple cell just by chance then Hoyle is right. That is not the case, for the following reason.

Order in Disorder

It is in the nature of randomness to throw up local pockets of order. If a million people each threw a coin ten times it is quite likely that there will be a sequence of ten heads in a row somewhere. Likewise, if you created an environment like the young earth just after its formation, with seething chemical activity going on in various localities, there could well be a small pocket somewhere that produced our XNA and sat with it quietly "breeding" away, and another that had some kind of metabolism in operation. Autocatalytic reactions could be important in both—these are reactions that, once started, generate their own momentum. Such reactions would particularly need the elementary control mechanism already mentioned.

However, order is relative. Chance pockets of order would be hopelessly vulnerable in this early melting pot of a world unless some kind of protective membrane could be placed around these primitive bits of chemistry. We must suppose, therefore, that one of our chemically active locations produces membrane-like bubbles of some description. The problem with the average bubble, though, is that it is not a sophisticated membrane capable of letting in the necessary raw ingredients and letting out the inevitable waste products. Without such a membrane, however basic, the life expectancy of a cell—a glorified globule really—must be short. Odd bits and pieces of metabolic chemistry, XNA chemistry and control mechanism are even more helpless than the helpless gene. It seems to me, therefore, that the primitive XNA, metabolism, cell membrane and control elements must have formed more or less simultaneously—another residual piece of irreducible complexity. Possibly the membrane could exist first, but the other three are certainly mutually dependent and would have needed refuge within the membrane. Simultaneously is probably a close enough description.

Building Blocks

Here it is impossible not to mention an iconic experiment that should probably rank alongside the three that I mentioned at the beginning of this section on science. In 1953 Stanley L. Miller and Harold C. Urey at the University of Chicago produced the first man-made primordial soup, in a glass flask. They showed that in a laboratory, under very specific conditions of temperature, pressure, electrical discharge and so on, amino acids—the "building blocks of life"—can be produced. There have been various questions raised about the experiment, and modifications made to it, but the basic thesis survives.

We also know that amino acids are found in meteorites; and there is some evidence that the high pressures produced by meteorite impact may cause these to polymerise into peptides, which are basically short proteins. As a bonus, some later versions of the Miller-Urey experiment have apparently also produced nucleotides—the units that link together to form RNA (and—in pairs—DNA). Let's make a generous assumption, therefore, that in the hadean world of the very early earth there would have arisen, by chance, micro-environments equivalent to the Miller-Urey flask. Without any supervising chemist, the vast majority of these would have ended in failure, but now and again some form of XNA could occur. There could also be some bursts of primitive metabolism. Eventually some of these micro-environments could settle down to form the pockets of order discussed above.

Reproduction

Once all this is up and running, there is now a crunch question. Does this first ever combination of XNA, metabolism and membrane, with suitable control mechanisms, have any reproductive capability? Nothing fancy, you understand, just an ability on the part of the membrane to stretch with the growing cell, pinch together to effect the separation, then join up around the two resultant daughter cells quickly enough to prevent the contents of both rejoining the raw puddle of primordial soup.

Our primitive cell, apart from this rather ingenious membrane, must also have some way in which the timing of the division is decided. If this is too early then the daughter cells will probably not have enough metabolic elements and XNA to survive. If the division occurs too late, then the parent cell will suffocate under its own size, as its volume becomes too great compared to its surface area. For similar reasons, there would have to be some way of distributing these fairly between the daughters—even on a Goldilocks planet there is no room for a Cinderella cell.

Abiogenesis

This hypothetical process of moving from non-living to living is known as *abiogenesis*. It all seems extremely unlikely, and it is well to remember that this genuine "spark of life" would be easily snuffed out. Even with a half-decent membrane life will be tenuous. All the elements involved in the process easily denature under even minor trauma caused by heat, acidity, or radiation. Many people, quite understandably, take refuge in the idea that God intervened to stack the odds in favour of the spark happening. Dawkins, of course, refuses to do this, but has no real alternative to suggest.

As previously remarked, the non-religious person can simply note that even if the envisaged process were as difficult as I am proposing, that's OK because, in the time available, this primal flask scenario could take place trillions of times—any life-friendly planet could host a vast number of opportunities for abiogenesis. That is an assumption, because very specific environments are needed—leading suggestions are deep thermal vents in the ocean floor and locations around volcanoes. Let us suppose that across every square millimetre of the earth's surface a thousand potential "genesis moments" took place every second, how many would that be in a year? Well, you can work that out in a trice I'm sure, but just to economise on effort I make it about 10^{30} or a million trillion trillion. Since we know that the "genesis moment" that succeeded took place within a window of about a billion years (probably a lot less but we're being generous here) then we have time for 10^{39} attempts at kick-starting life. That sounds like a lot of scope for success, but you may remember that the probability of putting together a suitable 100-link chain of basic units was only one chance in 10^{60} for each attempt. There simply isn't time for such an unlikely event, not by a very long way. It's a non-starter, both metaphorically and in a rather profound literal sense.

Yet we should persevere. On my scenario, what length of suitable XNA chain *is likely* to occur by chance in a billion years? Well, I make it 65 units. In other words, 4^{65} is roughly the same as 10^{39}. Incidentally, if you use a spreadsheet to check out my rather bumbling mathematics, be sure to click the box for "comma separators" to avoid the onset of migraine.

My stab in the dark figure of 100 units as the maximum possible length of XNA needs to be adjusted in the light of this further thought experiment. The question at issue now becomes whether such a small molecule—only 65 units long—could coalesce with and control primitive metabolic elements inside a suitable membrane, begin replicating, and successfully manage the splitting of the new cell into two viable units. This is incredibly unlikely, even though we might have to say, strictly speaking, it is possible.

As always, the devil is in the detail. My calculations are based on a thousand potential genesis moments per second per square millimetre of the earth's entire surface. I suspect that is very optimistic, as is the idea that only 65 bits of information could provide all the necessary functions. We also assumed that the four basic units already existed in profusion, and all that we know about the RNA existing today suggests that only very specific molecules could work as such units. Each would probably contain at least a couple of dozen atoms.

There are still, in addition, those critical factors that were necessary for any of this to get started. Even if there are huge numbers of "Goldilocks planets", in the sense of orbiting a star to give a temperature range similar to that which we enjoy, I wonder how many of those planets would have the special facilities that we required in our cosmic hotel. I mentioned gravitational strength, atmosphere, magnetic field, water, the moon and plate tectonics, but it's easy to add more. From a scientific point of view, how many such planets are there in our universe? Observation, the basis of science, suggests one.

From a statistical point of view, how many such planets are there likely to be? The answer is approximately none. If the chance of any one of these factors occurring is as high as one in ten thousand I would be surprised. Yet that would make the likelihood of them all happening to the same planet only one in a trillion trillion. (10^{24}). Incidentally, this figure is also known as a *septillion*. Dawkins claims that out of a billion billion planets in the universe, there are likely to be a billion planets on which life could start. Such a claim simply does not make sense—by a factor of at least a billion trillion. If, as suggested earlier, we credit Dawkins with being over generous to his opponents and suppose that there could be a billion billion life-friendly planets then we should still be adrift by a factor of a trillion.

Consolidation

Once the successful "genesis moment" had taken place all we had was a rather shaky "protocell" as I shall call it, rapidly increasing in number by division, with a handful of XNA genes which also possessed enzyme-like qualities—sufficient at least to keep the cell metabolism on the rails and contribute somewhere along the line to membrane functioning and cell division. There was a great need for consolidation of the hard-won ground.

Now it often seems to be assumed that once there is a cell it's all over bar the shouting, but that is certainly not so. The next major step involves the bacteria and their close relatives the archaea, but these typically contain 2–3,000 genes, now subsisting in DNA rather than XNA, and with the different versions of RNA performing a variety of functions. The whole updated paraphernalia also needs several hundred of those enzymes that bothered Fred Hoyle so much.

Lingering somewhere in the line of descent is our *last universal ancestor,* probably one of the organisms that flourished before the bacteria and archaea split up. Whether this was a bacterium, an archaeon, or something else is a matter of debate. If we regard the protocell as our *first* universal ancestor, it seems that to progress from first to last is a truly monumental task. I think that Hoyle's assessment is not entirely wide of the mark, but is exaggerated because not all the enzymes he had in mind were needed to get the process going, and the localisation of the chemistry into cells could allow an early, rather crude, form of selection to begin.

In case you are not familiar with the terms, the first universal ancestor was the first cell that was truly self-sustaining and replicating, and which survived long enough to become the start of the "tree of life". The last universal ancestor was the species from which the archaea and bacteria diversified, making it the last organism from which all life as we know it today is descended. Again, this may be over simplified and our knowledge is limited—there could have been many early branches that turned out to be dead ends—but the basic picture is still helpful. From our point of view now (i.e. ignoring the dead ends) this period from first to last universal ancestor is the very early "trunk" of the tree of life. At the bottom of the trunk is the simple protocell, with a handful of XNA-based genes and an *extremely* rudimentary metabolism. At the top is a complex bacterial type of cell with a sophisticated metabolism and thousands of DNA-based genes.

I'm not at all sure how we can even start to understand this transition from a handful of XNA genes to a few thousand DNA ones. My problem with development of systems explored in earlier chapters seems to apply here as well. In particular, the shift to DNA is difficult to envisage, because DNA by itself would be of little use—it also needs functioning RNA of different sorts in order to code proteins and to perform its new replication routine, together with the array of enzymes already mentioned. This seems just as complex as the evolution of the eye, but on a micro scale. Worse, while we may invoke exaptation as a major player in the evolutionary process from amoebae to hominids, it is hard to see how the protocell's successors could have anything much to exapt from.

Here's another problem. We are accustomed to thinking of huge strings of DNA in which mutations can often take place with no effect at all, but in our XNA chain, with only 65 links, one such change would appear to be almost inevitably catastrophic—with such a small genome everything counts. There is no room for neutral variation that might be useful later. Neither is there room for even fleeting accidental damage. Are we to suppose that the repair mechanisms mentioned in my previous chapter were already there in some earlier form suited to XNA? That's a very big ask.

Finally, there is the puzzle of the event often known as the "great oxygen catastrophe" which lay far in the future—probably by about a billion years—but to which these very early developments are highly relevant. Basically, once the early microbes took off they got along pretty well without the need for oxygen—they were anaerobic—and indeed oxygen would have been poisonous to them. Then along came the cyanobacteria that produce oxygen through photosynthesis.

This oxygen was mopped up for millions of years by a very simple process with which we are all familiar—all exposed iron simply rusted. Much of it became folded into rocks as geological change took place and can be seen today. Eventually the rate of oxygen production was too great and it accumulated in the atmosphere. Fortunately, aerobic bacteria and slightly more advanced organisms were able to develop—which was good for everything that came after that, because aerobic respiration is so much more efficient than anaerobic.

The point is that to make this change the very basic elements of cell metabolism such as the Krebs Cycle (or its predecessor) had to be modified— sometimes put into reverse—to fit in with the new order. It simply seems like yet another improbable coincidence that this could happen, a real joker in the pack. By the way, the oxygenation of the atmosphere probably took place in only a few thousand years, so if modification had been impossible there was no time to start again and wait for an all new *aerobic* "genesis moment" to come along. All in all, it seems to me that the transition to the elaborate metabolic mechanisms of the new DNA-based life model, even up to the level of our last universal ancestor, was a very unlikely business indeed.

Eukaryotic Cells

There is even more complexity when we introduce the formation of the eukaryotic cell—the fourth megafluke in my provisional list—once we have a suitable earth and some primitive life. Eukaryotes contain membrane-bounded organelles, the most universal and conspicuous of which is a nucleus. The archaea and bacteria do not have this luxury, with its benefit of much better and more specialised organisation of the cell. In particular, DNA is packaged inside the organelles, mainly in the nucleus.

Lynn Margulis has shown convincingly that a key factor in this step forward was the establishment of a symbiotic relationship between bacteria, such that eventually one cell would absorb the other, whose functioning would be adapted still further to produce the eukaryotic prototype. However, there is still the question of how this truly prodigious rearrangement of chemistry came about, and how each faltering step towards the new arrangement would have proven advantageous to survival.

Dawkins, in rather acquiescent mode, takes the view that this may have been even more improbable than the inception of life. Well, on this occasion I shall simply allow myself the luxury of agreeing with him.

Sexual Reproduction

The start of sexual reproduction deserves particular attention, since the type of cell division required (meiosis) seems to have an irreducible complexity all of its own. The sexual strategy was highly effective, leading to better DNA repair, faster elimination of deleterious mutations, more rapid spread of advantageous traits, and greater variation within the species, which in turn would accelerate evolution. The crucial element in meiosis that confers the benefits is the mixing of genetic material—in other words, maternal and paternal chromosome copies swap genes. Yet none of the benefits would accrue immediately after the first small step was taken. Even if meiosis developed from the normal process of cell division (mitosis) it is still complex.

This is, of course, no different from other evolutionary examples such as the eye, in terms of complexity, but it stands out as strategically crucial, because it is the main cause of variation, alongside mutation. It's obvious of course that meiosis in itself has little value if it is not followed by fertilisation. Here again we seem to have an outright demand for parallel co-ordinated developments, the intricate meiotic mechanism within the cell, and physical sexual characteristics and behaviour found at the organism level. There may be a simpler starting point in the ability of bacteria to exchange DNA, but the processes are very different and a long chain of exaptation would have to be proposed to link them together. In view of our lack of knowledge in this area I would not like to hazard a guess as to the probability of sexual reproduction beginning. I'll just call it unlikely.

A Chance in a Googol?

We have now done the basic work needed in order to estimate the probability of our existence. For tidiness I would now rearrange my points as follows, including the step from hominids to *homo sapiens*, even though we have not yet considered it in detail:

- Formation of a universe with fundamental physical constants suitable for production of stars.
- Development of the solar system, earth, biochemistry and protocell: the first universal ancestor.
- Development from protocell to a DNA-based organism that was the last universal ancestor.
- Development from the last universal ancestor to the highly-structured eukaryotic cell.
- Development from the early eukaryotic cell to the hominids.
- Development of *homo sapiens* including human consciousness and cultures.

With regards to the fundamental constants, people like Roger Penrose, Martin Rees, Harold Morowitz and Paul Davies all agree, following earlier thinkers like Hoyle, that if the universe we know is the only one there is, then our initial assumption is very simple: its suitability for life is staggeringly improbable, ranging from maybe one in a trillion to don't even think about it. I have already further argued that getting from the bare existence of such a universe to the first universal ancestor involves a probability of less than one in a septillion.

Moving on from there to the last universal ancestor needs the massive imponderable change to complex, DNA-controlled cellular life. The intricate DNA repair mechanism outlined in the previous chapter also needs to start up, if it has not done so earlier in a simpler form. In terms of the eukaryotic cell, even Dawkins thinks this may have been extremely lucky, which seems to mean for him about one chance in a billion. I also stick to my estimate for evolution producing a hominid with the potential for human intelligence as having a probability of one in a trillion.

Add up all these strings of zeros and the total comes out at 10^{67}. Since I have chickened out of putting a probability figure on the protocell to DNA step, and on sexual reproduction, and we have not yet looked at the final step to *homo sapiens,* a few more zeros ought to be added. If we took the highest possible figures we could probably get to a *googol,* my favourite number, which weighs in at 10^{100} but there is little point in such an exercise, for we reach the level of unimaginable improbability long before that. Rather than expend effort on adding or subtracting more zeros we should consider instead the significance of it all.

On the biological front, it seems we have explained the complexity that is apparent when we consider the present, but in so doing we have replaced it with a complex process in the past. Buried within that process are several phases where the complexity seems to be irreducible just as much as it initially seemed to be in the evolution of the eye. In particular there is that whole nexus of functions that had to be there at the point of formation of the protocell: short but replicable XNA strands, cell metabolism, membrane, and reproductive capacity. The DNA repair process had to be in place, at least in some primitive but workable form, not much later.

In Chapter 7 I suggested that it might be possible to translate the project manager function into a set of rules. That would reduce the element of randomness, and it may also suggest entities like my genetic filing cabinet that would increase the probability of long-term exaptations. Having examined the detail of what happened, as far as we know at present, there is now an obvious question, namely, "Where are the rules?"

If we consider first the rules of natural selection, they are fairly simple: variation in the genotype, expression in the phenotype, selection of the best adapted, and reproduction. Yet even these rules are not eternal, they are emergent. Just as the laws of chemistry emerged from the laws of physics once the universe had cooled sufficiently for chemistry to happen, so the rules of natural selection could not have emerged until there was a suitable biological context, in the form of a variable genotype exerting consistent control on a stable phenotype. Those early stages in abiogenesis were the products of random chemistry in the context of the specific state of the earth at the time, which again was the product of natural forces acting randomly. It is impossible not to conclude, therefore, that although the rules that govern evolution really are rules, they have arisen by chance. If there had been a different type of initial relationship between genotype and phenotype, there would have been different rules. There might also have been a different kind of evolution, but we have no evidence whatsoever for this occurring.

The same could be said of my supplementary rules that might govern the project manager function. I suggested that one rule in operation might be imposed by the limitations of the robot recyclers. Yet they too had to evolve, and the fact that those limitations arose is a matter of chance—unless there were other rules governing the evolution of robot recyclers, but then they would have to be determined by something else. We could regress for a long time until eventually we hit clear random chance. I would not be surprised if many rules evolved at different levels of evolution—I believe the "evolutionary developmental" people are keen on that sort of thing. The presence of these rules does not, however, radically affect the probability issues.

Once we take into account the detail of abiogenesis and the other matters discussed in this chapter, it is clearly fallacious to speak of natural selection as if it were driven by some kind of independent laws ranking alongside the major laws of physics. Those laws only came into existence when the circumstances were right. Similarly, although the project manager metaphor contains important possibilities, at least in my opinion, it too required a pre-existent set of circumstances—the raw materials created so far, surveillance apparatus, communication links with the manager's office, and so on. Finally, we can also see the deep-rooted fallacy contained in the Nilsson and Pelger model. In addition to the difficulties I rehearsed in Chapter 6, it had its own pre-existent conditions in the form of the initial algorithms fed into it and the software to run them. Without them the eye model would have done nothing.

Incidentally, if we want to take into account in any shape or form (i.e. with or without God) the "front loading" concept it makes sense to group together the first two steps listed above, and then group together the following three steps, so that there are now three "epochs" as we could call them. The start of each of these epochs requires its own set of information: the laws of physics, the initial DNA structure, and the specific mutations needed for human consciousness, which we have yet to discuss. Our summary would then become:

- Big Bang to protocell: process governed by starting conditions, laws of physics and chemistry.
- Protocell to hominids: process additionally governed by DNA initial structure and evolution.
- Hominids to *homo sapiens:* process additionally governed by mutations needed for human consciousness.

The starts of these epochs represent peaks of maximum improbability, or maximum divine activity, depending on your presuppositions. If we leave out divine intervention, we simply have to accept these massive improbabilities, even though they add up to an overall level of improbability that in normal life would simply be called impossible.

This has been a rather intense chapter and I apologise to the numerophobic. I suggest we unwind with a brief illustration.

A Big Round of Applause . . .

I find it difficult to imagine a probability like one chance in a googol or even one chance in a septillion. I keep trying to express it to myself in terms of how long one would have to play the National Lottery and win every time. (It has been said that the National Lottery is a tax on people for not understanding statistics.) One illustration that I like is as follows. A grain of sand is made radioactive in a lab where they can do such things. The purpose of this is that it can be detected in future. It is then taken away and just left, somewhere in the world. *Anywhere.* It could be in a Saharan sand dune, at the North Pole, inside someone's car in Singapore, on the deck of an Atlantic container ship, in the lounge of 594 Acacia Drive, Preston, on an eyebrow of the Statue of Liberty, or anywhere else on earth.

Each week the game show, maybe called *The Golden Grain*, gets under way at peak viewing time. This week's three lucky contestants stand on glistening golden podia, each accompanied by a glamorous assistant holding a golden envelope. After four advertising breaks, the first envelope is opened. Arnold from Nottingham has guessed that the *Golden Grain* is in Tenerife, on the roof of the *Los Gigantes* hotel, four metres to the right of the fire escape.

A giant screen now shows the scene live from Tenerife as a helicopter flies in the *Golden Grain* swat team, who abseil down to the hotel roof and scan the area with a golden Geiger counter. Has Arnold won a fortune? No. What bad luck, a big round of applause for Arnold. Likewise, the second contestant, Tracy from Romford, who guessed at the fire bucket on Platform 1 at Barking station; and the third, Karl from Highgate, who thought the *Golden Grain* was on the left boot of a security guard in Red Square.

However, there is even more excitement near the end of the show. On the phone-in (calls cost £1.50, mobile rates may vary) Shirley from Southampton wins the prize for *closest guess* with the top of the Great Pyramid. This week's *Golden Grain* was in fact on a piece of camel dung next to the Suez Canal.

This is all good fun, but if my argument is correct, then the minutely small chances of a lucky contestant *exactly* locating the *Golden Grain* are still much higher than the chances of us being where we are today. I reckon, by a strange coincidence, that the chances of locating the *Golden Grain* are somewhere around one in a septillion. It's a good round number and is *extremely* generous when it comes to the question of the likelihood of our existence. There were six crucial "milestones" along the road from Big Bang to modern humans, each of which might justify this level of improbability on its own. As always, generosity is my middle name.

Would you expect to win the *Golden Grain* game show? Would anyone? It's just too unlikely. The word *impossible* starts to creep in. Yet the atheist has little choice but to deny such slack use of words and say that everything did just happen by chance, even though unlikely. However, it is at this point that Dawkins makes his leap of faith. At the end of Chapter 4 of *The God Delusion* he gives a summary of his argument and states his conviction that one day his winch will come. Very well, I have put that enigmatically, but that is rather appropriate to the concept in question. A brief explanation will suffice for now, with more detail later.

Following the lead of Daniel Dennett, Dawkins pictures evolution as a crane. This crane hauled us from protocell to human. One day we will discover an even better version, a crane that will explain the constitution of the cosmos in the same way that evolution explains the development of life.

The conviction is profound, but where is there a shred of evidence that such a crane exists? What we have here is a leap of faith—but it's a faith that wavers straight away. Dawkins goes on to argue that even without this super-crane, "the relatively weak cranes we have at present are, when abetted by the Anthropic Principle, self-evidently better than the self-defeating skyhook hypothesis of an intelligent designer".

Really? If I were Voltaire's Dr Pangloss I think I should at this point be extemporising about the self-evidently self-defeating use of the concept of the self-evident. But there's no need. I've had years of experience with these arguments about things being self-evident. Not with atheists, but with overzealous fundamentalist Christians. There are some who, when their backs are against the wall, resort to the simple claim that the Bible is "self-evidently" reliable. It's basically a code for "evident to me".

I acknowledged earlier that clear-minded criticism of religion is a good thing in pointing out wishful thinking, but it seems that Dawkins is now veering in that direction himself. I should think we could broadly agree on the process that has taken place, a process that is extremely unlikely to have happened purely by chance. If you want to argue that it did then there is no way I can disprove your belief—I wasn't there when it all happened. We could pursue all the arguments and have a good debate. However, if I said, "I'm right because God told me so", I think you would feel short-changed. Argument from the "self-evident" is more or less on that level.

CHAPTER 9

Narrowing the Odds

In order to discuss life, the universe, and everything in a brief span I have not stopped off very much along the way to answer objections to my point of view. I should like to do that now.

My basic proposition is that we *could* exist as we do now, in the universe that exists now, purely by chance—but the probability of this is extremely low, certainly lower than one in a septillion, which was the probability of winning on *The Golden Grain*.

I hope you will agree that I have tried to be fair, even generous, not tossing around probability figures with too much abandon. There are some matters that I have mentioned briefly that probably could carry a lot more weight than I have placed on them up to now. For example, there are nasty little problems of how the protocell conserved its genes without the elaborate repair mechanisms found further along the evolutionary timeline, and how the initial reproductive process got under way just when it was needed. Linkages across time such as those necessary to prepare for the great oxygen catastrophe and later for the eukaryotic cell are particularly mind-bending. That whole coincidence of cell membrane, metabolism, control, and replicator could be far more unlikely than I have suggested, as could the journey from first to last universal ancestor. All in all, my *Golden Grain* illustration is very reasonable.

In order to avoid this conclusion, Dawkins and other atheists now tend to bring on their big gun in the probability debate, convinced that this will blow all enemies, especially religious ones, clean out of the water. Nothing could be further from the truth.

Bring On the Multiverse

There are distinct ways in which the word "multiverse" is used. The first use of this word is the most obvious, and is the one that particularly suits Dawkins' views. In this hypothesis there are simply a lot more universes than the one in which we live, maybe just too far away for us to see, possibly spread across an infinity of space-time, or perhaps existing as alternative space-time islands within "the void". The ideological purpose of proposing such a multiverse is to crank up the likely number of Goldilocks planets so high that it seems almost inevitable that somewhere conditions suitable for life would occur. As my chapter title suggests, the aim here is to narrow the odds against life getting under way.

In order to have any relevance to us, all the universes in the multiverse need to have the same physical laws as we have in our universe, because the evolution of life, as far as we can see, depends on those laws. In other words, we could call this the "plain vanilla" view—however many universes we have in this multiverse, there is only one basic flavour. In effect, we are talking about clones of the universe we know, which seems simple enough. However, there are three problems with this concept.

First, there is no evidence for the existence of this type of multiverse. Dawkins likes to mock belief in God as being similar to claiming that there is an invisible teapot circling between the orbits of Mars and the earth, a jolly jest that originated with Bertrand Russell. However, this multiverse hypothesis is a belief in the invisible teapot just as much as any form of belief in God. There is no evidence in its support. In fact, some physicists think it is ridiculous.

The second difficulty is that each of the universes in the multiverse might have the same physical laws as ours, but each would probably have different starting conditions. We tend to imagine that when a big bang happens and forms a new universe, we are bound to end up with something like ours. Not so. We have the type of universe we have because of a certain unevenness in the starting conditions. If the initial "microdot" had been totally uniform then the universe would be the same, with no galaxies, stars, or planets.

If you are an excellent cook, or alternatively are able to follow the instructions on a packet sauce mix, you will know the importance of starting conditions. If the ingredients are evenly mixed into the liquid before heating, a smooth Hollandaise will result. If there are lumps, the situation will only deteriorate until they are positively galactic. Liquidisers are mostly used to sort out such problems on a domestic scale, but on the cosmological scale the initial lumpiness is very important and should on no account be liquidised away.

Depending on the starting conditions, any particular universe could develop as a uniform sphere of gas or some other configuration with no planets at all. It might be necessary to have trillions of big bangs just to get one other universe like ours. How many invisible teapots can we propose before it becomes clear that we are simply making it up as we go along?

The third problem is this: if a universe is formed by a big bang, without which there is no space-time at all, why *should* it have the same physical laws (which are all about space-time) as our universe? It seems to me that we will inevitably end up proposing higher laws that determine how big bangs work, which leaves us with the question of why those laws should be as they are. The only way out now is to say that in fact there could be many such possible sets of laws, but we still don't need a higher law, or a God, to decide which one we shall have for our universe. There could be instances of universes with all sorts of higher laws, it's just that we happen to live in the one that we do, with the laws that it happens to have.

The Tutti-Frutti Multiverse

This kind of multiverse is the second possible type, which we shall call the "tutti-frutti" model. In this multiverse there are no restrictions on which physical laws shall apply to the universes within it. That sounds like a good idea, because it could solve the mystery of the apparent fine-tuning of things. If there are an almost infinite number of universes with different "magic numbers" then there's nothing really special—let alone God-given—about ours. Problem solved—except for a couple of difficulties.

As with the first type of multiverse, it's tea time again. There is no more evidence for this version of the multiverse than the first. Moreover, one multiverse cannot be both plain vanilla and tutti-frutti. If we want both, we will have to propose a new entity, the tutti-frutti multi-multiverse. This is a collection of multiverses, each of a different flavour (i.e. having a different set of physical laws). Each of these multiverses contains within it a large number of universes of the same flavour. The plain vanilla multiverse (which happens to be ours) contains a large number of plain vanilla universes, each with so many planets that at least one planet like ours is almost inevitable, probably a lot more, just by chance. Phew.

Within each multiverse, however, the problem of starting conditions remains. Yet that shrinks into insignificance compared to the "higher law" problem as we should apply it to our exotic tutti-frutti multi-multiverse. How many different sets of physical laws could there be? If there is no restraint at all on the six magic numbers, we would need an infinite number of multiverses to give any probability at all of our type existing. If there is no higher law, that seems to be the only conclusion.

Belief in a multiverse is often presented as scientific fact, or at least a strong possibility, despite the lack of evidence. Sometimes quantum mechanics is brought in—there are some heavyweight scientists that hold to the "Many Worlds Interpretation" (MWI) to tackle certain quantum paradoxes. But the MWI is hardly the kind of thing that helps with arguments about probability. The MWI is very dynamic, with new universes continually splitting off trillions of times a second so that indeed all possibilities do happen, even though we are only aware of some. Where exactly these universes exist is a good question; one answer seems to be that they exist in an infinite dimensional type of space known as a "Hilbert Space", named after the great German mathematician David Hilbert (1862–1943). This is, however, a mathematical construct, not something that has been shown to exist in the normal sense of the word.

Those who uphold the MWI are quite clear that their model is the best answer to quantum paradoxes. However, even if that is correct, this type of multiverse on its own solves little. For example, this multiverse can only have one set of physical laws, it's a type 1 multiverse. Otherwise, the number of possible outcomes from a succession of quantum events would rapidly escalate towards infinity. To put it mildly, we would end up with a terrible mess. So the problems that we thought were solved by introducing the type 2 multiverse are not solved by the MWI, whatever its other virtues.

Max Tegmark proposes a beautiful hierarchy of universes. It's rather like my tutti-frutti multi-multiverse with additional features such as an infinite number of sub-universes through which all starting conditions can be expressed. I think my point is made. Surely when we get into language about an infinity of sub-universes and infinite dimensional spaces we have moved far beyond our normal concepts of probability. With all these infinities around, *anything* can be pretty likely, even certain.

Infinity Blues

In an infinite number of universes all possibilities must be realised. Just imagine, this morning Jonathan Arkwright of 594 Acacia Drive, Preston, got out of bed and said to his wife "Oh heck, it's Monday". Somewhere there must be another universe absolutely identical to this one in every respect, except that Jonathan Arkwright got out of bed and said "Oh heck, it's raining". Somewhere else there must be two more universes, one corresponding to each of these awakenings in every respect, except that the rings of Saturn are purple. I suppose it could be so. Tegmark should have gone into marketing, for he sells multiverse ideas with such charm that they become not only believable, but a virtually certain truth. Sadly, a feeling of absurdity follows some time later—but then, I'm not a physicist.

This is all surely too high a price for Dawkins to pay, for the following reason. In this type of multiverse, in which all possibilities happen somewhere, there must be worlds similar to ours, with all the life forms that we have, but which have arisen instantaneously (complete with apparent fossil record) rather than through a long process of evolution. So how do we know that ours is not of this sort? If Dawkins pursues multiverses too avidly, he could end up a Creationist. Further, if all possibilities are realised, there must surely be a universe somewhere which is governed by an all-powerful being, or at least all-powerful within that particular universe. Again, how do we know that ours is not that one?

It is true, of course, that many physicists do not like the idea of infinity in the traditional sense because of the complications caused by the concept, particularly when used of anything that can be measured. Often the word is used in a modified way to mean simply a very, very large number. Perhaps "unlimited" would be a better word, so that if additional dimensions or universes are required, in order to meet theoretical or observational requirements, they can be regarded as possible, no matter how many might be needed. If that is what Tegmark means by infinite, then I should have to withdraw my previous two paragraphs. In one sense, I should breathe a sigh of relief, because my anecdote of the Arkwright family raises the particularly difficult philosophical problem of personal identity. However, in his television work, Tegmark revels in just that problem in his supposed multiverses, so I am not sure in what sense he himself uses the concept of infinity. In any event, my main points are not affected by the possible modification.

Gambler's Fallacy

This all seems rather esoteric—discussion about the multiverse idea always seems to end up with an infinite number of universes, with all the difficulties involved. It is neither scientific nor sensible to maintain multiverse hypotheses for which there is no evidence and which bring with them so many problems. I still believe it is quite a viable conclusion that if there were no intelligence involved in the whole process, then the probability of our existence would be extremely low. Multiverse hypotheses do not blow anything out of the water, and when it is apparent that their proponents are simply trying to avoid this rather obvious conclusion the whole thing looks rather like special pleading. Instead of hypothesising a multiverse, why not hypothesise the existence of God?

Alongside my arguments, however, there is a simpler reason for ignoring multiverse hypotheses in the discussion of probability, namely, there is a severe danger of "gambler's fallacy" creeping in. Suppose you are taking part in a coin tossing competition similar to the experiment I mentioned earlier, maybe with a few other people in your local venue. You are hopeful that you will score ten heads. However, the person next to you, a seasoned professional, starts a little early and throws very quickly. You are still hopeful since you have already scored three heads, but your dreams of fame and fortune are interrupted by uproar—your neighbour has scored ten heads. Suddenly, all hope has vanished—what are the chances of that unlikely sequence of coin throws happening *twice* in the same room at almost the same time?

The answer to this question is, of course, very small. Very many people would now throw their lucky coin to the floor in disgust and leave. Yet that is totally illogical, because your individual chance of success is precisely the same as it was previously, or without anyone else in the room at all. Similarly, if we look at the steep improbability of life as we see it on earth, how would it make any difference if it had developed on some other planet or in some other universe? It wouldn't.

Alien Life

The next attempt to narrow the odds is to make do with the one universe we know about, but to argue in one of two different directions. First, some of those who believe in *panspermia* (the view that life was seeded on the earth by microbes brought from space by meteorites) seem to believe it is some kind of solution to the problem of the origin of life on earth. Well, there is some evidence for panspermia, but from a probability point of view it makes little difference. The intricate process of development up to the proposed microbes would have to take place somewhere, and the necessity for this to then be transferred to earth is another additional link in the chain of improbable events.

Second, some argue that there could well be intelligent life on other planets (or their moons) that orbit stars other than our sun, the so-called "exoplanets". After all, we have only detected (at the time of writing) about 700 such planets in a universe probably containing billions, so it seems there's a long way to go before we can draw any conclusion as to whether life is to be found elsewhere. If life were discovered elsewhere, (so the argument goes), then that would increase the probability of life on earth having arisen simply by chance.

This complaint is based on a misunderstanding of sampling. In almost every type of survey—consumer, political or whatever—results to an accuracy of maybe 5% either way are frequently obtained on the basis of a sample of only a few hundred people out of many millions. The reason this works is that the population sampled is relatively uniform. Generally speaking, above 100,000 or so the population size is irrelevant. Since the universe is also fairly uniform, we can be 95% certain, even now, that no other life-sustaining planets actually exist. To get to 99% certainty we should probably need to check out around 10,000 planets, which could happen within the next few years given the potential of NASA's phenomenal Kepler mission and its probable successors.

People who run surveys generally use statistical tables to determine sample size and my assertion is based on such methods. Don't be fooled, however, by thinking only about surveys that attempt to predict the results of political elections, because a large number of people change their voting intentions after being interviewed by the pollster. Also, of course, much sampling is not random but selective, (including the star sampling carried out by Kepler), and follows well-established practice for analysing the data. I do not mean to over-simplify the issue—but sample size is not a long-term problem in determining the probability of the existence of extra-terrestrial life. Even now, on statistical grounds, the odds are stacked against it.

Sampling v. Analysis

The next objection may be that, even if my arguments hold for events such as the formation of planets, which happened many times, there are other things, notably evolution, that only happened once as far as we can see at the moment. We can surely learn nothing from a sample of one.

I have already dealt with this in my discussion of evolution, pointing out that sampling is only one approach to the assessment of probability. It seems worth noting, however, that it is possible to sample many types of event *within* the evolutionary process. For example, we can sample duplication of genomes and determine the number of mutations that normally occur in each new generation. We can also determine what percentage of mutations are normally beneficial, what proportion of new species, on average, are wiped out by catastrophe, and so on. We can take practically a 100% sample of mammals existing today and determine that only in one case out of 5,000 or so did a mammal develop into an intelligent life form like ours. The message of evolutionary theory remains, essentially, that variation and selection can produce novelty, but the development of human intelligence is still very unlikely.

My argument here does not rely on elaborate statistical hypotheses such as Dawkins attacks in *The God Delusion*. I think he is probably quite right to do so—but he ignores the rather simpler facts that I am portraying. Instead of considering these in any detail, he seems to veer towards gambler's fallacy, with the assistance of multiverse thinking, despite its many problems. He then seeks to sidestep these problems by his use of the Anthropic Principle, to which we now turn.

Anthropic Overload

The word "anthropic" simply means "relating to humans", and the phrase "Anthropic Principle" refers to the fact that we tend to view the universe from our point of view as humans. Unfortunately, the term implies different things to different people. Dawkins complains that the religious take it as evidence of the existence of God, whereas in fact (in his view) it is an alternative hypothesis. He ought not to be so harsh, for the various meanings given to the principle allow diverse interpretations. "Anthropic" has become a buzz word, and rather overloaded. Rather than getting bogged down in terminology and questions of who said what, I think it is more useful to consider the broadest possible spectrum of anthropic ideas and how relevant they might be to our discussion.

My *level 1* Anthropic Principle is the simple notion of *anthropic selection*. We are carbon-based life forms and as such we are bound to interpret the universe from our point of view. This doesn't seem very spectacular, so I shall spice it up a little. There could be other types of life in the universe that we simply *could not* recognise as such. Rocks may have a fascinating inner life (maybe on a very long timescale) but we cannot perceive this because we are not rocks. If these other life forms were to feature conscious beings then they probably would not be able to recognise us as a life form either.

The obvious difficulty with this view is that it is by definition non-provable, therefore it cannot be described as scientific. The same criticism would apply if these beings were held to be in a different universe from ours within a multiverse, or if they were held to be some kind of computer-based entity.

Next *(level 2)* is the idea of *anthropic bias,* which we could also call *anthropocentrism.* This is similar to anthropic selection but relates to the possibility of intelligent life elsewhere in our universe that we *could* recognise as such, if we came across it. This life would probably have a very different chemical basis from ours, having followed a very different evolutionary pathway.

Suppose, by way of example, that the earth had happened to develop with a surface temperature twice as high as we actually have and retaining an atmosphere of methane (i.e. no "oxygen catastrophe"), then evolution might have produced a thinking species with a skin like asbestos, a totally different metabolism from ours, and the appearance of a twenty-foot diameter green pancake. We should then be reflecting on how lucky we are to be green pancakes in a universe clearly designed for our existence. In other words, design is in the mind of the beholder. Doubtless our intelligent green pancakes would come up with an equivalent to the Anthropic Principle under some other name—perhaps the *verdibatteric* principle, from their word *verdibatteros* or "green pancake".

The *verdibatteroi* do not exist on earth, and they certainly don't live on a planet near you, but they could exist somewhere, and at least the idea is *in principle* provable. It could therefore be described as a scientific hypothesis—even though there is no evidence for it as yet, and our initial sampling of planets, as we have seen, is not encouraging. Once again, though, the danger of gambler's fallacy creeps in. The happening of an unlikely event somewhere else in the universe does not, in itself, affect the probability of another unlikely event happening here. There are, however, a couple of loopholes in my argument which require attention.

It could be that if we observed intelligent life that had developed independently of life on earth, it would show us new data about evolutionary development, and such data might give us a stunningly fresh insight into the evolutionary process as it has occurred on earth. In principle, that could lead to a reassessment of the probabilities involved in our evolution. Although I think it is unlikely that such a didactic opportunity will arise, until we have a candidate example it is impossible to say for certain.

Another interesting outcome would arise if the Kepler mission and its successors found that the generation of life is a common event in our universe. We could then imagine standing on one planet with the *verdibatteroi*, or on another planet observing Protoworm, or on yet another with some friendly Cybermen (hopefully subdued forever by a passing Time Lord). A Gallup survey would reveal that 70% of each of these life-forms believed the universe was created especially for their benefit. With our broader vision we could contemplate the wonder of life springing up all over the place, evolving inevitably as night follows day. With some advanced species we could maybe argue about the existence of an all-powerful zogg.

If this picture of all-pervading life began to emerge then, again, we might have to re-assess the probabilities surrounding our own existence. However, there is no evidence for life evolving inevitably all over the place, or anywhere at all apart from on earth. Indeed, there is no evidence for the existence outside our earth of anything more complex than simple organic molecules, including amino acids. As we have seen these are often hailed excitedly as "the building blocks of life", but a pile of bricks does not a building make.

The improbabilities remain, and I hope you will notice that in this and the previous chapter I have avoided broad assumptions about what can and cannot happen in any kind of mystical sense. I have sought to argue from what we observe happening on our planet, in our solar system in our own universe, which seems to me quite scientific.

Anthropic Principle *level 3* states that the universe must have developed in the way that it has in order to bring us or other observers into existence. In theory we could look at our own specific needs and track back to the fundamental values of the universe. We would not need any other observation, or knowledge of measurements made of the fundamental values. Whatever these must be in order to make our existence possible is what they are, otherwise we simply would not be here making our observations.

Some people, apparently, find this a profound thought, but I must confess that I find it distinctly underwhelming. Others have made similar complaints, which usually amount to the assertion that this version of the Anthropic Principle is a truism—it has to be true. It simply tells us that if things had been different in the past, things would probably be different now.

Level 4 is more interesting and states, in essence, that the universe had to develop in the way that it has *in order* to bring us or other observers into existence. In some shape or form, that is its purpose. This seems to me like a design argument, sneaking the idea of purpose back in under cover. Critics of the principle on these grounds are not hard to find.

Level 5 is the same as level 4 but with the proviso that, rather than an intelligent being shaping the universe to produce observers, the observers themselves bring the universe into being. This implies that the observers affect things that happened before their own existence, but this apparently implausible idea is held to be supported by quantum mechanics. A compromise view is that many universes come into existence but only those that create observers survive. In either case, it is not clear how the observers actually affect the universe. Speculation and circularity are the usual criticisms of this type of view.

Where, then, does Dawkins stand in all this? Having attributed such importance to the Anthropic Principle, how does he really believe it operates?

I know that Dawkins would not explicitly go so far as levels 4 and 5, which are often lumped together as the *Strong Anthropic Principle,* for if he did he wouldn't need even to think about multiverses—they are simply irrelevant if there is either a pre-existing designer or emergent designer(s). In any case, such ideas contradict at a basic level Dawkins' overall thinking. Since we have seen that level 1 is inherently non-provable, and level 3 is probably best described as a truism, that only leaves level 2.

The first three levels on my scale are often grouped together as the *Weak Anthropic Principle.* Discussion of the level 2 type of theory almost always seems to bring in multiverses and alien life forms. The reason for this is simple—it is the only use of the Anthropic Principle that is easy to understand and which is also true to the original thrust of the whole idea, which involves selection.

It is now obvious why Dawkins, in *The God Delusion,* runs through all the difficulties of assessing the probability of extra-terrestrial intelligent life, yet still comes to the cheerful conclusion that "there are very probably alien civilizations that are superhuman". The panache is as breathtaking as it is illogical. It seems he simply must get to this conclusion somehow so that he can attach to his views the label "Anthropic Principle", which sounds much more convincing than "My Pet Theory". It is interesting that while he makes this point he refers to four science fiction writers, but very little science.

Having established his anthropic credentials he continues, "we could only be discussing the question in the kind of universe that was capable of producing us. Our existence therefore determines that the fundamental constants of physics all had to be in their respective Goldilocks zones".

What does the phrase "had to be" mean? If it means that the fundamental constants were determined by some *necessity* that humankind should eventually exist, then this implies the existence of God as a cause of this necessity. If it means that, *as it turned out,* the fundamental constants must have been as they are or we wouldn't be here, then this merely implies the extremely unlikely fluke that we have been discussing. It seems that this verbal ambiguity is an attempt to smuggle in a stand-alone purpose for the universe without the need for a designer. In other words, it's a fudge.

We saw earlier that Dawkins argues, following the imagery of Daniel Dennett, that evolution should be regarded as a "crane" that can elevate our understanding of other areas at present beyond our grasp. We saw that he also supplements this with the Anthropic Principle as a stop-gap until the cosmic crane that explains everything is revealed. Those who disagree with him need their consciousness raising by understanding natural selection.

We seem to be in an area that can only be termed mystical. I call those who subscribe to this view "cranies" because the term is mildly disrespectful and, appropriately, has something of the feel of a cult about it. Although I can understand the psychological drive here, the whole thing seems somewhat patronising and hardly scientific. I could equally well argue that cranies need their consciousness raising by Morris Dancing—or, for that matter, theology.

Erasing the Epitaph

It often seems that we might need an epitaph to theology. I mainly have in mind natural theology, since it is so often claimed that Darwin and modern science in general has discredited the whole subject. I now feel strongly that the argument from design has not been overthrown by Darwin, or, for that matter, by Dawkins.

In the two centuries since Paley wrote, our detailed understanding has grown, in fact many times over, extending to the minutiae of physiology, cytology, genetics, and biochemistry. In particular, we have become aware of the systemic nature of the earth and its biosphere—that network of interlocking systems that depend on each other. Even accepting evolutionary theory in terms of the process that happened, this all reduces down, as I have tried to show, to the question of the extreme improbability of human life existing as it does without a designer. Dawkins' illustration of *Mount Improbable* is ingenious, and very few of us would entirely deny its validity with regard to some aspects of evolution, but it is just not sufficient, and all the smoke and mirrors of multiverses and Anthropic Principles fail to undo that fact.

The problem for atheism is that once a designing mind is admitted into the picture, the other main arguments for the existence of God tend to come alive. If there is a designing mind behind the universe, it makes sense to regard that mind as the first cause of everything. If we are a product of that mind, then it would be strange if our minds were mere illusion, or bore no relationship to the divine mind. If that relationship is admitted, then the moralities found in human cultures are best explained by their common origin; and if we have an intuitive concept of God as supreme being then that is validated as experience of a real, not imaginary, deity. Even Anselm may yet have his day! The epitaph should be erased.

The epitaph should be erased for another reason—not for the comfort of the faithful nor to keep theologians in employment, but to avoid long-term disappointment for atheists. There is, I think, an atheist misapprehension, which is that the abolition of belief in God would automatically abolish superstition and all such primitive nonsense. We have seen that such a sea-change did not take place as a result of the Enlightenment, yet the misapprehension persists—just one more push and the goal will be reached.

The reason this does not happen, and is not likely to happen, is that these "primitive" understandings of how the universe works do not arise from monotheism at all, as I hope to illustrate.

The Great Irony

I do not expect to convince everyone of the legitimacy of natural theology, and many atheists will undoubtedly remain in lucky fluke territory—our existence is simply the way it all happened, by chance. Using multiverse theories to claim the opposite is too problematical, and we lack any evidence to show which (if any) such theory is correct both mathematically *and* as a representation of reality. The Anthropic Principle should only really be deployed if we can point to intelligent life springing up in many places in the universe or multiverse, and we can't currently do that.

However, if we deny any divine initiative or influence and also claim that our existence is simply a fluke, (i.e. we acknowledge the huge improbability of things being as they are) then a fascinating thought follows on. I am not convinced that atheists really take this on board, hence the potential for ultimate disappointment.

Supposing I were to suggest that, in our universe, under very special circumstances, now and again, miracles happen. For example, I claim there are certain exceptional conditions that can arise in which matter on a larger scale than subatomic can behave with particle-wave duality (we already know that this happens at the subatomic level). It could become an interesting after-dinner diversion. Let's all think very hard and focus on Harold. We see shimmering, reminiscent of the transporter bay on the Starship Enterprise, and suddenly Harold is gone. A few seconds later there is a clattering of plates and dishes in the kitchen, from which Harold duly appears, smiling sheepishly and wiping leftovers of the main course from his jacket.

Why couldn't our world be like this? All it needs is a slight modification to the one that we've got, or always thought we had. Let's suppose that this extra little bit of flukiness is extremely unlikely—maybe one chance in a billion. No problem. All we need to do is add a few more zeros to our improbability calculations. While we're at it, what else would we like to exist? A solar system somewhere with planets shaped like sugar cubes, perhaps? We could accommodate practically anything if we wanted to, because everything is massively improbable anyway.

I trust, though, that you have spotted the deliberate mistake. I gave the impression in my dinner party illustration that everyone is quite sure the experiment is going to work. If that were so, two things would follow. First, the guests would focus on getting Harold to land somewhere much safer than the kitchen, say, on a sofa or a bed. Second, it wouldn't be much of a fun thing to do, because if it were predictable it would be mundane, no more exciting than playing *Trivial Pursuit*. In other words, and this is the serious point: *no-one claims scientific predictability.*

Let's suppose that the after-dinner game catches on. Most of the time in these postprandial sessions, Harold (or whoever) goes nowhere. Over a couple of years, with thousands of Harolds, two are seen to go transparent for a few seconds, one is knocked off his chair by a mysterious force, four claim to have had an out of the body experience, eighteen claim they saw their kitchen vividly in their minds, but in black and white, and three claim to have actually moved, as verified by the other guests, all of whom passed lie-detector tests. One of these paranormal events took place in Thetford, another in Cowley, and another in a village near Aberystwyth. Only Harold from Cowley actually ended up in the kitchen, the other two were seen to move towards the kitchen door and then back to where they were before.

It seems that the likely success rate for this teleportation experiment, according to the tabloid press, turns out to be about one in 10,000. This cannot, of course, be disproved by scientific observation, because no one is claiming it happens every time, or that it's possible to replicate the same conditions to make it happen again in Cowley or one of the other "hotspots". It's just one of those things. Even if you could have permanent observation everywhere and nothing happened, it would be reasonable to suggest that the observers (or the knowledge of being observed) upset the concentration of guests, so they couldn't focus properly.

What reply is there to such an assertion? If it's so unlikely that we should be here, yet we believe it came about just by chance, why should we not also believe in other very unlikely things—at least given a hint of evidence?

The Good Old Days

This is a tricky one, so let's put it another way. In the good old days the scientist could simply refute the red-top newspapers' sensationalism in a clear way: these things just don't happen, they are against the laws of nature, and we understand the laws of nature pretty exhaustively—mechanics, thermodynamics, optics, electromagnetism, and so on. End of argument, exit boffin. The "old days" ended some time after the Michelson-Morley experiment, probably around the beginning of the twentieth century. Although up until then many, of course, had abandoned belief in an interventionist God (it's that power of deism again), there was still a sense of stability, a sense of the inherent *understandability* of things, just *as if* the whole universe had been created and set in motion by a creator who fixed the rules and made them unchangeable, permanent, immutable. God remained, in effect, as the great orrery maker in the sky.

It was easiest to carry on with this "safe" outlook, because without it there is no backstop against anyone who wants to claim that there is variability in the laws of nature, a variability which could occasionally lead to strange events such as the teleportation of Harold.

In the end, then, the probability of the earth existing as it is without some kind of designer is extremely small, but from an atheistic point of view that's just the way it is. However, by some sort of extreme irony, the atheist has also thrown away any guarantee of predictability. People like Copernicus, Kepler, Galileo, and Newton believed that the laws of physics and mathematics were there because they believed in a perfect God. The perfect God communicated via the Bible *and* via our understanding of the physical and mathematical principles that he laid down—and he laid them down as unchanging and invariable rules. Nature was *necessarily* reliable and immutable because God was reliable and immutable.

The atheist who wishes to be consistent is in a somewhat fraught position. If the whole of our existence is just a fluke, it would be quite reasonable to suggest that there are pockets of added flukiness that, like Harold, we may experience on rare occasions. In fact, there is no logical reason to suppose that nature always behaves in the same way. It could behave differently while we aren't looking, and for all we know its behaviour might change with time.

In case you think I should have stuck to writing sermons, you'll be glad to know that my assertion finds support from the great eighteenth-century Scottish philosopher and (probable) atheist, David Hume (1711-76). He pointed out the most forcefully that, having sceptically eliminated God and miracles on the grounds of lack of verifiable evidence, then logically we should also eliminate those archaic ideas of uniformity on the same grounds. We cannot be certain that the laws of nature are consistent, or that they will be tomorrow what they are today.

Humean scepticism is very popular within the atheist community, and his assertion that the existence of God and the reality of miracles can never be proved scientifically is quoted endlessly. Yet those same sceptics seem less keen to dwell on Hume's equal scepticism concerning natural law. We believe that the laws of nature are the same everywhere and throughout time, but we cannot know this for certain. Eliminating God, therefore, does not rule out the possibility of extremely unlikely things happening, even though it's part of our nature to believe that those things we observe frequently are more probable and we adopt such beliefs out of pragmatic necessity.

Emergence

The danger with the assumption of uniformity is that it ignores the possibility of emergence. We know that the laws of physics are a bedrock of the universe as we see it today, but until the universe cooled to the point where atoms could form and begin to interact with each other there was no chemistry at all. The laws of chemistry emerged when the environment allowed it.

Eventually, with the formation of a protocell, biochemistry emerged, with its own laws. The crucial factor here was the presence of a genome, however simple, which governed the cell according to the information contained in its early RNA and later DNA. In turn this led to evolution with its own laws. We may similarly note the emergence of consciousness and the emergence of human consciousness.

This still leaves the alleged teleportation of Harold looking rather different from these ancient and large-scale events, but it might help to look at the actual process of emergence one more time. Suppose for a moment that you were around at the time when abiogenesis was about to get under way. There you are, observing one of those chemically active thermal vents—I suppose you would have to be an angel, but let me stress this is not a religious assertion, merely an illustrative device.

Apparently meaningless chaos has been going on at this location for thousands, maybe millions, of years, when suddenly a patch of colourless slime appears, but vanishes soon afterwards. At the next team meeting of the Heavenly Host you recount the strange episode. Several others have seen similar things on rare occasions all over the world, but no one knows what to make of it—until the "genesis moment" finally happens and eventually there is protocell slime around every corner. It is only when the emergent phenomenon has taken off that the previously mysterious forerunners make sense.

Harold, fortunately, is of a fairly balanced personality and ignores the crank e-mails that tell him he is forging a new way for mankind that will release the full potential of the human brain, heralding the dawn of a new age. I am not putting forward such theories myself, merely pointing out that emergence might involve, for a time at least, the incomprehensible.

We shall hear later Harold's full story of what happened at the Cowley dinner party. In the meantime, as he himself quite often remarks, "It makes you think!"

CHAPTER 10

Quantum Quirkiness

The quantum world—the world of the very small, inhabited by sub-atomic particles—is quite beyond our power of understanding in the normal sense of the word. Yet there are some broad principles of quantum mechanics (sometimes also referred to as *quantum theory*) that have become well known and influential. The purpose of this chapter is to look at some of these broad principles as they impact on the issues under discussion, but without going into a kind of quasi-religious mysticism, which is always a potential pitfall.

Why Quantum Mechanics Matters

The ideas of quantum mechanics have, to put it mildly, significant implications for our day to day world. To begin with, the theory explains why the whole shooting match is prevented from imploding. Apparently the *Pauli Exclusion Principle* is the reason that everything doesn't shrink back together in a kind of reverse Big Bang. You'll appreciate what a Bad Thing this would be if you saw the superb BBC series *Atom*. At one point the presenter, Jim Al-Khalili, holds an apple and simply says that if you removed all the empty space contained in all seven billion people in the world—that's to say the space within and between the atoms of which they are made—then the resultant matter would be about the size of the apple. Wow. So that's at least one way in which the very small quantum "world" affects the world as we know it, by maintaining structure and preventing implosion. We're talking here about the foundations of physics.

Quantum mechanics explains the properties of atoms, why they behave consistently in the ways they do—oxygen is always oxygen, and ever more shall be so. Without this little trick, life would be very confusing; in fact, impossible. So there is another fairly important connection between the small and large scale models of our universe—consistent chemistry.

One would think that something that lies behind the laws of physics and chemistry would possess a simple, easily understood grandeur. If only it were so. Our awareness that reality is not so obliging started off with Max Planck (1858–1947) when he attempted to explain the frequencies of light emitted when we heat an object such as a lump of metal. His basic discovery was that energy is conveyed in packets, called "quanta" (singular "quantum"). This was gradually extended by others—but then the nightmare began.

Uncertainty

Courtesy of Werner Heisenberg (1901–76) and his uncertainty principle it seems that uncertainty is everywhere. For example, we cannot determine the position of an electron, we can only estimate the *probability* of it being in a certain location in relation to the nucleus of the atom to which it belongs.

One way of imagining this is to think of the traditional picture of an electron orbiting a nucleus. We shall call the distance of the electron from the nucleus d. At low speed you can point to the electron and where it is. You can put in a very small tape measure and check that d hasn't changed. At high speed, however, it just becomes a blur. Since the electron is always the same distance from the nucleus this blur is a hollow sphere or shell. You can be pretty certain that the electron is somewhere in the shell, but not at all certain as to where.

Mathematicians and physicists dislike pictures, but love equations. The *Schrödinger wave equation* describes in mathematical terms the shell that we have visualised—but why is it called a "wave" equation?

This is not an obvious matter, but an extension of my simple shell picture might be worth a try. Suppose I started at the nucleus of my hypothetical atom and gradually moved out from it, I would certainly not detect anything until I got close to distance d from the nucleus. However, if I were moving too fast I might miss it—crossing the electron's path while it was somewhere else. Remember also that we are talking about a shell, not a circle. I might be at a distance d from the nucleus, but standing, as it were, on the equator, whereas the electron has gradually changed its orbit so that it passes a bit further "north" and again I miss it. Alternatively, d might not be constant—the orbit might be slightly elliptical.

In this sort of scenario, taking up a position of distance d from the nucleus means that there will be a probability, but never a certainty, of being hit by my pet electron within a certain length of time. But I might also be hit if I take up a position a bit less or a bit more than d from the nucleus. It's less likely, but still possible. The likelihood of it happening will depend on how elliptical the orbit might be, and the extent to which the electron circles in one plane or deviates from that.

What seemed like a simple task—start from the nucleus, move out and report when you get hit by an electron—would actually have to be repeated, maybe thousands of times, to get an overall picture of the electron's behaviour. You could plot a graph of how many times you were hit by the electron when standing at each distance from the nucleus. Early on in the journey it would be exceedingly rare to encounter the electron; at distance d the score might be 70%, then it would drop off again.

In order to get a full picture of the movement of the electron you would have to repeat this whole operation moving out from the nucleus each time in a large number of different directions, one after the other. Putting all the graphs end to end would give you a complicated series of ups and downs, in other words a kind of wave indicating probabilities. Repeat this total process over and over again and the wave would repeat itself over and over again. This would not be easy to interpret, however.

At this point I would go along to my friendly local university and get a maths professor to tell me the equation that describes my series of graphs. I would be thoroughly reprimanded for sticking my measurements end-to-end, a much more sophisticated method of integration of all the data is called for. The resulting equation would be my own personal wave equation for the electron I had studied.

In 1926 Erwin Schrödinger (1887–1961) set out a much better equation covering all particles everywhere. Considering his "interesting" personal life involving, in effect, two wives simultaneously, this was no mean feat. Uncertainty must have been for him a day-to-day experience.

Larger atoms have up to 118 electrons and extremely lumpy nuclei compared to hydrogen. When atoms join together into molecules they share electrons and things get even worse. Applying the word "genius" to Erwin Schrödinger is a huge understatement.

My treatment here can only give a tiny flavour of the subject which I hope will not cause too much derision among any readers who happen to be physicists. But some interesting thoughts follow on, even from this simple treatment. For example, since the position of our token electron cannot be exactly determined, is there a possibility that it could be a ridiculously large distance from its nucleus—say, five light years away? The answer to this question is "yes", although as you might guess the probability of this is exceedingly small. In the quantum world, the electron is not exactly situated anywhere, it is simply more likely to be detected at a certain distance from the nucleus (which we called d) than anywhere else.

This points us to another interesting quantum factoid. Supposing our electron is located behind a barrier that, in conventional terms, would not allow it to pass. Is there not still a probability that it might be detected on the other side of that barrier? Again, the answer is affirmative. In the right setting some electrons will perform this feat, which is known as *quantum tunnelling*. The phenomenon is applied particularly in electronics. More important to most of us, however, is the fact that without quantum tunnelling the sun (or any other star) would not shine. Hydrogen nuclei (protons) do not have enough energy, despite the massive temperature of the star, to overcome the repulsion between them and fuse with each other, this fusion being the process that produces energy. Nevertheless, some do tunnel through the barrier, so the stars do shine.

Entanglement

According to the exclusion principle that I have already mentioned, many subatomic particles in an atom cannot have certain properties the same. If the property known as "spin" of one of the particles changes, another "partner" particle will immediately change as well. This also applies, for example, to a pair of photons—even if they are separated by a distance of many miles—provided they are *entangled* with each other. This entanglement can be produced by some method such as ensuring that they stem from the same event at atomic level.

In an experiment conducted by the University of Geneva in 1997 photons were sent several miles in opposite directions, but still exhibited this peculiar (to us) behaviour. In principle (i.e. on the basis of the maths) two particles could be on opposite sides of the galaxy and still show the same behaviour. You can find details of the experiment in question and other bizarre happenings on the *gap-optique* web site (see Bibliography for link). Some of it is not easy reading, but the more accessible articles linked to the site are fascinating. Their results have been confirmed by further experiments in Geneva and at other centres.

The new holy grail appears to be teleportation. It's important to note, however, that it's *information* that may be transferred. Even then, although there seems to be non-local correlation between properties, which can be deduced retrospectively, it is not possible to pass information instantaneously between two points by tweaking those properties at one point and observing what happens at another point. It does seem to be possible, however, to transfer the characteristics of a photon from one place to another by a process known as *quantum teleportation*.

If you really want to get into this subject then read *The Non-Local Universe* by Robert Nadeau and Menas Kafatos and also *Entangled Minds* by Dean Radin. The latter gives a simplified but particularly good illustration, originally devised by physicist N. David Mermin, of the phenomenon explored by the Geneva team and others. The illustration is quite long, but if you read Radin's account I think you will find it as startling as I did and worth the effort. If it's really not your thing, however, here's a summary.

Imagine two identical boxes about the size of, say, lunchboxes. Each has a red light, a green light, and a switch, and the switch can be set to three positions, labelled 1, 2, and 3. These two boxes are in labs miles apart and there is no direct connection between them. However, both are connected by optical fibres to a third box in another lab, between the first two. This third box simply has one button on it. When the button is pressed a photon is sent simultaneously along each optical fibre, both photons originating from the same light source in such a way that they are entangled. The photons are detected by the remote boxes, which flash either red or green.

Nothing goes back along the optical fibre—yet there is correlation between the colours of lights that flash. When the switches have the same setting (1,2, or 3) the lights flash the same colour, either both red or both green. When the switches are on different settings they *may* happen to flash the same colour but often do not. Overall, if you just looked at one box in isolation, it would be flashing red and green at random. Yet when you set the switches the same, there it goes again—the same colour flashes on both. How do the boxes "know" when they have the same switch settings, and how do they "know" what colour the other box is going to flash? How can information be transmitted instantly from one box to the other if they are miles, or light years, apart?

On reading about this while sat in a convenient coffee shop (I was supposed to be at a meeting but tragically it was cancelled) I grabbed some serviettes and tabulated all possible combinations of switches and lights. I must admit that by the time I finished my serviette scribbling my cappuccino was stone cold, but it was worth it—the greatest "a-ha" since the dogfish and the Plank's constant experiment way back in my school days.

Although this illustration corresponds to a real life experiment, the complicated physics and maths is, of course, concealed in the fictional boxes and described to give us a layman's impression of what is happening. Nevertheless, the result of this experiment was truly "spooky"—and it has been repeated and verified several times.

The key point is that there is indeed non-locality—that is to say, an effect that is remote from what we normally regard as the location of a particle. But it is not possible to set the switch on one box and produce a predictable result on the other box. That sort of instantaneous signalling device would be very useful, but would break the rule that nothing—not even information—can travel faster than the speed of light. The same applies to quantum teleportation, because some information has to be sent by conventional means (i.e. slower than the speed of light) in order to set up the actual teleportation. Of course, if the recent claim that neutrinos *can* travel faster than the speed of light is verified, this paragraph would have to be re-written. So would a lot of scientific literature, but the phenomena of non-locality and entanglement would remain unscathed.

Complementariness

Wave equation thinking raises another interesting question. Is our sample electron a particle or a wave? That same question can be asked of other entities, particularly light, because of another classic experiment that goes back to the early nineteenth century and has been performed in many versions since. This is *Young's double slit experiment,* in which a light shines through two slits, beyond which is a screen. The screen shows a banded interference pattern, as would be expected from a wave. But if the screen is removed and replaced by two small telescopes, one pointing at each slit, then you see light coming through one slit or the other, not both.

We're assuming here that the light source is turned down very low so that only one photon at a time is moving towards the screen or telescopes. In other words, light appears to act sometimes as a particle and sometimes as a wave. It seems as if somehow the photons "know" about both slits, even though they only travel through one of them, and then "decide" in cooperation with the other photons where to hit the screen in order to make the interference pattern.

We tend to think of physics and maths as giving a single explanation of reality. With the advent of quantum mechanics, all that changes. We require *complementary* understandings of scientific data. Thinking of light as a wave is part of the explanation of what light is, thinking of it as a particle is another part, and neither is complete on its own—even though we cannot observe both at once. Now of course that is not very satisfying to many scientists, for whom their whole *raison d'être* is to provide definitive explanations. The frustration is that the sought for understanding may, by its very nature, be unattainable.

Observer Effects

The double slit experiment raises yet another intriguing aspect of quantum mechanics, namely, *observer effects*. It seems as if the behaviour of photons is affected by how we observe them. One way they seem like a wave, another way they seem like particles.

Another type of observer effect goes back to my opening illustration in which we were tracking an electron. You could only detect the electron when it ran into you, or at least into some kind of detector. But that would immediately slow it down—it would lose momentum. Any observation has some effect like this, and these effects are significant in the quantum world, although far too tiny to register in the day-to-day world. Yet another observer effect arises in connection with quantum events, which inevitably bring us to the most famous cat ever apart from Dick Whittington's, Puss in Boots, and the Cheshire Cat.

Schrödinger's cat is a paradox. In case you don't know, the scenario is that the unfortunate cat is placed in a closed box, which also contains a very small speck of uranium, a Geiger counter, a vial of cyanide, and an electrically operated hammer device to break the vial, which would kill the cat. When the uranium emits radiation (i.e. decays), the Geiger counter will trigger the hammer device. Farewell feline friend.

The half-life of any radioactive element is the time it will take for half of its mass to decay, but no one can predict which particular atoms will decay and which will not. For a particular atom, it could be now or never. Or any time in between.

That may seem simple enough—if the uranium in the box emits radiation immediately, Tibbles will die immediately; if it takes a year then the cat will die in a year's time, assuming of course that it's remotely fed and watered in the meantime. The tricky bit is that as long as the box is closed we don't know whether the uranium has emitted or not, and according to quantum mechanics we have to regard it as both decayed and not decayed. This is called a *superposition* of two states. Therefore, we also have to regard Tibbles as both dead and alive, which is a bit odd.

Please note: it's not the religious fundamentalists or the scumbag theologians who are saying this, it's the scientists. Why? Because superposition is part of the theoretical structure that provides quantum mechanics with its vast power. The problem is that it's difficult—maybe impossible—to understand what it actually means.

The most frequently given response to this problem, as worked out by the good and great of the physics world, is known as the *Copenhagen Interpretation*, which is that once the box is opened and an observation occurs there is a resolution of the uncertainty and the uranium becomes either decayed or not decayed, with the state of the cat being determined accordingly. That may not sound like much of a solution, because the next question is obvious: how could my observation make any difference? It sounds like a kind of voodoo. It even sounds as if my mind (which makes the observation) is affecting the material process of atomic decay.

All this means that the famous cat invokes the question of mind influencing matter, in a similar way to the double slit experiment. The distinction between mind and matter is a dualism with a long history in human thought, and contemplating its removal is somewhat vertiginous for many. The Copenhagen Interpretation involves observer effects with bells on.

You will notice that the response outlined above is fittingly called an interpretation, not an explanation. An alternative interpretation, which we have already encountered in connection with the multiverse hypothesis, revolves around the idea of parallel worlds. It is often known as the *Many Worlds Interpretation (MWI)* and originated mainly with Hugh Everett (1930–82) in the 1950s. According to this hypothesis, for any quantum event there are two universes running in parallel, one in which (in this case) the uranium has fired the Geiger counter and one in which it hasn't. So Tibbles is actually dead and alive at the same time, but in different worlds. Proponents of this view maintain that it also makes the sums work out. Do not, however, try to visualise what it means, for therein lies insanity. It's like *Sliding Doors* multiplied millions of times over. Perhaps in some feline world beyond the stars they've made a film called *Sliding Catflaps*.

The Copenhagen Interpretation has found the greater acceptance, so observer effects have remained a subject of great discussion. The important thing, it seems to me, is not to make mystical assumptions about mind influencing matter but to dig deeper into the issue of what an observation really is. That is a philosophical question to which we will turn later.

Schrödinger's cat is a paradox because it links together the very small, where we know that quantum rules apply, with the normal-sized world to which we generally relate. It seems that there must be a touch of illicit process going on, because we know that Geiger counters, relay mechanisms, and cats are not subject to quantum mechanics, but the paradox makes it seem that they are. Yet it is difficult to show where the logic of the paradox is faulty. For now, let's simply note that uncertainty, entanglement, complementariness, and observer effects are well-established principles.

We should also note, perhaps, that at first sight quantum mechanics tends to introduce a dualistic way of thinking. Things that are exceedingly small operate according to quantum mechanics, while everything else operates according to classic Newtonian rules. This dualism raises the obvious question: when do things get small enough to exhibit quantum behaviour? We could fire a stream of tennis balls at a wall with two gaps in it, but we would not expect to see something like the results of the double slit experiment. Likewise with half-inch ball bearings. But what about sand grains? Or single-celled algae? Or heavy carbon-based molecules? Or helium atoms?

Angels and Pins

I can't resist referring back to those medieval theologians we looked at earlier, who, we are always told, argued about how many angels could dance on the head of a pin. Actually, they didn't, that's a second-hand misquote of a derisory remark, involving the point of a needle, made by others much later. But those medieval chaps did have some pretty arcane stuff going on. For example, St Thomas Aquinas wanted to know whether an angel could move from one place to another without passing through the intervening places. He came to the conclusion that sometimes it could. He would have had no problem with Harold from Cowley moving from one room to another, provided that Harold became temporarily angelic.

The angels and pinheads caricature represents quite a lot of things that people like Aquinas found interesting, such as the question of whether there was an angelic substance that was not material and therefore did not occupy space like the matter which we can see. It sounds like madness—until you get into quantum mechanics. The parallels had struck me before, but I was delighted to have them confirmed recently by Robert Bartlett in his excellent BBC series *Inside the Medieval Mind*. Once again the theologians were asking the right questions before everyone else, this time 700 years ahead of the game.

Quantum thinking has re-opened the basic question of what the world around us actually *is*. Once we get beyond atoms, sub-atomic particles, and waves, what is everything made of? This is the traditional field of philosophy known as *metaphysics,* which literally means "after physics". Are there two sorts of stuff in the world, mind and matter? Is there another possible division between small quantum stuff and big normal stuff?

These are not unimportant questions. The mathematics underlying quantum mechanics may work, and one day it may all be drawn together into one completely unified theory of everything. But as Stephen Hawking famously asked, what breathes fire into the equations? I can use Pythagoras' theorem to verify that the partition wall under construction in my garage is at right-angles to the outer wall. However, the fact that the theorem is mathematically correct does not prove the existence of my garage or the wall. Even if you knew of their existence by other methods, the fact that Pythagoras was obeyed wouldn't tell you anything about what the garage, or the wall, were made from.

To what, then, would a great mathematical theory of everything actually refer? Metaphysics is sometimes dismissed as old hat, but the most modern science demands that the discussion be re-opened. This discussion is highly relevant to the probability issues raised in the previous chapters.

Re-inventing the wheel is one of the least satisfying pursuits available to the agile mind. It will help us therefore if we take a very brief look at how discussion of these matters has been pursued in the past. We need just some basic bullet points, so if you're not into philosophy, don't panic. By the way, you can also think of this little excursion as a stepping stone to understanding epistemology—the question of how we know things—so it's a doubly worthwhile exercise.

Welcome to the Philosophical Forum

Down an alleyway off a bustling main road there's an old doorway, with a look of jaded splendour about it, bearing a brass plate. Brushing aside some slightly overgrown ivy the plate reads "Philosophical Forum. Members Only." Fortunately, we have day passes, provided we don't make too much noise. Having signed the guest book we head for the room marked "Mind and Matter". On a plinth just inside the door is a plaster bust bearing the name "Descartes 1596–1650", so we shall first see why he has the place of honour.

Starting from the obvious, you can say that there is either one basic kind of stuff in the universe (a view called *monism),* or more than one *(pluralism).* It might strike you as odd to talk about such an abstract question, but it's the sort of thing philosophers talk about a lot. Common sense tells us that the universe is made of many kinds of stuff such as rock, wood, air, and toothpaste, to name but a few. We very early learn, however, that this is just an appearance, because everything is composed of atoms, which in turn are made of sub-atomic particles, which in turn are made of a few basic very small sub-atomic particles. We also know that we have many thoughts, and that these thoughts are somehow connected with the brain, which in the end is material and therefore is made of the same very small sub-atomic particles.

On a practical day-to-day basis we (thankfully) know the difference between wood and toothpaste. We also know the difference between the thought of toothpaste and the actual tube lying on the bathroom shelf. Yet it's possible that in the end wood, toothpaste, and the idea of toothpaste are all just sub-atomic particles put together in different combinations—that would be an extreme kind of monism. On the other hand, we could maintain that these things are totally different from each other, which would be pluralism. So the whole question that we are considering isn't so daft after all, although it might seem irrelevant to normal life. I sympathise with that feeling but ask you to run with the idea for now.

If we go for pluralism, then we can choose anywhere between two and a lot, but mind and matter are generally enough for most normal people. Dualism of this philosophical variety says that the mind, the world of ideas (such as the thought of toothpaste), is a separate reality from material things (such as the toothpaste that is there on the bathroom shelf). Obviously the brain is material, but for the dualist there is something else, commonly called "mind", as well. Discussion normally revolves around mind and matter because experience of both is absolutely fundamental to our human lives.

So far, so good. Let's be dualists for a moment—just like René Descartes. He was quite happy with the body being like a machine, with the mind being an immaterial something that could affect the body and could also be affected by it. The problem is, if mind and matter are so different, how can they affect each other? It's like wondering how a light beam could move a boulder. And where is the mind located? It's impossible to deny that we experience both mind and matter, but exactly how they are connected has baffled a lot of Very Clever People. Descartes thought they interacted through the pineal gland just underneath the brain.

In order to get round this problem, the clever-clogs monist claims that *either* mind *or* matter is the ultimate stuff, one or the other, you can't have both. If you go for the first you are called an *idealist*, and this is one of the big philosophical classifications. Some idealists believe that the material universe is illusory, although most wouldn't go to that extreme. It's certainly not a good lifestyle option to live as though that were true; people think you're barmy.

If you go for the second view, that *matter* is the ultimate stuff, then you are what's known as a *materialist,* claiming that minds and thoughts are just processes within a material substance such as the brain, or at the most they are merely a kind of spin-off from those processes.

Materialism in the philosophical sense, by the way, is nothing to do with the popular use of the word, as in being concerned only for making money and spending it. Similarly, idealism in the philosophical sense is nothing to do with the popular use of that word, as in striving for some great goal. No, the words materialism and idealism are purely neutral words about how we view reality. Note also that philosophers do not normally use the word "stuff", which is rather unsophisticated. They use the word "substance"— which to most of us is quite confusing. In philosophical circles we have to put out of our minds the ways in which we normally use that word. Substance is to do with the reality when we get behind the sub-atomic particles and get down to what everything is.

You might suppose that, after a couple of thousand years or so thinking about it, philosophers would have come up with a definitive answer to these problems, but you'd be wrong, although their efforts line the walls of the *Philosophical Forum* and some of the books are getting a bit faded. The most common view from the "new atheist" camp is materialistic, in which the mind is just a spin-off of processes in the brain. The pineal gland theory didn't last long.

Mind and Body

Whether we're inclined to make mind or matter the most basic, in a practical sense we're stuck with both. The so-called *mind-body* problem which arises from this fact can be stated as follows: if someone stands on your toe, you don't feel an electrical stimulus in your brain, you feel a pain in your foot. Why?

Of course, neuroscientists can point to the part of the brain that has been stimulated, and I would guess that by stimulating it artificially they could induce the pain without standing on your toe—some people think it's fun to do that sort of thing, but you would still feel the pain in your foot, not in your head.

Things become yet more surreal when we consider not just receiving information but processing it, making decisions, and acting upon them. You can decide whether to ignore the person who stood on your toe (the Stoic way), apologise even though it wasn't your fault (the English way), or punch the offender on the nose (the night-in-the-cells way). If you go the third way, the magistrate is not likely to accept the excuse that you couldn't help doing what you did, because it was all caused by electrical circuits in your brain. That would be a view called *determinism* but in real life it's generally regarded as stretching materialism too far. As with the extreme idealist the word "barmy" tends to be invoked.

To summarise, then, we're stuck with our experience of mind and body. The idealist says that mind is the ultimate substance, while the materialist says that the body is ultimate. Whichever view you take, the problem is to figure out how the mind affects the body, and vice versa. Let's be more specific, since we know a lot about how brains and neurons work. How does the mind affect the electrical signals that pass across the billions of synapses (nerve junctions) that make up the human brain, and how, in turn, is the mind affected by the brain's electrical activity? How can material and non-material things affect each other?

These are important questions because a consistent materialist will automatically dismiss the idea of God, since God is by definition non-material. Any concept of God *must* therefore be a delusion! Similarly, the idea of abstract moral principles means nothing to a consistent materialist, because all ideas are unreal compared to the material world; therefore moral principles must be derived from concrete phenomena, as in consequentialism. The idealist, on the other hand, has no problem with such abstractions and might point out, for example, that mathematical truths are clearly real, even though they are immaterial—and so the argument continues.

If you happen to be a lateral thinker, you may already be entertaining thoughts like "relativity tells us that energy and matter are interchangeable, so perhaps mind and matter are interchangeable as well". Or perhaps, "if the Copenhagen Interpretation is correct then it seems that mind and matter are connected whatever the philosophical problems attached." These are the right sort of questions—but let's finish our day trip before we pick them up again.

Attempted Solutions to Ignore

Moving on through the *Forum* we come to the seventeenth-century philosopher Gottfried Leibniz (1646–1716), he of the "Best of All Possible Worlds" theory mentioned in Chapter 1. Leibniz is represented by a rather large oil painting showing him with two clocks. The painting is allegorical. He held that mind and body are like two clocks that are completely separate, but both keep perfect time so they always correspond. God has set things up this way—it's called a *pre-established harmony*. The fact that when my toe is stood upon I feel a pain is not caused by any connection between the two things, it's just that both happen at the same time.

Nicolas Malebranch (1638–1715), a French philosopher of the same period (smaller portrait with eyes raised slightly heavenwards) maintained that God synchronises the mental and material worlds whenever they appear to interact, a view known as *occasionalism*. For the most part, however, the mind-body question remains unanswered among the great philosophers of centuries past. Those answers that were proposed often seem today clumsy and contrived, sometimes bringing in God as a quick fix.

What Have we Learned?

Well, we can't stay here all day, so let's leave the *Forum,* hopefully armed with a better understanding of the major issue under discussion and some of the answers that have been tried and found wanting. To test whether this hope is justified, let's ask the first obvious question: does quantum quirkiness support a real dualism of mind and matter? I think the answer to this question has to be negative, for if mind and matter were separate there could be no question of observation affecting a quantum event.

Now this verdict will seem to some rather trite, since the paradoxes of the quantum understanding of things may not actually indicate mind influencing matter, but mind perceiving or interpreting things in two different ways. Even with this view, though, it is still clear that observation involves a dialogue between mind and matter. It is no longer possible to say that things happen in the material world "out there" and are definitively observed by our minds "in here". As the veteran physicist and philosopher Bernard d'Espagnat put it in an article in *Scientific American (November 1979):* "The doctrine that the world is made up of objects whose existence is independent of human consciousness turns out to be in conflict with quantum mechanics and with facts established by experiment."

Having voted for monism (i.e. just one reality), does quantum quirkiness now point us in the direction of idealism or materialism? My answer to this key question is: neither. It remains useful shorthand, of course, to refer to mind and matter or to mind and body as statements of our experience that we cannot deny, as long as we also hold that ultimately there is only one reality. This is not a new idea philosophically, but you won't hear it mentioned by the "new atheists". Sometimes it's called "neutral monism" or "double-aspect monism". The second term is more descriptive, underlining that there is only one underlying substance to everything, with two complementary aspects, mind and matter. We don't need a mind-matter interface in the pineal gland. Once we have grasped this integrated view of the universe many other intriguing thoughts follow on, three of these being particularly relevant to our discussion.

First, we saw by way of introduction to this subject that quantum mechanics upholds the structure of the universe and the laws of its operation. If there were a universal mind, then there would clearly be no great problem in such a mind interacting with the quantum level of reality and thus determining how the universe will operate, including its starting conditions. Materialism cannot allow the existence of such a mind. Pure idealism is problematic because it is difficult to imagine that there is no real material world. Dualism has the problem of how the realm of mind could possibly influence the material. Double-aspect monism cuts through these difficulties, by providing us with the most intuitively plausible account.

Second, entanglement could obviously affect DNA mutation and the fate of our helpless genes. Yes, of course, mutations are random events, but then so is the behaviour of the lights on the boxes in the "spooky" experiment outlined earlier in this chapter. It's just that the randomness is somehow co-ordinated between the two. Who knows what could be happening elsewhere in the universe that could affect DNA duplication at critical moments in evolutionary history? When it comes to entanglement, distance is no object.

The biologist Rupert Sheldrake believes that there are "morphic fields" which contribute to cell development and the ways in which the genetic code is expressed in organisms, and his claim no longer seems to me incredible. His views are given in two works, *A New Science of Life* and *The Presence of the Past*. There is some overlap in his work with the psi phenomena discussed elsewhere in this book and covered objectively by Dean Radin. I was intrigued to find on reading Radin, incidentally, that some (agreeing with Susan Greenfield's "continuum") propose that earthworms possess a form of consciousness. Let's hear it for Protoworm.

Third, quantum tunnelling takes place in the nervous systems of vertebrates in the electrical synapses, which are particularly numerous in the retina and cerebral cortex. Quantum events are, therefore, fundamental to human consciousness. Some highly qualified academics such as Brian Josephson, Roger Penrose, and Stuart Hameroff have put forward hypotheses involving quantum brain theories, but the whole field is very much a work in progress.

The broader idea of mind-matter complementariness is being applied by some from the point of view of neuroscience. Mario Beauregard and Denyse O'Leary in *The Spiritual Brain* make a strong scientific case for the existence of a non-material dimension to human beings, in deliberate contradistinction to the materialist understanding of the mind. We have not yet discussed the question of the brain and development of human consciousness and culture, but once again there is no reason to think that a universal mind could not institute the specific developments that we may suppose were necessary.

Narrowing the Odds: a Reprise

Dawkins, naturally, pays scant attention to the subjects raised in this chapter. He prefers to get bogged down with multiverses, hypothetical alien life forms, and the Anthropic Principle, with the aim of narrowing the odds in favour of human beings existing purely by chance. Yet there is a much easier way of narrowing the odds, by acknowledging the possibility that at least in the three crucial areas listed above, a universal mind is at work.

Dawkins' aversion to such ideas is highlighted in *The God Delusion* by his remarks about "God's bandwidth", which show a lack of understanding of what theists really believe, or possibly little awareness of entanglement, according to which the mind-matter matrix is already potentially in communication. It does not require a set of cosmic routers and fibre-optic cables.

Intriguingly, my proposal has some parallels to the ideas of Alfred Russel Wallace that I referred to in Chapter 5, ideas that caused him to be allocated second place to Darwin in the evolutionary hall of fame. Although Wallace lived until 1913 and was almost the only surviving supporter of the role of natural selection at that time, quantum mechanics was not, at the time, sufficiently developed or understood for the connections I have made to be put forward. Wallace's view that the action of "spirit" was necessary to abiogenesis, the development of consciousness and the development of the human spirit made him seem like a throwback to a pre-scientific age. At the very least, it was easy to portray his views in such a manner. In retrospect, this seems unfair.

By a further happy coincidence, there is a parallel with the three "epochs" that I suggested in Chapter 8, which were as follows: Big Bang to protocell; protocell to hominids; hominids to *homo sapiens*. I demarcated these epochs as I did because there was a need for an information input at the start of each: the laws of nature, the initial DNA structure, and the mutations necessary to human consciousness.

Dawkins naturally has a general wish to avoid any concept such as mind influencing either the cosmos or evolution. It also seems to me, though, that a further reason for Dawkins' attitude could be the mutually supportive relationship he enjoys with Daniel Dennett, whose thinking exalted Darwinism in the 1990s in support of atheism. His crane illustration, already noted, appeals greatly to Dawkins, and he also supports the concept of memes, which we shall discuss shortly. Since Dawkins is not a philosopher it is hardly surprising that he takes on board somewhat of a Dennett "platinum package" deal.

However, although Dennett's thought covers a wide range of specialities, his views on the mind-body question are particularly important. He is very much influenced by the philosophy of Gilbert Ryle (1900–1976), as expressed in the latter's seminal work *The Concept of Mind*, which was published in 1948. The influence is hardly surprising since Dennett studied as a post-graduate under Ryle at Oxford, receiving his PhD there in 1965, and he himself acknowledges the importance of his mentor.

Ryle's work is most famous for its verdict that there is no "ghost in the machine", whether we call it mind, soul, spirit or, for that matter, astral effulgence. For Ryle, descriptions of the mind such as "intelligent" are just coded ways of saying that someone behaves in an intelligent manner. On this view, our experience of mind as something separate from our physical selves is illusory. Further, we cannot know the self by somehow looking inwards, because there is no independent part of us that can carry out such introspection.

To be honest, I found Ryle hard going when I read him many years ago, and my reason for doing so is now lost to my illusory mind. I think it's true to say, however, that the need for complementariness now renders one-sided monism (whether materialist or idealist) redundant, for as we have seen we may need complementary descriptions even of a single reality. I see no reason why mind and matter should not be considered such descriptions. We can uphold the real existence of mind and matter equally and still be good monists—materialism is not essential. Recognition of the holistic aspect of reality would be another useful step in resolving the "Post-Enlightenment Gridlock".

George Wald (1906–97) was a Nobel prize winner in physiology and medicine who specialised in study of the eye. His well-known quote sums up much of my own feelings *(International Journal of Quantum Chemistry 26, 1984)*:

> The consciousness problem was hardly avoidable by one who has spent most of his life studying mechanisms of vision. We have learned a lot, we hope to learn much more; but none of it touches or even points, however tentatively, in the direction of what it means to *see*. Our observations in human eyes and nervous systems and in those of frogs are basically much alike. I know that I see; but does a frog see? It reacts to light; so do cameras, garage doors, any number of photoelectric devices. But does it *see*?
>
> ... The second problem involves the special properties of our Universe. Life seems increasingly to be part of the order of nature. We have good reason to believe that we find ourselves in a Universe permeated with life, in which life arises inevitably—given enough time—wherever the conditions exist that make it possible. Yet were any one of a number of the physical properties of our Universe otherwise—some of them basic, others seeming trivial, almost accidental—that life, which seems now to be so prevalent, would become impossible, here or anywhere... It has occurred to me lately—I must confess with some shock at first to my scientific sensibilities—that both questions might be brought into some degree of congruence. This is with the assumption that mind, rather than emerging as a late outgrowth in the evolution of life, has existed always, as the matrix, the source and condition of physical reality.

You might recollect from my first chapter that one of the founding fathers of modern atheism was Baron D'Holbach in eighteenth-century France, and that D'Holbach was an early materialist. As usual, the ancient Greeks had anticipated the modern world, Democritus (460–370 BCE) and Epicurus (341–270 BCE) being well-known examples, but there were occasionally other materialists in the East and, later, in the Muslim world. The French Catholic priest Pierre Gassendi (1592–1655) attempted to reconcile Epicurus with Christianity, but from then on materialism was (and still is) almost invariably linked to atheism, and logically so. Wald shows that one can have great knowledge and understanding, and yet come to the realisation that something critical is lacking in the materialist viewpoint.

Two Historical Coincidences

I noticed recently a coincidence which I thought rather poignant. Gilbert Ryle's grandfather was the celebrated J. C. Ryle (1816–1900), the first Anglican Bishop of Liverpool and a staunch Victorian leader of the Evangelical party in the Church of England. That transition over a couple of generations, from deeply committed faith to an attitude of scepticism about any non-material reality, seems symbolic. The story has been repeated millions of times over.

A second coincidence is even more interesting. When Gilbert Ryle returned to Oxford after the Second World War, C. S. Lewis was in full flow. At the end of Chapter 3 I appended an "extended footnote" on Lewis even though he fell outside the time frame under discussion. I cited him as a culmination of that type of Christian scholarship that adopted a positive attitude to evolution, scientific knowledge, and the human dimension of the Bible, yet still believed that its message supported a broad Christian orthodoxy. I called this "core orthodoxy" to distinguish it from both Liberalism and Fundamentalism.

Ryle and Lewis overlapped as Fellows of Magdalen College for about eight years. Ryle was one of the debaters at the famous Socratic Club in 1952 while it was under Lewis' enthusiastic presidency; many of the Oxford good and great had their turn, especially from the fields of philosophy, theology, and associated subjects.

Now of course this is all merely historical coincidence, but again it is rather symbolic, a microcosm of the post-war debate in general. Did we want to follow the faith sketched out by Lewis, orthodox, but shorn of objectionable irrelevancies, obscurantism, and institutional arrogance? Or did we want to turn to a new way of thinking in which language about God and the soul was either irrelevant or meaningless? Our cultural elite, if I may use that phrase, predominantly chose the second. Oxford, of course, held its breath, awaiting the arrival of Dawkins and Dennett in the early sixties to carry the flame forward still further.

Secularisation

Under the influence of materialism, secularisation became the norm and the long-standing Christian denominations became marginalised. Those who rejected both materialism *and* Christianity were quite likely to experiment with the irrational lines of thought that we saw becoming increasingly popular during the preceding century, later overlapping with the "new age" movements and Eastern religions. Secularism expanded across Europe, except sometimes in countries that retained strong Catholic loyalty and practice. The free-market religions of the US fared much better, allowing the upsurge of fundamentalism that troubles the "new atheists" so much. Ironically, the nation that most fervently proclaims freedom of belief seems to be one of the most religious, while the UK, with its national churches and bishops in the House of Lords, is one of the most secular.

Having held their peace for forty years, it's a puzzle as to why this particular group of atheists suddenly became so aggressive as the new millennium dawned. Perhaps the success of Christianity in some parts of the world sounded alarm bells; perhaps there was a sudden awareness of the growing influence of Islam; perhaps the liberal children of the sixties began to feel they were running out of time; perhaps there was a group wish to deny the role of atheism in twentieth-century suffering by using religion as a scapegoat.

Peter Hitchens in *The Rage Against God* points out that our new bellicose atheists seem to have not only a belief but a *burning need* that there should not be any God. On my reading of their works I think he could be right—we may never know the full story. We do know, however, that the materialistic outlook has had an enormous effect on our culture, even though quantum mechanics has made the basis for holding to it ever more difficult to justify. Secularism does not, however, appear to be troubled by the facts, it simply propagates its views as if there were no real alternative.

CHAPTER 11

Harold from Cowley Reveals All

Secularism made the idea of God seem like a historical relic, a sentimental attachment to bygone days. Materialism turned the idea of looking for God into, if anything, a vague quest for "something out there". To complete the set, *scientism* became accepted as a natural fit with both of these tendencies.

Scientism is the assumption that science can objectively explain everything and therefore (probably) resolve all human problems. Anything that it cannot explain is regarded as unimportant or, preferably, non-existent. I do not believe that scientism is the way forward, for the simple reason that it is not scientific. There is no scientific proof that science can discover all knowledge.

We saw in the last chapter that there is no problem with a universal mind relating to the universe, especially in light of quantum mechanics. The laws of nature, DNA mutation, and the operation of the brain and nervous system are locations where this might be particularly relevant. Such thoughts lead naturally on to another, namely, can such a mind affect things in our ordinary lives at the scale on which we live?

In traditional terms, does God connect to the world—and us—by revealing himself in sacred texts, or perhaps through miracles? Is prayer a real dialogue, or merely talking to oneself? Is the idea of a relationship with God just a manner of speaking, or can there be a reality to it? Doesn't suffering show that, even if there is a God, he is not concerned with life as we experience it? This is not a new discussion, but the "new atheists" are recycling the old arguments once again as part of their current strategy, and scientism is the order of the day.

In order to move things forward I should like to consider first and foremost the question of miracles. This is the pivotal issue, because if we believe in the possibility of miracles then revelation is also clearly possible. On the other hand, if God doesn't really get involved in our world then revelation, prayer, and spirituality seem to be either pointless or a purely emotional exercise. From now on, for the sake of brevity, I shall use the word "miracle" to include other aspects of divine involvement with the world we know.

More feeble spirits might attempt to consider an easy case—perhaps a claim to minor healing, or a remarkable set of circumstances that occurred at an opportune moment in someone's life. I have chosen to recycle the tale of Harold from Cowley. Here we have potentially a full-blown miracle, but without the complexity of initial presuppositions—Harold is a secular person, not big on religious experience which might sway his interpretation of things. That's appropriate, because all we are asking here is whether the miraculous is possible—yes or no.

In case you have forgotten, or, heaven forbid, skipped the relevant chapter, Harold was the one clear, undisputed person that was genuinely transported, according to all reports, from the dining room to the kitchen, purely by the power of the dinner guests' thoughts. There were a couple of near misses in Aberystwyth and Thetford, but Harold was the real thing. I used Harold's experience to illustrate the scientific point that if there's no one minding the shop, so to speak, then how can we be sure that the laws of nature are consistent? How can we know that there isn't some flukiness built into things—not manifest every day, but just now and again under very specific circumstances? If that were so, why should it not be possible for Harold's experience to be genuine? If it were, should it be treated as a miracle?

As you can imagine, Harold became quite a personality because of his claimed experience; even strangers in the street would shout "beam me up, Scotty". Then, on the second anniversary of the event, he accepted the invitation to appear on a TV chat show. Viewing figures were high that night, such was the curiosity about his experience.

The Happy Medium

As Harold sat in hospitality he could hear the preceding guest, this week's occupier of the *Happy Medium* slot, adding his comments about the teleportation phenomenon. According to this guest, the area was particularly strong in psychic events on account of the intersection of three ley lines nearby, which also explained several UFO claims made in the area over the years. After the mandatory contribution from the musical guests it was time for Harold. The first question was a general one about what actually happened on the night in question. He replied:

"Thank-you, Jonathan. Well, it was very strange. All the others were staring at me. One of our friends, whose name is Fiona, seemed to be kind of, er, daydreaming I suppose you could call it—I just thought she'd had too much wine. Suddenly—I know this sounds stupid—I seemed to be looking down on everything. I could see things on top of the dresser like an old Christmas card that must have just been left there. Then, to my amazement, I found myself in the kitchen".

"But a lot of people would say you actually just walked there..."

"No, no, I definitely didn't, because all the others would have seen that. As far as they were concerned I gradually vanished, just like in the transporter bay on *Star Trek*. In any case, I don't think I would have walked in there, broken a couple of plates and thrown chicken bones all over me for a laugh. Do you?"

"No, that would be a little strange just to fetch the coffee." *(Laughter from audience).*

"I definitely felt myself land and that's when my arm hit the plates that were piled up next to the dishwasher. I also realised my left foot was in the cat's drinking bowl." *(Laughter from audience).*

The questions now follow a predictable course—too much wine, magic mushrooms in the starter, a publicity hoax for pecuniary gain, and so on, all easily de-fused by Harold because he's heard them so many times before.

"None of us have been the same since. Fiona's been writing a book. The others carried on much as before apart from meeting a couple of times to try to repeat "the phenomenon" as we call it. One, Gordon, got religion of some sort. I've lost contact with him I'm afraid, but the rest of us still see each other now and again."

A few more jokey winding-down questions, and Harold finds himself back in hospitality enjoying a glass of warm Chardonnay with nibbles. To his surprise, a somewhat extrovert, expensively-dressed woman makes a beeline towards him and introduces herself as Shirley. She's due on in a few minutes to tell the world what it's like to be a game-show celebrity living in a psychical vortex in Southampton.

"I thought that what you said was *fan-bloody-tastic . . .*" she bubbled enthusiastically, touching Harold on the arm, ". . . it's a miracle if you ask me." With that she's whisked away by the producer's assistant deputy PA and the trainee floor manager, who hands her a golden model of a pyramid.

Like the above little story, the question of miracles combines the areas of improbability and of personal experience. Atheists are, of course, total disbelievers in miracles, dismissing any credulity in regard to them as superstition. Harold used to be of exactly that frame of mind, but has become, in his words, "open to the idea" of the supernatural because of his experience. Not that these things happen every day, but "it makes you think".

The sceptic hearing Harold's narrative is quite clear as to what actually happened. Altered, trance-like psychological states are a known feature of situations where impressionable people are under pressure from a strong personality, or as the result of drug use. Accounts of out-of-body experiences are also common. Put the two together and you have a miracle-free explanation.

Harold is quick to counter this, however, on several grounds. First, if it was all just in the mind, how did he come to know about the card on top of the dresser, which he could not have known about by normal methods? Second, the other reports of people trying the teleportation experiment, although not so complete as Harold's, are consistent with his. There's clearly *something* going on, even if we can't explain all the facts. Third, he has no memory at all of walking into the kitchen, but does remember his attention being rudely caught by plates crashing around him and a wet left foot. Fourth, if it was all in the mind how could all the other guests have agreed so closely on what happened and tied it in with what he says happened? Remember, everyone passed the lie-detector tests.

As a clincher, Harold has also watched interesting programmes on the serious TV channels, and has come to believe that it's possible, in very specific and *extremely rare* circumstances, for matter to take on wave-like qualities and be transmitted somewhere else. He's heard about quantum teleportation of course, and regards it as backing up his view. Michio Kaku believes major teleportation will be possible in the future, so why not now, given, perhaps accidentally, the right circumstances?

There are many people like Harold—not with exactly the same dramatic claim, but with tales of out-of-body experiences, ghosts, premonitions and so on. They have become aware of a "Big Picture". What I like about these people is that usually their experiences were unsought and unexpected. They are often willing to talk about them only with some diffidence. There is an ambiguity about their experience.

Clear Ambiguity

In order to clarify matters, let's first look at Harold's experience in the light of that fundamental principle of science, Occam's razor. What is the minimal explanation of what happened? Well, I have already given one possible sceptical account—the whole thing was caused by trance-like states, possibly due to something in the food. Perhaps Harold was the most severely afflicted, leading him to go into the kitchen as if sleep walking, suffering at the same time the sense of watching himself that happens in out-of-body experiences. He actually had seen the card on top of the dresser on some other occasion—perhaps when changing a light bulb—and forgotten about it. As for the lie-detectors, well, it's possible to fool them, and in any case the guests, as far as they were concerned, were not lying and would therefore be less detectable.

That seems to have solved the whole thing. However, we should also be sceptical about the scepticism. What is the likelihood of seven people having the same rate of ingestion of, and response to, a toxic substance such that each goes into the necessary altered state, and out again, precisely on cue? How likely is it that they *all* could fool the lie detectors? And what actually happened to Harold? Attaching the label "out-of-body experience" isn't really an answer, because such experiences themselves are not well understood. What could have brought it on, right at the necessary moment? Why did they all see the same *Star Trek* effect when two of those present had never even heard of transporter bays?

Because of the ambiguity, someone eventually would come up with a new theory—for example, that what happened at the dinner party was an example of telepathy, of which there are many well-attested claims. These suggest that our perceptions can be influenced by something external to us of which we cannot be aware through normal sense experience. If that is so, should we not fall back on such an explanation for the Cowley dinner party experience? There might be more evidence for such a thing than for synchronised trance states. I doubt that the latter could be any more easily verified retrospectively by conventional scientific method than a telepathic hypothesis.

Bringing in "psi phenomena" like telepathy makes the whole situation more complex. Dean Radin in *Entangled Minds* and *The Conscious Universe* summarises that these effects, detected by *scientific* studies, are spasmodically real. However, although they are stable when a large amount of data is analysed, they are *weak* effects. Curiously, the "real but weak" view was a conclusion I reached a long time ago on the basis of worried parishioners and personal experience.

If there is any truth at all in such theories then Occam's razor would suggest that some form of telepathy, communicating a shared—but possibly flawed—image of what was happening, is a more rational explanation of the Cowley experience. It is a simpler explanation than some kind of simultaneous and rather tightly choreographed problem with toxic substances and instant recovery from their effects.

Evaluation of the story of Harold becomes instead evaluation of the many claims about telepathy. This kind of ambiguity is highly likely with any claim to the miraculous, because no event happens in total isolation, and no interpretation is free of presuppositions. Someone would come up with a theory about electromagnetic fields. Others might have a theory revolving around out-of-body experiences. The "happy medium" would talk about ley lines, and of course, there's always hypnosis.

The real problem is that in a situation that is not claimed to be repeatable Occam's razor eventually turns out to be rather blunt, so trying to disprove miracles by science is, in the end, futile; yet sceptics keep trying to do this, failing to accept that those who believe in the possibility of miracles generally acknowledge the power of science in its own field. Sceptics are disputatious because what they are wedded to is not just science but absolute regularity, the conviction that if things *usually* happen a certain way then they *always* happen that way—which (as pointed out by Hume) cannot be a certain conclusion, although it is very much part of the *zeitgeist* or "spirit of the age" within some parts of our culture.

Shirley from Southampton, however, is not unduly troubled by her *zeitgeist*. Or shall we say it's a different *zeitgeist* from that which influences the rationalist, or even the open-minded Harold. As far as "Shirl the girl" is concerned, every rumour of the unexpected is grist to the mill. She is, of course, a dedicated member of the *Most Haunted* types of network, and always phones in to the live programmes when she sees a dark shadow on the screen. One of her favourite expressions is, *"it was obviously meant"*. What the rationalist sees as gross superstition is a pretty normal way of looking at things as far as our Shirl is concerned.

Here we have, then, three different attitudes to the inexplicable. At the extremes the attitudes are "never" and "often", with the middle-of-the-road Harold wanting to say something but always struggling with his experience. If ever he becomes a Christian he will surely join the Church of England.

Naturalism

The view that *by definition* nothing apart from the purely natural can ever happen is known as naturalism. Upholders of naturalism would regard Shirley from Southampton as naïve and unduly superstitious, merely acting out her misguided assumptions about cause and effect. Yet the follower of naturalism is equally guilty for assuming an absolute law of regularity that in fact does not exist. The assertion of regularity is statistical—this is what happens in a large percentage of cases. We cannot say "all cases" because we have not observed all cases. *There is no law, standing alongside the laws of motion, gravitation, optics, and so on, that forces an absolute regularity on everything else.*

Rather than speak of the natural and supernatural I prefer to speak of the usual and the unusual, because such language is simply descriptive of what we or others claim to observe. Looking at Harold's alleged experience, if we put it down to some kind of telepathy that would have to be classed as unusual. However, there are probably far more claims to verified telepathic experiences than to precisely-timed instant-on and instant-off food poisoning, which would also have to be classed as unusual. If, like Shirley, we went the whole hog and accepted that Harold really did de-materialise and then re-materialise next door, we should certainly have to call that very unusual indeed, since we would be short of other instances at any scale larger than that of a proton.

The kind of reckoning that we would have to do on hearing Harold's account is very similar to the kind of reckoning carried out by adherents of any religion that upholds miracles as genuine. All three of the main monotheistic religions have to evaluate the miraculous elements of the Hebrew Bible or Old Testament. Christianity has to do the same, in addition, with the miracles surrounding Christ. Islam must do the same with all of the above plus the revelations to Mohammed. All three—like most other religions—make further claims, to varying degrees, concerning the powers of lesser prophets, saints, mystics, and healers.

Probably the most weighed-up account is that of Jesus' resurrection. The evidentiary aspect is well known—the records feature two complementary strands (empty tomb and resurrection appearances), each being witnessed by different combinations of people over a period of time. They look like independent witness statements, with minor differences such as one would expect. The writers knew about grave robbers and ghosts, so it wouldn't have been *that* easy to trick them. Finally, the religious and civil leaderships would have had a huge vested interest in simply producing the body of Jesus, but they couldn't, despite unlimited powers of search, bribery, interrogation, and intimidation, backed up if necessary by the threat of further crucifixions.

The evidence here is much stronger than in Cowley, but of course so is the unusualness of the claimed event, which means that many "believers" are like "doubting Thomas". It is only atheists who imagine that "believers" simply sail through life on a cloud of naivety with no doubts about anything. Strong evidence about a trivial event is easy to accept. Flimsy evidence about an unusual event is easy to reject. But what do we do with very strong evidence about a very unusual event? The answer is that we generally reject even the very strong evidence and let regularity rule. In order for this not to happen, we need something independent, beyond the event itself, to provide a clinching argument. In the case of the resurrection accounts in the New Testament, that something is the whole story developed in its various books.

A parallel might be something like this. Supposing that following the Cowley event news gradually leaked out that one of those present was a Nobel Prize winner, a dignified scientist and a much-honoured professor at a local university. It further transpires that the said professor's award-winning research had been in the field of "cascaded quantum tunnelling, with special reference to organic molecule energy states". Would we still be unshakeably certain that *nothing* unusual had occurred that night?

Consideration of miracles is always difficult because they are ambiguous and not repeatable on demand. We should still employ Occam's razor to eliminate as much nonsense as possible, but we should not expect it to give a judgement on whether an account of a miracle is true or false. It cannot do that. Neither can science. The deciding factors lie beyond the event itself. As if that were not enough, for monotheists there is a major paradox at the heart of their faith.

A General Regularity

Having criticised those who believe in an absolute regularity, I now have to meet them half way. The tricky issue buried in monotheism is the view of creation, which we have already examined briefly, in the ancient text of Genesis and other parts of the Bible. Ultimate power lies with God, yet there is enough space between God and creation to allow for belief in a *general* regularity, which excludes belief in capricious forces and many of the other features of "non-organised" religion like Shirley's. I have already pointed out that to speak of the miraculous assumes that there is such a thing as natural law—without which the word "miracle" means nothing. Shirley, in fact, despite her enthusiasm, does not believe in miracles at all. What she really believes in is an arbitrary and fragmented universe.

It is the belief in a *general* regularity about things that stops the middle-of-the-road types from settling down with the more naïve upholders of the miraculous. As we have seen, this belief in a general regularity was an important basis for the development of science. It is also an important basis for life as we experience it—too much divine intervention could be a very mixed blessing. I feel an illustration coming on.

Let's consider what the Americans call the "fender bender", which we could call a "bumper thumper" but, for some reason, don't. As I sit patiently waiting for a break in the traffic, what divine act will prevent the careless person behind running into me? Presumably a mysterious operation of his brake system, together with the instant installation of very high friction tyres. Which is fine except that the car behind his now requires the same treatment, and the cyclist further down the line is going to need something extra special to avoid going over the handlebars.

Perhaps it would be simpler to ensure that the driver immediately behind me wasn't so tired when he set out on the commuter run. So, in the new divine plan, everyone who drives to work is overcome by a strange narcolepsy at around 10.30pm the previous night. Others don't understand why this is, but find it puzzling that when they attempt to drive anywhere unplanned their cars won't start—the angel of road safety has intervened.

Following this through, even at this trivial level, it soon becomes obvious how unworkable the divine intervention scenario really is. Solid materials have to instantly turn soft to avoid injury, which then requires that buildings be temporarily held in place by angelic action. A wall made of foam rubber is not fit for purpose, even for a few seconds. Any human action that might prove injurious has to be limited—sometimes the law of gravity is suspended, to benefit flying cyclists.

Science cannot exist in this world, because there are no reliable rules. Any thoughts in people's minds that might prove harmful to themselves or others are instantly scrambled and experienced by the thinker as a memory lapse; some people only remember half of an average day. Free will is severely restricted. There is no right or wrong, because nothing is any more significant, morally, than anything else. In other words, life in this hoped-for utopia is a kind of 24/7 divine magic show, just one continuous round of miracles performed for people who are ultimately irresponsible puppets.

Most of those brought up in monotheistic cultures do not, of course, verbalise matters in just this way, but the general presupposition of regularity, as the norm, is there. That is why mainstream monotheistic religions are normally very slow to validate any particular claim of the miraculous, while at the same time upholding its possibility.

A Clash of World Views

The question of how a general regularity and occasional very unusual events can be reconciled depends on our world view. Atheists argue that in the case of a reported miracle it is always most likely that evidence has been falsified, observations mistaken, or reports corrupted. Intervention never happens because there is no one to intervene. Deists admit to the existence of a deity but deny the element of intervention because that would be against their view of how God works. Both parties should in theory be open to the unusual as part of the natural order, but they generally are not, preferring to keep things simple.

It's the theists who have the most difficult task. Some simply accept that God made the rules and therefore God can break them—regularity is sacrificed in favour of intervention. The main argument against this "tinkering God" view, as I have called it, is that if God can break the rules in this manner why does he not do it more often, to alleviate suffering—particularly if he is omnibenevolent? There is also the common-sense argument, shown in my motoring illustration, that once this type of intervention starts—the "breaking of rules" type of intervention—it is very hard to see where it can stop.

The more common theistic view is that God does not break the rules but works with them at a deeper level than we can understand, in order to sometimes bring about unusual results. From our point of view this may often be inexplicable, but from God's point of view it never is. Neither regularity nor intervention is sacrificed. This is the type of view put forward by C. S. Lewis in *Miracles*, still a classic, and the starting point for a great deal of religious thinking today. In traditional Christianity this view is summed up in the concept of *providence*. This sees the world of natural law as consistent within itself, including its own causes and effects, but with God nevertheless fulfilling his purposes *through* this process, not against it.

Dawkins and his colleagues regard this, of course, as a monumental cop out, but I think that what they often have in mind is the deistic-leaning liberal religious attitude which denies that the unusual can happen, but retains a significance for whatever did happen—perhaps as a sign pointing to God. It is true that miracles in the Bible are regarded as signs, not as magical phenomena in their own right. Even so, *they were only signs because they were unusual.* If we had been present at the resurrection we would have been just as astonished as were the witnesses described in the New Testament. We may freely allow that there were psychosomatic factors at work in the healings and exorcisms carried out by Jesus, but would still wonder how he was able to work in that context in a way that we are unable to do with our advanced medical skills.

I believe that the providential view is correct. Adding it to my earlier observations we can define a miracle as follows. A miracle is generally an unusual event, often ambiguous, which points to God's activity whether or not natural factors can be seen at work.

Providence and Suffering

The question of miracles is part of the wider question of how God connects with world as we know it. The "providential" world view is, therefore, also significant when we discuss the problem of suffering.

One of the most frequent questions thrown at me as a vicar was along the lines of, "How can there be a God when you see all the suffering in the world?" Sometimes this would be narrowed down to a particular type of suffering or a particular individual. The general assumption was that if there were a God he would be able to remove the suffering that we experience. That does not happen, so there cannot be a God.

I believe that religion should address such questions and not simply challenge us to have faith. Before going into detail, though, let me request that you don't interpret my attempt to provide answers as implying insensitivity to suffering. Such answers are not intended to replace pastoral care, love, and practical help to people who are suffering. Most of us have needed to give or receive in those ways at some time.

As far as committed atheism is concerned, suffering is not a philosophical or religious problem, only a personal and private one that hopefully can be ameliorated by medicine, psychotherapy, and euthanasia. The word "suffering" for the atheist is really just shorthand for things we don't like. Suffering cannot be avoided, because the universe itself is simply like that.

Atheists generally also claim that if there were a God then he would be the source of all suffering. They do not, however, look into the question of God's purpose for and involvement in that suffering. They delight in Voltaire and the background of the Lisbon earthquake, but never ask what Leibniz actually meant by the "best of all possible worlds".

At times atheists give the impression that religious people are smug and complacent about suffering. Yet many years ago a friend introduced me to the verse of G. A. Studdert Kennedy, often known as "Woodbine Willie" because of his habit of giving out cigarettes in the trenches of the first world war—he was an army chaplain. In one poem called "Missing—Believed Killed" he parodies the famous words of the apostle Paul which celebrate the victory of Christ over death. Kennedy's version reads as follows:

> O Grave, where is thy victory? O Death, where is thy sting?
> Thy victory is ev'rywhere, Thy sting's in ev'rything.

No atheist could have put it better, and these words have stayed with me since the day I first read them.

C. S. Lewis gives still one of the most-read analyses of suffering in *The Problem of Pain*, and his points are echoed and supplemented by others such as Alister McGrath and Richard Swinburne, together with a huge number of popular and religious devotional writings. Complacency is no doubt always a danger, but I don't see a lot of it in the religious thinkers that I've come across.

Theodicy

The word *Théodicée* was first employed by Leibniz to mean, in effect, justification of God, and much discussion since has followed his line of argument, particularly in terms of free will. This follows on the need for regularity in the universe that we discussed in the context of miracles. Without that regularity we are left with no free will and no responsibility. Accidental and pathological suffering is clearly necessary to allow regularity, but the ability of humans to willfully inflict suffering on one another is similarly inevitable for the same reason. Not only do human acts directly cause suffering, they often exacerbate suffering caused by natural events. If the human race were consistently constructive, co-operative, and caring, it would be much easier to endure suffering.

I think most of us would agree that lower life forms, perhaps those with no developed nervous system, do not suffer, while higher vertebrates often do. Yet even in those animals closest to us the suffering is generally limited to a relatively brief period, leading to death. Also, as far as we can tell, animals are spared the psychological suffering that comes from being able to predict death or loss in the future, or to imagine what might have been in the past. Animal suffering is by no means to be ignored, although it is perhaps less overbearing than human suffering.

Related to both human and animal suffering, and linking back to Darwin's well-known puzzlement over parasitism, we perhaps need to add another category, namely, *evolutionary* suffering. Suffering in both animals and humans appears to be a necessary part of the evolutionary process, whether (in our case) we look at infection, genetic disorders, or merely our inherent weaknesses. When the Apostle Paul wrote in Romans 7:22 that, "the whole creation has been groaning in travail together until now", he surely spoke better than he knew.

The problem we instinctively feel is that if we were God we wouldn't have done things this way. However, we would also say that if we were God there are many other things we would have done differently as well. I mentioned Victor Stenger's claim that he would have done a much better job, but we have probably all thought the same at times. In our heart of hearts we think it was a poor idea to create the universe in the way that religions claim that God did. Suffering is just part of a very big package, and it seems that we are faced with a clear threefold choice.

If we take the atheist route, each human life simply comes and goes; any other significance is a delusion, for we live in a vast universe that we can never fully understand. I was talking about cosmology with an artist friend the other day, and he remarked that he didn't find space at all inspiring, because its sheer scale makes it a prison. In the immortal words of *The Eagles*, "You can check out any time you like, but you can never leave." We can't actually get anywhere apart from where we are. The enthusiasm for finding hope in space is not shared by all, and in the hands of atheists appears to be a consolation prize once the hope of a benevolent God is gone.

If we take the deist route, then maybe there is design in the universe, and in some sense we are destined to be here, perhaps in accord with the Strong Anthropic Principle—the cosmos has to be as it is, as part of this destiny. I'm not sure what sense it makes to think of God starting off the whole show, with the intention of producing us as intelligent beings, then just turning his back on us. There are, however, some deists who regard the divine absence as temporary—a condition of the created order, but not one that persists when we finally meet with God outside of that. If such a dimension is brought into the debate, then it seems quite likely that God would rebalance the injustices that we perceive. It could even be that evolution and the final development of humankind is just one of many purposes in the divine mind. Perhaps God was into multitasking long before it became fashionable in the world of computing.

If we take the theistic route, then the transcendent view of God is balanced with a sense of *immanence*—the belief that God is as close as the air we breathe. Once this element is brought in, the possibility that God himself may suffer in the sufferings of the world becomes more real.

We have already looked at the specifically Christian view of this. Within the need for atonement, for which "the Lord will provide", there is the ultimate suffering of God in Christ. Atonement rehabilitates a God of love and purpose for us humans. As we saw, one can take either a conservative or liberal view of this. Whichever view is taken, if I were inventing a new religion I would not have my main leader uttering the words "My God, my God, why hast thou forsaken me?" The fact that those words are enduring shows a profound level of understanding on the part of the gospel writers.

Belief in an ethical, personal, suffering, and atoning God, whether put into a liberal or a conservative context, indicates that to portray the only options as either a cruel universe or a cruel God is unbelievably narrow. Yet this is the choice so often portrayed by atheists and the choice which the Dawkinsian underpinning team is keen to promote.

Hype and Hope

The "providential" world view allows the possibilities of revelation, the miraculous, and prayer because it is unnecessary to place the mind of God, the minds of humans, and the material world into separate lead-lined boxes such that they shall never interact with each other. This is not something to do with becoming a religious fanatic, it is everything to do with exercising a reasoned acceptance of the holistic world view I have put forward. Such a view is anti-scientism but not anti-science. It is a view that generates for many a sense of hope, instead of a sense of apathy or even of despair.

Intriguingly, even though the logic of atheism would imply that in the end nothing really matters all that much, atheist writers and presenters still like to enthuse about the future and present their own version of hope. Despite the negative actions of human beings they seem to maintain a belief in some kind of inevitable progress. If that fails, there is the hope of space travel, perhaps to allow us to escape from an Earth caught in a downward destructive spiral, due to either warfare or ecological disaster. Why they assume that we would do any better somewhere else than we have done here is not explained.

Then there are the transhumanists. The essential belief of transhumanism is that science will eventually allow us to live for as long as we want. Even now it is possible to be frozen immediately after death, in the hope of being resuscitated once that is possible and the necessary life-prolonging technology is in place. Brian Appleyard comments in *How to Live Forever or Die Trying* that even if the technology eventually succeeds, we would be very different human beings from what we are now. I agree—the boundary of death is an essential part of our humanity.

Leibniz is, I think, greatly misunderstood. He did not say that the world as we know it is the best of all *imaginable* worlds. There is much that we can imagine that is not actually possible. It might be better, even for atheists, to accept that the world we have is the best possible, as a working hypothesis, and focus on how to further realise its potential. That would be more productive than dreaming of a future which, at the very best, will only be available to a select few. In any event, is it really likely that ten billion people (the likely plateau population of the Earth) will stand by as the planet becomes hell, and allow resources to be diverted into sending a select few into space, or producing for them an elixir of life v2.0?

To conclude this chapter: the story of Harold from Cowley is fiction. Even if it were not, and there were a real Harold that was teleported I would not call it a miracle. Why? Because, even though unusual, it would signify nothing in particular. On the other hand, show me an alleged miracle that is a sign, part of a big picture, connected to claims about hope, healing, revelation, and human destiny, and I will certainly weigh up the evidence without the assumption that such things cannot happen.

CHAPTER 12

A Pause for Reflection

To summarise the story so far, in my initial historical chapters I delved into the origins of atheism, evangelical Christianity, liberal Christianity, and the various strands of irrationality that followed the Reformation and Enlightenment. We ended those chapters with what I called "PEG"—the "Post-Enlightenment Gridlock". Darwinism and its twentieth-century developments did not affect this a great deal in itself, but it appeared to fit well with the philosophy of materialism, the view that only the material world is real. In the West we find ourselves today still in the gridlock, notwithstanding the independent pathways to be found in conservative elements of Roman Catholicism, Judaism, Islam, and other groups with a strong cultural identity.

The "new atheists" have recycled many of the old arguments about religion, in my view in a highly unbalanced way considering the appalling results of atheistic movements in the twentieth century, and the many benefits that religion has brought, even though it has often failed. I tried to correct this imbalance. To add additional value, I attempted to show why the traditional arguments for the existence of God have some merit, particularly the argument from design and the moral argument.

Dawkins has made neo-Darwinism the weapon of choice for the "new atheist", but I maintain that, despite his undoubted expertise, his approach to evolution is too narrow to account for the development of complex interlocking systems, in which I include consciousness. There are broader alternatives held true by others with equally undoubted expertise, but they cannot be made subject to simple laws in the way that straightforward variation and natural selection can. We can propose rules for evolution, but the rules themselves have arisen from random processes. Difficult questions about fine tuning, abiogenesis, chicken and egg situations, the development of DNA, reproduction, and eukaryotic cell formation are not answered. Put all that into the cosmic context, and it seems to me inescapable that our existence is either the work of a universal mind, or an unbelievably improbable lucky fluke.

Quantum mechanics makes twentieth-century materialism redundant. It has thrown new light on how mind and body may relate to each other, and how a universal mind could relate to the universe, to evolution, and to human beings. Further, while we should be utterly rigorous in examining claims to the miraculous, there is no logical reason to declare miracles (including revelation) impossible, or necessarily contrary to the laws of nature.

Moving the Goalposts

There could be useful debate here, on all sides. However, this is threatened by a further hypothesis which has gained some traction of late. I refer to the idea that the universe simply arose out of nothing. As far as the debate about religion is concerned, this is certainly moving the goalposts and demands a response. In the process we shall start to veer back to that earlier question of epistemology—how we know things—because it still needs an answer.

The notion of creation from nothing has been given much publicity by Stephen Hawking and Leonard Mlodinow's recent book *Grand Design*, which surprised me since I thought that this idea was already a common talking point among cosmologists. As early as 1973 Edward P. Tryon suggested that the universe originated from a quantum fluctuation in a vacuum. In Tryon's celebrated words, "our universe is simply one of those things which happen from time to time". Perhaps the *Grand Design* media ripple was caused mainly by Stephen Hawking's name and the occasional religious undercurrent of the book. It is reviewed well by the usual suspects, including Dawkins, but meets scathing criticism from almost everyone else, including Roger Penrose, Paul Davies, and Susan Greenfield, to whom I have previously referred.

What we actually know from the evidence is that particles do appear from nowhere in a vacuum, but these particles only exist for a very short length of time. They are particle-antiparticle pairs, sometimes referred to as "virtual particles", and are to be expected under the laws of quantum mechanics.

For myself, I think that Victor Stenger puts the atheist viewpoint the most comprehensively, so I shall take him as definitive. Stenger's arguments are also generally more logical than those of other atheists. For example, he points out—as I did in discussing abiogenesis—that it is quite possible to have certain regions of increasing order within the whole, without breaking the second law of thermodynamics (that in a closed system disorder always increases). The increasing order locally is offset by increasing disorder elsewhere. That seems blindingly obvious to me, but has often been overlooked by some with a religious agenda. Stenger also seems to have less time than others for alien life forms.

Stenger is not afraid to say that extremely unlikely things *can* happen. Even if there *is* just one configuration for a Goldilocks universe, and the process of evolution as it happened was *very* unlikely, it could simply be that we struck lucky. We won in the cosmic *Golden Grain* competition. Again, I have to agree. It could have happened. Stenger further points out that, although it could indeed mean the end of everything if we tweaked just one of those "magic numbers" by a small amount, it might be possible to throw them all up in the air and have a completely different set of values that would produce a life-supporting universe. This seems improbable, but to be fair there is no alternative universe with which to make a comparison. If we could throw the whole lot up in the air and start again, we might learn a lot, but we can't do it, not even once. Even if we could, the health and safety people would complain.

I like this no-nonsense approach. However, Stenger is not consistent. He agrees with Dawkins that the world looks just as we should expect if there were no designer. Yet there is nothing to compare it with in this respect, no benchmark in the form of some other world definitely designed. Similarly, he makes comments, and quotes others in similar vein, to the effect that if there were an infinite God he would have done things very differently. Yet again, with what is he comparing? We don't have a quality assurance statement of how a world created by an infinite God should behave, and we all feel at some time that we could have done a better job.

Organised Spontaneity

What, then, of Stenger's contention, along with the other "spontaneous creation" advocates, that the existence of the universe just happened? He deploys the concept that the laws of physics come from the symmetries of the "void" out of which the universe spontaneously arose. Those that didn't arose from a process of "spontaneous symmetry breaking". The answer to the question, "Why is there anything?" is simply "Why not?" The transition from "nothing" to "something" is purely natural, because "nothing" is an unstable condition compared to "something".

Smuggling in the word "spontaneous" in generous quantities doesn't solve a lot. How would we go about proving *this* assertion scientifically? Stenger is keen to press home the claimed lack of independent corroboration of many religious claims—for example, concerning the Bible. Well, it would seem to me that to corroborate a claim like his, experimentally, one would have to take a decent number of examples of "nothing"—let's say, a hundred and seventeen—and observe them for a very, very long time, maybe forever. Even if there were no change for millions of years, all of our samples could spontaneously switch to "something" while we were taking a coffee break.

The word "spontaneous" can be used in two ways. Take, for example, a large number of uranium atoms and leave them in peace for a certain period of time, corresponding to the half-life of that particular uranium isotope. We know that half the atoms in our sample will decay—but we don't know which half. We saw with Tibbles that if you looked at one atom in isolation it could decay at any time, or not at all, so if it does decay we could call that a spontaneous event. However, this kind of spontaneity occurs as a result of physical laws that already exist, so it cannot apply to the debate about the start of the universe and fine tuning. What Stenger has in mind is a spontaneous event by which the universe came into existence, *including* its physical laws. It just happened.

It is obvious here that words are being used in strange ways. Our image of instability is usually based on the picture of unstable equilibrium such as exists if you have, for example, a ball bearing sitting on top of a cricket ball. The slightest nudge in any direction and off it goes. Yet what can "unstable" mean in relation to "nothing"? We generally think of a void as nothing, yet this kind of void can "spontaneously" give rise to "something". This is a strange kind of entity, perhaps best described poetically:

> Dark void beyond all senses lying, potent source of life and light,
> Needing no cause to work your wonder, self-sufficient, emergent might.

Or, as Walter Chalmers Smith put it more succinctly,

> Immortal, invisible, God only wise,
> In light inaccessible hid from our eyes.

I make the parallel because we seem to have here a first cause regardless of whether we refer to it as "the void" or "God"; I have tried to work out the difference, but cannot. Stenger seems to be using a cosmological argument in disguise.

Ironically, it also seems that he is falling into the error that is most commonly levelled at the ontological argument as stated by St Anselm. You may remember that the great saint generally stands accused of treating existence as just one more property of things, whereas in reality something that does not exist has no properties at all. Similarly, using words like "nothing" or "void" and then attributing to them properties such as "unstable" may make grammatical sense, but what do such concepts mean?

Stenger claims that his view is a valid interpretation of the evidence, but what we actually have is a mathematical deduction from very indirect evidence. That leaves me with a strange, uneasy feeling that I can best explain with a paradox.

Mirror Mirror on the Wall

This puzzle first occurred to me about fifteen years ago, but apparently is a well-known paradox. The question is this: *When you stand in front of a mirror you see an image of yourself reversed left to right. So why is your image not also reversed top to bottom so that you seem to be upside down?*

The first answer given is often that the lens of the eye crosses over the light rays as they pass through, but then it dawns quickly on most people that this also puts the image upside down. All circular convex lenses do the same. The second answer may be that our eyes are arranged side by side, with the implication that if they were one above the other then we would indeed see things in a mirror upside down and not back to front. This answer is easily proven wrong, however, by just shutting one eye. No change.

Further answers generally come down to issues of the brain and perception. We find it relatively easy to see ourselves reversed left-to-right in mirrors and get used to it—after all, we are more or less symmetrical about a vertical axis so it's not that odd. In contrast, seeing oneself upside down would be bizarre, so the brain learns to compensate and we see ourselves the right way up instead. However, this can't be the whole story, because the same effect occurs if we are looking at objects, not merely people. We have all had the experience, I should think, of looking into a mirror set into a wall in such a way that we thought we were looking through a window into, say, an adjacent room in a restaurant. It's only when we see a chalkboard bearing the word "unem" that we realise our mistake.

Finally, there are technical explanations from those with some knowledge of optics. Apparently the mirror does not reverse anything vertically or horizontally, but in depth—that's why, when you move towards the mirror, your reflection appears to move in the opposite direction, which is also towards the mirror. Again, it is difficult to see how all this would act differently in a vertical as compared to horizontal direction.

So what is the answer? I think it's as follows. The key thing is that we don't have transparent heads. Therefore, although the image from a mirror is heading towards us according to all the normal laws of optics, in order to see it we have to turn round. If we had transparent heads (and eyeballs for that matter) we could stand facing into the room (like the mirror is) and the light reflected from it could pass through all the intervening tissue and hit our retinas from the back. Everything would then be correctly orientated. In the absence of transparent heads, however, we have to turn round.

In the name of scientific investigation we could turn around vertically by performing a handstand in front of a large mirror. I haven't tried it for fear of precipitating a seizure of some sort, but I strongly suggest that you would then appear upside down and not flipped left to right. However, we normally don't do handstands in front of mirrors; if we did, the changing rooms of *Marks & Spencer* would form an entertaining and near-perfect experimental environment. We normally just keep our feet on the ground and turn horizontally. In fact, we are so accustomed to mirrors that we don't think of it as turning round at all. But we do turn round and the image is reversed horizontally *relative to us*. If you get tired of trying to dematerialise your least-favourite dinner guest into the kitchen you could test out my little puzzle instead—you may even get people doing handstands in front of mirrors. Anything to avoid *Trivial Pursuit*.

Know Thyself

You may wonder what all this has to do with evolution, cosmology, quantum mechanics, and the discussion about probability. Well, if we weren't aware of our observational restrictions we would probably be inclined to propose a theory that gravity somehow stabilises the vertical dimension in a reflection, but not the horizontal dimension. Those given to particle physics would no doubt invent a new particle, perhaps to be known as the "reflektark". String theory would discover a process—maybe called "photification"—that can happen in certain dimensions. Fortunately, all this is unnecessary because, in this case at least, we are aware of our observational restrictions and assume that there are reasons for the way we see things.

This little puzzle is of course an illustration of anthropic bias. Our conditions as observers affect what we see, but there is an important difference from the familiar picture of "carbon-based human observing the universe". Obviously that basic anthropic bias is still there. Even if we *had* transparent heads we would still need the Goldilocks environment and might still wonder how things had turned out to our benefit. However, my illustration adds another factor, namely, that we don't just observe or not observe, but that when we do observe the universe it is biased by our own observational apparatus—our sensory organs, our brains, and the consciousness that interprets everything.

The argument from design is often dismissed as a proof of the existence of God, because our sense of design could be illusory. *The Blind Watchmaker* tells us that it is—teleology is just about the way we see things, and to insist otherwise is for the most part not regarded as reasonable. It would be like going into the aforementioned changing room and then calling the shop assistant to complain that the jacket has been made to button the wrong way round. "It's just the way you see things, sir, when you look into a mirror". Continuing the argument would be a sure way to end up in compulsory therapy. As the product of physical forces in the universe we turn round to look at where we've come from, and inevitably see things in reverse—*as if* everything were geared towards our eventual existence.

However, I have not been arguing from a *perception* of design, I have been discussing mathematical improbability. Ironically, I would argue that the Anthropic Principle, as espoused by Dawkins, doesn't go far enough. We are not mere observers, we are highly *biased* observers. Only a super-observer—such as God—could observe everything and observe it perfectly. Bishop Berkeley (1685-1753) pointed this out a long time ago. We'll be meeting the good bishop later when we return to the *Philosophical Forum*.

Lost Horizons

My little riddle illustrates a feature of our observations, even at the normal everyday level on which we operate. In this case we can puzzle over it and eventually draw a conclusion because we can look at optic nerves and human brain function in enough detail to draw a scientific conclusion. We don't invent elaborate theories about ultimate reality because they are not necessary. Supposing, however, that there were an observational bias buried deep in the mental constructs somehow related to our brains, maybe hardwired into the neurons. How could we know of any such bias? In general, with what unbiased mind could we observe our own minds in order to detect our observational restrictions? Even if, hypothetically, there were no such horizons to our knowledge, how could we *know* that for certain?

This is a fundamental point at many levels. Let's take, for example, the whole arena of string theory, with its compactified dimensions and such like. My admiration for those who come up with such theories, and then piece them together into an all-embracing membrane theory, is (like the membrane, I believe) unbounded. Yet how do we know that the maths tells us truth about the underlying reality? It could merely represent, albeit in an ingenious way, that version of reality of which we are aware, as filtered by our observational restrictions. That seems a real danger when we bear in mind that string theory deals with a scale of things only a trillionth the size of that dealt with by the more conventional particle model.

Of course, these theories are said to be vindicated by the fact that they fit with our observations obtained from particle accelerators and so on. They allow predictions to be made, which one would often regard as the clincher. However, Ptolemy's system of epicycles did pretty much the same thing for the great puzzle of his time, the movements of the heavenly bodies. Yet Ptolemy's model of the solar system had the earth at its centre, so it wasn't 100% correct.

It is easy to think that these problems have been overcome by technology. Tools such as particle accelerators and all the instrumentation that goes with them can look much more deeply and with greater objectivity than any human being. That seems obvious—until we remember that they can only look for phenomena that we have designed them to look for, using technology based on the science that we have developed using our minds. If we designed them to look for something else, they might find something else. The reports that they give us have to be analysed according to the criteria that originate in our minds, assisted by the computers for which we write the software—using those same minds.

The Large Hadron Collider begs to be mentioned in this context. Let us assume, until further evidence becomes available, that Eloi Cole, the gentleman recently arrested at the LHC, is *not* a time traveller from the future who has come to warn of our impending destruction. That being so, we can look in amazement at the data now pouring forth, showing the tantalising hints of the Higgs boson. What is not often realised, however, is the sheer amount of information involved, needing an international network of thousands of computers to perform the analysis. The question is obvious. If this network had been configured differently, if the operating systems had been different, if the custom software had been different, would the results have turned out the same?

Please note an absolutely crucial point, namely, that observational restrictions are nothing to do with experimental error. Such errors can be detected and compensated for, even in a system as complex as the LHC. No, observational restrictions are to do with what is observed accurately, repeatedly, and verifiably—just as our cranio-ophthalmic anatomy gives us a mirror image accurately, repeatedly, and verifiably.

No matter how accurate our observations, then, there is always a horizon to our knowledge. We cannot see beyond the perceived edge of our universe because light from there (if there is any) has not yet had time to reach us. We cannot see beyond the edge of a black hole because the gravitational field of the black hole prevents light, and everything else, escaping from it. These "event horizons" are generally acknowledged. There must be, however, an equally real horizon in our minds, a boundary that we cannot cross. Ultimately this is no more than we should expect, unless we are to believe that we have unlimited intellectual capacity. We could call this the "thought horizon".

The existence of such a horizon does not mean that there is no real truth, and it is important not to fall into that bottomless pit. What it does mean is that assertions such as those made by Hawking and Mlodinow, Stenger, Tegmark, and others which are inevitably removed from observation can only be regarded as *interpretations*, in the same sense as the Copenhagen Interpretation and Many Worlds Interpretation of quantum mechanics.

Avoiding the Issue

You may remember Arnold, who acted as cannon fodder for the *Golden Grain* competition. Let's rewrite the script and imagine that Arnold had won the competition outright. What would be the average viewer reaction? I suggest that it would settle along a spectrum between two extremes, assuming that all possible ways of cheating have been eliminated.

The first extreme view would simply be that although it is vanishingly unlikely that one would correctly guess the *exact* position of just one grain of sand left anywhere in the world, it *could* happen. No alternative hypothesis has been vindicated, so best of luck Arnold, have a good life. Presumably Stenger would follow this line. Dawkins might argue that even though we can't see them such competitions actually happen frequently all over the universe, so it's not that unlikely that there should be a winner somewhere.

The other extreme view would be that the chance of Arnold winning is so small that there *must* be an alternative explanation. Even though all attempts to find such an explanation have failed, something will be found one day. The money should go to charity, not to Arnold. In desperation the TV production company sets up a panel of judges to decide the destiny of the prize money. Some judges claim to be utterly scientific and simply accept that what had apparently been observed—a very lucky fluke—was what happened. Others focus on its sheer improbability. A lawyer states that if Arnold gets the money she will petition for the release of several people convicted on the basis of DNA evidence, which has a recognised failure rate of around one in five million.

There is no question that in the orrery type of situation, based on large-scale observation and deduction, science has been spectacularly successful. In the *Golden Grain* type of scenario, however, we seem to be in the domain of the uncertain, just as much as if we could shrink ourselves down to the size of an electron to test out the wave equation. Numerous theories would spring up as to what had actually happened, none of them supported by any evidence. People would take sides and debate would continue for a long time, tossing around their interpretations. Why? Because weighing up vanishingly small probabilities takes us to our thought horizon, which is frustrating. It's much less frustrating to champion one interpretation and argue about it. Suddenly, everyone's an expert.

One thing that is quite striking about the "new atheists" is that they often do not stick to their areas of real expertise. They broaden out their attacks to cover the impossibility—as they see it—of there being a God who could influence the world as we experience it. Superstition, claims to the miraculous, prayer, examples of bad design, suffering, and the logical paradoxes of the (non-existent) God, are all drawn in to support their argument, often with little understanding of other points of view. The common feature of these writers is that they normally decide first what God must be like, and then decide that they do not believe in him (or her, or them, or it). This is an interesting method. It smacks of frustration, and I would suggest it is the same frustration as that felt by the pundits for and against Arnold, the frustration of coming up against our inevitable thought horizon.

It could be replied, of course, that religious people, equally, offer merely an interpretation when they resort to arguing from design, causality, or morality. There is, however, a very big difference between the two lines of argument. Design, causality, and morality are phenomena that we observe and about which we draw conclusions. One can have serious debate about such matters—they are within our thought horizon. However, arguments about spontaneous creation are not within that boundary. Their upholders cannot point to the occasional object that simply appeared from nothing. If over a period of maybe a year we heard of a pebble that suddenly appeared from nowhere, then a mushroom, a piece of coal and a smoked haddock, the whole idea might be more believable.

I have already made two suggestions as to how we should progress the debate about science and religion, and re-state them here by way of consolidation, before adding a third.

Firstly, I suggested that we should accept the term *implicit design* as a neutral description of something that actually exists, but which may be explained by invoking a designer or in some other way. It could be simply coincidence, even though the likelihood of that coincidence is extremely small.

Secondly, I proposed that we should accept the fact and implications of the holistic universe pointed to by quantum mechanics, particularly bearing in mind that this is highly relevant in certain crucial areas such as the foundation of the laws of nature, gene mutation, and the functioning of nervous systems.

I would like to add a third suggestion, which is this: that we recognise and try to define more clearly the thought horizon within which we are compelled to live.

These three proposals would form a good "tripos" for contemporary discussion. We might even find some new directions. Unfortunately, the "new atheists" generally prefer knee-jerk responses in preference to the pursuit of such ideas. We have seen this tendency in regard to historical events, the miraculous, the question of suffering, and the supposed science-religion conflict. Now we shall need to add to the list something like, "science has proved that creation simply happened". If one has the temerity to speak of the thought horizon, then that will be immediately classed as "god of the gaps" thinking, which it is not. What we see developing through the dogmatic "new atheist" approach is a new religion, and that is the subject of my next chapter.

CHAPTER 13

The Big Yellow Crane

Religious people are often accused of believing the unbelievable, after the manner of the White Queen in Lewis Carroll's *Through the Looking Glass*. Lewis Wolpert takes up this theme in his book *Six Impossible Things Before Breakfast*. From Wolpert's point of view, as an atheist, the accusation is, of course, justified, and he writes in a refreshingly amiable spirit, with entirely appropriate warnings against superstition. However, the majority of religious people do not believe the unbelievable, they simply have a different concept from Wolpert as to what makes something believable. They fully accept that science is believable within its own sphere of activity. However, they do not believe that science tells us *everything* that is true. Why should it? There is a thought horizon.

Wolpert's accusation is more fittingly levelled against atheists than against most "believers". We have looked at the belief that the universe came into existence spontaneously from nothing. That seems impossible within the normal meaning of words. Next, the atheist calls on us to believe in a set of circumstances and events that, while not technically impossible, are so incredibly unlikely considered as a whole that we should normally call them that. Here we are in *Golden Grain* territory. We have looked, under this category, at major themes of evolutionary biology and cosmology. Put all this together and it seems that atheism—at least as expressed by the "new atheists"—is just as dependent on "believing the impossible" as is any religion. It also has to be said that those who pursue the hope of alien life forms with religious zeal, despite the total lack of evidence, ought to fall under Wolpert's condemnation.

On the other hand, there are some ideas about reality that are distinctly possible yet seem to carry little weight in atheist thinking. *Quantum quirkiness* raises new possibilities of the interaction of mind and matter as two aspects of one reality. Parts of this marvellous whole can be entangled, regardless of the physical distance between those parts, and I proposed that quantum transactions may affect the large-scale world through the gene mutations lying behind evolution and within the complex activity of nervous systems.

Within this view of reality, the idea of a mind underlying everything, and accessible to human minds, is neither impossible nor ridiculous. The same applies to interactions between that mind and the world we know, leading to the "providential" understanding that does not see miracles round every corner, but does not deny their possibility. Along with that understanding comes a re-assessment of suffering, and a sense that it may be profoundly part of a divine plan.

If Wolpert is right that religious people can be a little too quick to believe in the impossible, I will complain in return that atheists are reluctant to consider alternative ways of assessing what is possible.

The Biological Crane

Dawkins claims that evolution through natural selection is like a crane that explains the diversity, complexity and (in his view only apparent) design to be found in the living world. Over millions of years this crane hauled life from its most primitive mono-cellular form to the incredible phenomenon that is the human animal. Now he wants one that will explain everything else as well. As previously noted, he is following here Daniel Dennett's terminology in *Darwin's Dangerous Idea*. Cranes are good because they show how apparent design developed from the ground up. "Skyhooks", on the other hand, are bad, because they suggest that there is design from an outside source such as God.

In the North East of England there's not much we don't know about cranes. One of the more interesting examples, to be found on the north side of the river Tyne, is a massive yellow beast with a horizontal jib. Diligent research has revealed that it's known as a "hammerhead" crane, yet even within its type it's an interesting design. The jib has a level top side and on this is a small crane that runs along on rails. This illustrates Dawkins' analogy quite well. The small crane represents biology, driven by evolution, and the large crane on which it sits represents cosmology; Dawkins would like this to be driven by some kind of evolution as well, even though the laws of physics do not point in that direction.

This piece of local industrial heritage symbolically fits the "new atheist" aspiration so well that it could become a shrine for cranies. As part of the informative recorded narrative, available free in the visitor centre, it would have to be pointed out that this is another example of the fallacy of illicit process. Just because one proposed explanatory model may move from simple to complex via variation and selection doesn't imply that all others must do the same.

The Cosmological Crane

As we have seen, evolution could never have started without a cosmos possessing suitable physical values. Stephen Hawking's words in *A Brief History of Time* provide a good summary: "The remarkable fact is that the values of these numbers seem to have been very finely adjusted to make possible the development of life. Most sets of values would give rise to universes that, although they might be very beautiful, would contain no one able to wonder at that beauty." His latest work puts him alongside Stenger in the "spontaneous creation" camp, but this interpretation doesn't contradict the basic fact that he points out in my quote.

Fred Hoyle abandoned his atheism as a result of such considerations—I briefly mentioned his views in Chapter 8. The renowned lifelong atheist Antony Flew, who died recently, moved from atheism to deism for similar reasons to Hoyle, although focussing additionally on abiogenisis and DNA. His views can be found in his book *There is a God*. Now I am not saying that these changes of conviction happen all the time—they don't. Yet these luminaries and others highlight the problem, from the Dogmatic Darwinist point of view, that in this complex pre-biological phase there is not the remotest semblance of anything that could be naturally selected. Not a single gene—selfish, helpless, or otherwise—in sight. There is development, as the forces of the Big Bang unfolded and continue to unfold. Of mutation, adaptation and selection, however, there is nothing. What we do have is a holistic quantum universe in which every part is related to the whole. As we have seen, far from pointing away from the existence of God this all opens up new possibilities in our understanding. It is a rather different crane from the one required by Dogmatic Darwinists—the people for whom Darwinism must explain everything.

Meet Dave

It's time now to meet the crane driver, Dave, who sits in a cab at the top of the whole shebang. Dave can pick up from a low loader on the quayside a generator set weighing several tons and deftly place it on the deck of an ocean-going barge moored nearby, to an accuracy of a couple of inches. Yes, he might have the benefit of modern technological devices involving two-way radios, computers, GPS, and maybe a laser or two. Nevertheless, it's not the kind of job you would entrust to a chimpanzee, however highly trained. Despite sharing 98% of his DNA with the chimp, Dave has a conceptual apparatus that the chimpanzee does not have, an apparatus that has developed over about the last 150,000 years—a mere split-second in the grand scheme of things.

If you've followed my valuable social suggestions throughout this book and had folk round to attempt teleportation, or figure out why we don't appear upside down in mirrors, this next question will seem easy. It is: what has Dave got that a chimpanzee hasn't? Leaving out the initial ribaldry, the answer given will probably be "a bigger brain". You may get "opposable thumb" but that's not thought so important nowadays because, notwithstanding its usefulness in handling tools and so on, other species apart from our own have one in some shape or form. "Opposable thumb" is just *so* twentieth century.

However, although the "bigger brain" answer is correct, there are certain puzzles attached. For example, the human brain is not actually the biggest in the animal kingdom, nor is it the brain with the most neurons. There are also many instances where people who suffer brain damage adapt remarkably well with, effectively, an abnormally small brain. Size alone is not the key.

What makes Dave suitable for his job is a particular form of brain development which allows him to understand concepts and to reason things out in very complex ways. Without this ability Dave would have to work out from scratch, by trial and error, what to do each time he had to load a generator set. Hard hats would be scant protection for those working below.

This may seem overstated. Thousands of species have learning abilities and communicate using rudimentary sounds to co-ordinate their activities. However, their learning is accounted for by instinct and mimicry; they don't build complex languages, and that seems to be a key factor in distinctively human consciousness. A word is a particular kind of symbol, and the linguistic abilities we have are also the key to the manipulation of other symbols such as those used in mathematics. The result is that we have an ability to conceptualise, reason, draw conclusions and to act on them, which is unique to us.

An intriguing point brought out by Nadeau and Kafatos in *The Non-Local Universe* is that this ability to conceptualise and communicate through words and other symbols is not just a matter of plugging in another module to an existing design of brain. Many parts of the brain are involved. When it comes to auditory and vocal functions, unique developments in other parts of the body also had to have happened, probably over a long period before the arrival of modern man. These are some of the reasons that our immediately ancestral hominids were so important. Jumping to a *homo sapiens* equivalent from the kangaroo, crow, dolphin or octopus would have been impossible.

Susan Greenfield, in her television work and in *The Private Life of the Brain* gives an intriguing picture of the high level of *plasticity* of the human brain. It is always on the go—doubling in size during our first two years of life, and then doubling again by the time we reach sixteen years. However, this multiplication in size is not caused by an increase in the number of neurons, which is more-or-less fixed at around 100 billion, but by growth in length and complexity of the connecting "wires" which are part of each one. New connections form by the shed load, each with its own synaptic chemistry, until we have a staggering 100 trillion or thereabouts.

How these connections in our brains form is largely governed by experience—areas of the brain that are used more than others develop more connections. This plasticity continues to a lesser degree throughout life, which is the reason that those suffering from damage of one part of the brain can adapt, to some extent, to use another part instead. Incidentally, brain plasticity is found in all mammals, but it appears to be particularly significant in *homo sapiens,* for reasons that will become clear later.

Language Learning

Probably related to plasticity is an even greater mystery than language itself, namely the ability of children to learn different languages, and the rules that apply to them, at a very early age, without formal teaching and without massive amounts of trial and error. It seems that this ability is somehow pre-installed in the brain, possibly in the form of a system of understanding the rules for language generally, so that after birth (starting almost immediately) the child begins to match this understanding to the linguistic environment. In some cultures children learn two or even three languages at once without even breaking into a sweat.

The development of our mental abilities, of course, became a crucial factor in survival—the ability to out-think became more important than the ability to out-fight or to out-run. Fortunately, once the ice had finally departed, about 10,000 years ago, we were able to launch more and more into settlement and then agriculture. Whatever level of consciousness was present in the dog, goat, sheep, ox, ass, and horse was sufficient to allow their domestication, and staple crops were established throughout the world. By a happy coincidence, we had the ability by then to work out techniques of husbandry and much else. The rest is history. Literally.

Our higher level of consciousness includes, along with the language package and probably closely connected with it, abilities to think conceptually and hypothetically, with different systems of symbols for different needs. We have the ability to speculate and plan, to analyse and synthesise data, to form complex and flexible social structures and so on. Where did all this come from, on such a short timescale, much too short for normal evolutionary explanations? Even if the biological crane gets us *almost* to the end of our evolutionary history, I don't see how it can account for this last spectacular transition.

Since this critical ability needs so many factors to make it possible, it seems that to designate the emergence of this higher consciousness a further "megafluke" is fully justified. In Dawkins' view, of course, the brain simply evolved by a series of small steps, just like everything else, and there is no doubting the huge survival advantage conferred by human consciousness. It is the short timescale involved that seems highly problematical.

Dave's View of Things

Dave knows little of the matters discussed in the last section. Apart from getting on well with his workmates, he's a member of his family, he's part of a local community that he meets "down the club" on Friday nights for a pint of *Rivet Catcher,* and he goes fishing with a life-long friend on Sundays. He takes a passing interest in football, fixes cars, and listens to *The Moody Blues* and *Pink Floyd.* As far as religion is concerned he is very taken with the views of sunsets sometimes obtainable from his high vantage point and thinks there is a God, but can't understand suffering. He used to go to church now and again when the kids were little, for special events. If pressed he would probably say that religion is mainly about knowing right from wrong. In other words, he is part of a culture, of which one element is religion.

One could, of course, write sketches like these for the whole human race, and all seven billion would be different. There would, however, be some common elements such as security, family, friendship circles, local community, national identity, and so on. Abraham Maslow (1908–1970) is still valuable in understanding these features of human life. He arranged human needs in a pyramid, with physical and safety needs at the bottom (food, water, security, and so on). Above these in the hierarchy are the needs for love and belonging such as friendship, family, and sexual intimacy. Further up are the needs for achievement, confidence, and self-esteem. Finally, at the top, is what Maslow calls "self-actualisation", the ability to live a creative, moral, and honest life, open to facts, unprejudiced and geared towards problem-solving, sometimes with respect to the problems of others.

According to Maslow, we need fulfilment of these different layers of need in order, starting from the bottom. If, for example, we are in danger of starvation, it's difficult to think about achievement. If we are struggling to achieve some essential goal of our own, it's harder to focus on solving other people's problems. Even though Maslow has been criticised for making his hierarchy too rigid, this seems to fit well with everyday experience.

The problem with this hierarchy is that it can easily become a hierarchy of power. Some will increase self-esteem by damaging that of others. Some will make themselves more secure by making others more insecure. Not everyone attempts to live by the golden rule, and no one lives by it perfectly. Why should people disadvantage themselves for the sake of others? We noted earlier that altruism in human beings is much more complex than the programmed self-sacrificial behaviour patterns of ants or termites. How is the urge to altruism developed in human communities? When it fails, how is conformity—a necessary form of damage-limitation—procured?

Well, the most obvious suggestion is simply this: within any group certain practices are frowned upon and other practices encouraged. It's unlikely, for example, that one of Dave's workmates would have an affair with his wife, which would of course be a blatant theft of self esteem. Too many taboos concerning family, friendship and group solidarity would be broken. It would be useful to debate whether these taboos originate from God via some innate ethical system (the stance of many religions) or whether they have evolved because of their advantage in survival (the stance of many evolutionary psychologists and sociobiologists). Dawkins, however, is in no mood for messing about. As part of his overall strategy he railroads the discussion into one about "memes", so we shall need to look at this subject next.

The question is, even if we could have been hauled up to the present by the supposed cosmological and biological cranes, what *psychological crane* do we need to account for the phenomenon of seven billion individuals linking together into a range of cultures that together form our global culture? How do we understand the diversity that we see, and how do we understand the features held in common or shared by many—such as morality and belief in God?

The Psychological Crane

A meme can be initially understood as a persistent idea. The term was not invented by Dawkins, but he coined the word (together with "memeplex"— a number of connected memes) and popularised it. He now tries to use it to explain cultural evolution, including religious belief. However, it's over 30 years since the meme concept was first mooted, and it simply hasn't caught on, apart from among a small band of disciples. I doubt there are many more than twelve. Even without a deeper consideration, that should perhaps alert us to the fragility of meme theory. In a similar vein, we should also note that meme theory, as put forward by Dawkins and his associates, is *not* a popularisation of views held by a large number of scientists. It is a new way of looking at things, a philosophical lens if you like, although popularly expressed.

The ball was set rolling in *The Selfish Gene*, but the most crucial distinction is made in *The Extended Phenotype* Chapter 6, which asserts that memes are not *merely* persistent ideas but replicators (like genes) that are passed between people. However, there is no evidence for the existence of memes as replicators, certainly no equivalent of DNA that works for memes instead of genes, and any idea that there is such a thing is pure conjecture. In the Dawkinsian view, however, the meme is more or less parallel to a gene. If a meme is passed on faithfully, then in effect a copy of the meme will be planted in the brain of the recipient.

Moreover, this theory seems crude compared to the practical use of human language. Meanings are determined by context, which includes the pre-conceptions, ideas, areas of knowledge, and the overall culture in which people live. For me, *Rivet Catcher* is the name on a beer pump (honestly, it is) whereas Dave's granddad *was* a rivet catcher and could have told you how it all worked before ships were stuck together with superglue. Context radically alters meaning.

Meme theory seems unable to explain the use of metaphor, allusion, and paradox. In the centre of Newcastle upon Tyne there is a camping shop that some time ago held a New Year sale, but instead of the usual day-glow poster there was a tastefully designed sign which read, "Now is the winter of our discount tents". I thought that was fantastic, but how can it be reduced to hard-edged memes?

The propagation of ideas is constantly encouraged, diverted, modified, and restricted by human beings, for many reasons. We are not helpless slaves to whatever other people tell us or in making decisions about what we pass on. Yet meme theory is extremely atomistic to human thought. Is this why *The God Delusion* sorts religions into two piles, monotheistic and the rest, in such a primitive manner? The monotheistic meme, on this reckoning, is clearly present in all three monotheistic religions and not the rest—but why should there be a meme for "monotheistic God"? There might be one for "Judaistic God", another for "Christian God" and yet another for "Muslim God". How would we really tell?

If meme theory were correct, surely it would apply to all knowledge, including the scientific. As Alister McGrath points out in *Dawkins' God: Genes, Memes and the Meaning of Life*, even meme theory itself would be a memeplex. Of course, the dedicated "memeticist" would say that science is different from religion because it is subject to rigorous scientific method. But that itself would be under the influence of "scientific method" memes. In any case, what scientific test exactly has been applied to meme theory?

The main reason that Dawkins wants to hold on to memetics, despite all its weaknesses, is that it allows him to propose a Darwinian mechanism for cultural development. Just as it was proposed that the cosmological crane should be Darwinian in some way, so it is now assumed that the psychological crane should be the same. Why? There is no objective reason for either assumption. As I hinted at the end of my previous chapter, this seems to be a new religion.

The New Fundamentalism

I've referred from time to time to the "born again" experience which is at the heart of Christian fundamentalism, in which the new believer comes to a fresh appraisal of a proclaimed belief such as atonement. Here are some words that could easily be describing that belief. "It is beautiful because it is so simple and yet its results are so complex. It is counter-intuitive and hard to grasp but once you have seen it the world is transformed before your eyes."

Now you wouldn't be surprised if that quote were from a mid-west evangelical preacher talking about religious experience, and in fact such language is often used in the devotional life of religious groups. However, the quote is actually taken from *The Meme Machine* by Susan Blackmore (p10), and she is referring to Darwinism, leading on to her discussion of "Universal Darwinism".

Within the "new atheist" faithful this seems to be a new fundamentalism. Blackmore's conviction that Darwinism will explain all, following Dennett and Dawkins, is actually dogma, which is why I prefer the term "Dogmatic Darwinism" to "Universal Darwinism", although it amounts to the same thing. While the Dennett-Dawkins' crane is a fairly vague concept, Blackmore is highly specific and goes beyond memes to "temes".

In Blackmore's view the teme is the "third replicator"*. A teme is a *technological meme*. At the moment it can't be done, but the day is apparently coming when pieces of technology will replicate themselves and spread abroad, just as genes have spread through biological evolution and memes have spread through cultural evolution. It may possibly be that one day the temes will set off to explore the universe. Whether they will have any use for us is a moot point; they may be totally independent, leaving us to perish in the ruins of the planet. On the other hand, humans may be modified by the use of implants, drugs, and nanotechnology so that they merge with temes.

This new school of ultra-Darwinism has a dogma known as the "evolutionary algorithm" which holds that if you have variation, selection, and heredity then you must get evolution, i.e. design out of chaos. No great mind, no "skyhook" is required. Now it is easy, of course, to model this principle on a computer. Running algorithms, after all, is what computers do. You will guess my objection immediately, which is, "does it work like that in the real world?" I have already argued extensively that it does not, because such rules as there are to evolution arise out of the process by chance. Many well-qualified people, notably Stephen Jay Gould, objected to this algorithm when it was first proposed by Dennett.

As far as Blackmore is concerned the algorithm is a given, not open to argument. Almost as deeply held seems to be her belief in ET; apparently one reason we have not heard from extra-terrestrials is that the transition to the third replicator is dangerous, so the number of civilisations that make it through that transition might be smaller than would be suggested by the famous *Drake equation*. You may also have noticed an element of transhumanism creeping in, the belief that we can somehow transcend human frailty and live forever, or at least for a very long time.

All this owes more to science fiction than to science. I have great respect

---

* See her video talk archived at *www.ted.com* for details

for Seth Shostak, the senior astronomer and main PR man at the SETI institute (SETI stands for "Search for Extra Terrestrial Intelligence"). He has the unenviable task of promoting his cause while there is still absolutely no supporting evidence—which requires a kind of faith. However, Shostak carries this burden with great charisma, and also spends some of his media time debunking the wilder UFO ideas—both plus points. He seems like a calm senior bishop by comparison with Blackmore and her fiery brand of fundamentalism.

For my money the best approach would be to think of memes as hierarchies, so that some characteristics could be inherited while others varied. This is, of course, a familiar concept in the computer world so beloved of the "new atheists". The "God" meme would be a top-level meme, with monotheism, polytheism, and so on being "child memes" carrying within them the top-level meme. Within monotheism there would be a Christianity version, in effect a "grandchild meme" with parent and grandparent memes wrapped up in it. In the same generation there would be a Judaism version, an Islam version, and so on.

This idea might start to answer my complaint about the crudeness of the meme idea compared to actual human discourse, but it goes nowhere in answering the other objections to memetics. Moreover, it seems likely that with any further development the basic meme concept would die the "death of a thousand qualifications"—it would become so fragmented into different generations and relationships that the basic idea would be lost.

The concept of the meme is useful in pointing out that *some* ideas are *somewhat* atomistic and make their way through cultures unaided once they have been set going. Advertising experts have been aware of this for a long time, and have strategies for starting the meme such as advocacy, multi-channel tie-ins, the problem-solution formula, sponsorship, and the new kid on the block, social networking. And of course, it works—for a time, for a slogan. Music and catchy lyrics work—for a while. Humour works—until it becomes old hat. Then it's on to the next fad. One week it's cars, the next it's who has the best iPod. Most examples of memes given by those who believe in them appear to be in this league—rather trivial.

The concern to explain human cultural development by postulating the existence of memes is part of the wider attempt to explain everything by science. In *Understanding the Present* (p228) Bryan Appleyard put it like this:

> Science now answers questions *as if* it were a religion and its obvious effectiveness means that these answers are believed to be the Truth—again *as if* it were a religion. But it confronts none of the spiritual issues of purpose and meaning. And, meanwhile, its growing power enables it to drive the very systems that did confront those issues to the margins of our concern and, ultimately,

out of existence.

This is another excellent description of scientism. Appleyard gets a brief mention in the early pages of *Unweaving the Rainbow*, but his points are then ignored throughout the rest of the book, perhaps the very place where one would have expected them to be answered. To attribute major cultural changes to memes is speculative. That's not necessarily to deny validity to all the claims made by sociobiology or evolutionary psychology; those controversial ideas deserve thorough debate, not funnelling down into a concept which, though convenient, is deeply flawed.

What makes Dave the individual that he is? Evolution, certainly, but that applies equally to all of us. His culture has clearly added much to that; indeed, culture is a defining feature of *homo sapiens,* spanning art, music, symbolism, and story telling from our earliest days, then developing into the literary and post-literary cultures of which ours is one. The major function of culture is to provide a sense of purpose and meaning, and historically it has relied on religion.

Pathways to Purpose

The "new atheists" wish to demote religion from its position of cultural influence. Their presupposition is that if we get the science right everything else will fall into place. This may not *necessarily* lead to the hypothesis that science explains everything, but that seems to be the trend, and Appleyard is right—issues of purpose and meaning are driven out. At the very least, alternative non-religious pathways are sought in which some sense of purpose and meaning are felt to reside. Some of these such as sexuality, family, and community are basic to our existence, and we can certainly see their evolutionary significance. Others are much more variable and culture dependent. They exercise a moulding and modifying influence over the basics, for example:

Consumerism took off in the USA of the 1920s, building on the increasing prosperity brought about by people like Thomas Edison and Henry Ford. Partly seen as a key to peace, it was an alternative outlet for the aggressive instincts of humans, and this idea was reinforced by Edward Bernays, now generally recognised as the father of the modern PR industry. Bernays was a double nephew to Sigmund Freud, who became deeply pessimistic about human nature, particularly with the rise of Nazism. Ironically, Bernays' work on manipulation of the masses was read, and acted upon, by Joseph Goebbels, the Nazi propaganda minister. We ought, perhaps, to distinguish that interpretation from benign consumerism, with which we are all familiar, although some would question the use of the word "benign" since consumerism inevitably validates selfishness to a degree—otherwise there would be little economic growth.

Hedonism as a principle is easy to summarise in its popular sense: "If it feels good, do it." This latest incarnation took root in the sixties. However, the general problem with avowed hedonism was that only the rich could afford the rehab and divorce costs. As living standards increased, moving into the seventies, it became more of a general principle in a diluted and less ambitious form. Eventually the Reagan-Thatcher years transformed the whole concept into mainly financial terms and the "yuppy" was born. Once the translation into financial cost took place the majority of people realised that there just wasn't a big enough cake for everyone to indulge. Hedonism may then remain as the icing on the cake, but not the central purpose of life. It hardly seems able to create values from within itself, and easily becomes absorbed into consumerism.

Narcissism is obsession with oneself—most obviously in appearance or physical prowess, but perhaps also transferred to the intellectual and emotional. A degree of narcissism is no doubt necessary for a proper degree of self-respect. That fact feeds back, like hedonism, into consumerism—as health club owners, personal coaches, beauticians, cosmetic surgeons, herbalists, trainers, therapists and gurus everywhere will confirm, backed up by their accountants. Unfortunately, the narcissistic person is highly vulnerable to the passage of time—Wilde's *A Portrait of Dorian Gray* says it all. While others simply get on with life, the narcissist always has one eye on the mirror, and perhaps remembers goals not achieved, acknowledgement not received, or opportunities for self-fulfilment gone forever. Purpose and meaning must be elusive at best for the truly narcissistic.

Romanticism is an incredibly broad concept. Although the feel good factor is important, as in hedonism, it tends to be connected to a longer-term sense of rightness rather than some immediate fulfilment which is quickly gone. Sacrifice for that longer-term goal is noble, whereas for the hedonist such sacrifice would be simply a waste of the present moment. Unfortunately, romanticism of any sort is vulnerable to the actions of others who may not fulfil romantic expectations, to political and economic movements, and the reality of passing time—all is flux, as Heraclitus said around 2,500 years ago. The delighted lovers' song can become a tragedy of operatic proportions. National pride can become national humiliation. Joy in nature may be subverted by its cruel indifference at times to our needs. The loss of the dream can easily lead to the negation of purpose and meaning, so derivation of these things from the romantic is always hazardous.

These "-isms" and no doubt others account for much of human life, as reflected in the arts, media, sports, workplace, education, community and the general cultural context in which we live. The question is, can they produce purpose and meaning? And where do memes enter the picture, if at all?

The lead "-ism" today appears to be consumerism, which tends to swallow up everything else. The network of business and financial institutions which supports it often appears to be a value-free zone. That's not to deny (for example) the great humanitarian instinct of Bill Gates, or the pioneering spirit of the late Dame Anita Roddick, or the achievements of many other innovators in areas of "social entrepreneurship" such as Appropriate Technology, Fair Trade, and Microfinancing. Such enterprises do undoubtedly deal with purpose and meaning—but I am certain their values are initially brought to them by the founders and stakeholders. To wish it were otherwise might be noble, but fraudsters from Maxwell to Madoff are obvious contradictions of such a hope, and their behaviour is exceptional only in scale. Maybe I'm just mixing with the wrong sort, but it does seem to me that any attempt to glean purpose and meaning from consumerism is misguided.

In the nineties we talked about Francis Fukuyama's thesis of "the end of history"—a thesis that with the fall of communism the whole world would now march happily to the beat of capitalism. Unfortunately, history did not end in the anticipated manner. Disintegration of a great power bloc simply revealed the underlying tensions, resulting in civil wars, unrest, and the growth of organised crime. We gained the impression at the time that some underlying values were emerging, but the pessimism of John Gray, prophetically expressed in *False Dawn: the Delusions of Global Capitalism,* seems more credible in the light of our current financial turmoil. We need to learn how purpose and meaning can be *brought into* our global systems.

Management guru Charles Handy says in *The Empty Raincoat,* commenting on Maslow, "Perhaps his hierarchy did not reach far enough. There could be a stage beyond self-realisation, a stage which we might call idealisation, the pursuit of an ideal or a cause which is more than oneself. It is this extra stage which would redeem the self-centred tone of Maslow's thesis which, for all that it rings true of much of our experience, has a rather bitter aftertaste. Maslow himself was to acknowledge this towards the end of his life".

Handy's comment reflects the idea of "self-transcendence" expressed in 1969 in Maslow's "Theory Z" and also by the psychiatrist Viktor Frankl (1905–97) who focused directly on the search for meaning. I suggest that this something "more than oneself" is essential in any culture to hold in place the various "isms"—all of which are good servants, but very bad masters. This is the role of tradition—that unseen narrative which a culture recites to itself over the years, a narrative which sets individual and group responsibilities, extols that which is regarded as good and condemns that which is regarded as bad.

Memetic Overload

Dawkins has a habit of overloading concepts. I noted this with the Anthropic Principle, and it seems to be the same with memetics. I do not see how memetics can possibly take on the burden of cultural narrative. Memes seem more suited to the advertising slogans, logos, and strap lines used by consumerism and its other attendant "-isms".

Folk sayings and proverbs could, I suppose, be classed as memes, but they hardly convey purpose and meaning. My grandmother used to say, "many a mickle maks a muckle", and although I had no idea what it meant, it is still useful for stopping an otherwise tedious conversation anywhere south of Leeds. I think it must be an example of "memetic drift" from over the border and probably means the same as "Look after the pennies..." Not very revolutionary.

Some famous quotations or pearls of wisdom may have some influence, but most are simply quoted to support an existing point of view or to add emotional impact to an argument. Use of foreign or classical words also adds a certain *gravitas* to any statement. We play many such language games. Apart from showing off linguistic skills and intelligence, which could be a kind of preening, there's often the affirmation of belonging to a certain group or "inner circle", a giving or taking of security and esteem. There could be memes in the sense of the actual sayings and slogans, but the use of this material in practice is subtle, malleable, analogue, and greatly influenced by context.

The memetic model fails to give us a psychological crane that will explain to us how we came to be culturally where we are, and where purpose and meaning might be found for the future. Where else can we look?

Story Telling

Every culture has its myths (timeless stories with a continuing message) and its legends (stories of significant historical events plus their interpretations). Legends are often concerned with how the tribe or nation came into existence, how the gods or God work and why the situation of the present (good or bad), or certain features of the present, have come about.

I have these days only a few of my old college books left—a strange sentimental attachment I suppose. Yet they sometimes come in useful, and a vague memory can be resurrected. Ringgren and Ström in *Religions of Mankind* make the following comment: "Ritual, the action, forms a unity with Myth, the spoken word. Myth—relating the creation of the world, the death of the vegetation god, etc.—explains the ritual, which in turn illustrates the myth and heightens its effect."

In other words, the actions and the story reinforce each other—but we are not talking here about memetics, we're talking about religious tradition. Monotheism, being historically orientated, centres mostly on legend rather than timeless myth, but the connection with ritual is still made. Notably, Judaism re-enacts its "salvation history" through the yearly festivals such as Passover. Christianity re-interprets this in the light of the "Christ event", focussing especially on episodes in the life of Christ, re-enacting them through its own rituals. Official or unofficial stories of important figures down the ages fill out the main story and bring it up to date. It is the decline of that story that has left the way open for alternative pathways to compete for dominance.

It is not obvious how atheism in its own right can function in this cultural arena. The Big Yellow Crane is essentially a mechanical device, illustrating a mechanical view of how we come to be here. It's hardly inspiring in itself, and neither is the simple claim that there is no God. Adding some stirring invective about the evils of religion, and some rather aspirational claims about the inevitable future progress of science, provide, perhaps, a little colour. Personally, I don't want to be taken over by nanobots but I suppose that's a matter of individual taste.

In any event, crane-driver Dave doesn't much buy into all this new mythology. Even if it were all possible, which he doubts, it has little impact on his daily life, or on the lives of those around him that he cares about. A bit of common-sense morality, with the occasional tinge of Christianity, is just about all he can take. If Dave is the latest product—to date—of the Big Yellow Crane, then he has yet to be persuaded of this final great leap into a cosmic wonderland.

This is emphatically not just a matter of social class. I know plenty of young, and even not so young, entrepreneurial types who are totally non-religious as far as one can tell, but they don't devote themselves to finding the meaning of life through science. The more bohemian types who buy their working-class look from very expensive shops are more likely to be involved in alternative therapy than a grand vision for the future. Genuine bohemians seem more focussed on being bohemian than on the future of scientific endeavour. Meanwhile the middle-fliers of suburbia concentrate more on the housing market than on the possibility of travelling to Mars.

The Internet and thousand channel television seem to enable a significant number of people to get by with hardly any real vision of anything, let alone utopian scientific daydreams. My various "-isms", and the basic human drives, are much more relevant. It is also fairly obvious that the ethnic and religious minorities in our society have their own, very strong, cultural defence mechanisms against *any* imposed mythology.

The "new atheist" narrative alone, then, won't satisfy many, and seems to be designed with a scientifically-orientated elite in mind. However, once we add the concept of memetics into the mix it seems that anyone who doesn't go along with the cranies can be dismissed as suffering from a memetic "infestation" (one of Daniel Dennett's less felicitous terms) or possibly a "thought virus" (the more Dawkinsian phrase). It doesn't take a master logician to recognise that such an accusation could be levelled by members of any group against any other group that they didn't happen to like.

Somewhat frighteningly, it seems that, for Dawkins, the human mind is merely a bundle of virtual reality software that runs in the hardware of the brain. We can re-programme it so that it will no longer only run "utilitarian reality" but will enable us to live in future worlds according to taste. It appears to be of minor importance whether there is any truth in the new worlds of the imagination, as long as we can enjoy our "meme dream"—one of Blackmore's terms. Yet without truth, science and technology cannot themselves survive. What seems to be on offer is an updated *soma* for the brave new world—or maybe it's just the same old bread and circuses tarted up with electronics.

An abridged version of these ideas can be found in the final chapter of *The God Delusion*. They are a logical conclusion from the philosophical tendencies we looked at earlier. You may have wondered why I spent so much time talking about the mind-body problem, monism, dualism, and so on. Here's the reason: our modern atheism has defined itself unequivocally and aggressively as materialistic. That is to say, only the material is real. As a result, any inner conviction concerning values, aesthetics, or an unseen reality, however widely shared, is ephemeral.

Perhaps this is why space mythology is so appealing to the "new atheists". If it's material stuff that turns you on, the universe is, to all intents and purposes, an infinite playground. Much more interesting than dusty old documents that speak of ideas like God, justice, love, forgiveness, redemption, and eternity, documents that have formed civilisations for thousands of years. To the modern atheistic *illuminati* such things are hardly worth the parchment they are written on.

I've pointed out the shortcomings of atheist mythology and memetics rather like two points of a sermon, so traditionally that brings me to the third, where I thump on the pulpit for effect and declare that the whole method of materialism is faulty.

What's so Wrong with Materialism?

The fundamental problem with materialism is that we all experience our own minds. We are convinced that we know our own thoughts, we understand to some extent the thoughts of others, we can at least understand the idea of the mind of God. Yet materialists cannot really make any comment on mind at all. Logically, as scientific people, they can only make such statements on the basis of examining themselves (normally called *introspection*) or on the basis of their observations of other people.

Now I've already admitted that my understanding of the influential philosopher Gilbert Ryle may be inadequate, but I think one thing that I did pick up correctly is that there is no "ghost in the machine". There is no "I" buried in the brain or elsewhere that can examine what "I" am. That would be like trying to use a microscope to examine its own workings. Introspection is definitely impossible for the materialist.

That only leaves observation of other people, and I freely admit to the brilliance of Dennett's *Consciousness Explained*. Using only a "third-person perspective" he thoroughly takes apart the dualism of Descartes and any concept of "mind-stuff". There is no "centre of consciousness", in the pineal gland or anywhere else, which reviews reports from the senses and co-ordinates them into a coherent stream. His picture is that of a state of pandemonium in which different sense impressions and meanings subsist in "multiple drafts" in different parts of the brain, some drafts being short-lived, others more enduring, all clamouring to influence other parts of the brain which will produce words, actions, memories, and everything else that we regard as mental objects or events.

All in all it's a brilliant performance. The problem is that in escaping "unscientific" views I fear Dennett leaves himself exceedingly circumscribed as to what he *can* say about the mind. Yes, our minds make mistakes and can be subject to suggestion, illusions, and all kinds of other things; but how do these facts draw us to the conclusion that the mind is "only" an aspect of the brain, or an "epiphenomenon", or anything else? I just don't see that they do, and I don't see how the materialist can say anything about the nature of mind beyond that which is apparent in the outward phenomenon. The jibe that Dennett's view does not explain consciousness as much as explain it away often seems justified.

Ryle's Wheelbarrow

You may well have heard the old story about the workman who lives on one side of the border between two countries and works on the other side. (There are apparently versions from many parts of the world involving different borders.) Every morning the workman crosses the border, sometimes with his wheelbarrow, goes to work, and returns in the evening. The border guards are sure he's up to something since smuggling is endemic; they routinely search him, take his wheelbarrow apart, slash the tyre, probe down the hollow handles, spit on him and say nasty things about his mother. Always the result is the same—nothing. It transpires, of course, that he was smuggling wheelbarrows.

The concept of the "ghost in the machine", perhaps, is also a smuggling operation. We search for the ghost and find none, without realising that a machine has been smuggled into the discussion in broad daylight. If the question were put in the form, "Is there a ghost in the person?" then we could immediately retort, "Is there a machine in the person?" Eventually someone might suggest that there's a person in the person.

Purpose and meaning, then, are excluded from the modern atheism–scientism axis by definition, because in effect the person—the "I"—has been eliminated. That fact points to the main logical problem with materialism, in my opinion a decisive point. If materialism were true, then our thoughts would be determined, just like everything else—including the belief that everything is determined. So how could we claim that materialism is true? It's a vicious circle famously pointed out by the evolutionary biologist J. B. S. Haldane in 1927, but ignored by his successors.

There are so many subjective features of us such as awe, appreciation, love, loyalty, hate, affection, likes and dislikes which make up our sense of purpose and meaning. Whole areas of the arts and humanities are to do with our subjectivity, and what's more that middle layer of Maslow's hierarchy, connected with family, community, and belonging, seems to reside here. To be a person is to be subjective. About this, however, the consistent materialist can say nothing. For him this is all trivial, merely a mistake we keep making about our own selves. I'm not arguing for dualism, I'm arguing for a monism that is not exclusively materialistic, but recognises mind and matter as complementary and equal descriptions of a person. Unfortunately, Dawkins appears to rely upon the Dennett analysis with unlimited enthusiasm.

Incidentally, Greenfield's neurological approach may lend some support to Dennett's vision of multiple drafts and the "pandemonium" of the mind. As I read them, however, there is a huge difference between the two writers: Greenfield's model is far more inclusive and supported by scientific evidence. She sees the mind as arising from the incredible development of the human brain, with its unique complexity and plasticity—factors we noted earlier. However, while the brain is physically distinguishable from the body, the two are intimately connected through the rest of the nervous system and through the hormonal system. Greenfield also brings into the picture the role of peptides and possibly even quantum level transactions as already discussed. This inclusion of the whole body's chemistry and physics is a parallel to the place she gives to feelings in our moments of consciousness.

In my humble opinion, Dennett's views are too much based on the computer, while Greenfield's are more consistent with what we actually are. A person is not a disembodied head, nor an isolated brain cleverly kept alive in a vat of chemicals, but a phenomenal mind-body complex. Dave and the seven billion others huddled at the top of the Big Yellow Crane need more than anything a narrative that recognises them as human beings, including their subjectivity and including their need for purpose and meaning. Dawkins and Dennett reduce them to exclusively material entities, for the sake of a philosophical smuggling exercise.

A Driving Force

The driving force behind human cultures is far more obvious than the shaky hypotheses of memetics—people need a sense of purpose and meaning and will strive incessantly to achieve that. It is not enough for us to have sufficient food and drink, warmth, sex, and security. There is always the quest for more. I mentioned in Chapter 1 Nietzsche's fear of the eternal recurrence, answered by the striding forth of the Superman, and this should be a reminder that war is always one way to gain purpose and meaning. What materialism cannot accept is that to avoid such boredom or *ennui* requires something for its resolution in addition to the material.

To close this chapter, one of Greenfield's astonishing examples of brain development is in relation to London taxi drivers, who have to learn a huge amount of route information in order to qualify for a licence. One area of the brain, the hippocampus, is particularly responsible for such navigational skills, and this area has been found (through MRI scanning, a solid third-person method) to be particularly well developed in the taxi drivers studied, compared of course to control subjects who are not cabbies. That difference must be a tricky thing in itself for materialism, since mind is clearly influencing matter in a rather graphic way.

I call this astonishing because of its implications. Let's take one of the taxi drivers, Fred, as an example. Fred had to choose at some point in his life to become a taxi driver. He could have chosen, instead, to become, say, an electrician, a mechanic, or a chef. Clearly, in the event of such a choice, his brain would now be different from what it is today. That seems far-fetched, but the most modern research has shown such effects to be real, with different parts of the brain developing in response to different types of mental activity over a period of time. The types of mental activity that have been shown to produce such an effect include prayer and meditation.

It follows from this that the human brain is uniquely impressionable to cultural influence. The neurological facts are telling us something that we already know, which is that the long childhood required by our species, with its brain development, growth of language, and unfolding of derivative skills, allows us to develop as individuals, within the context of a culture in which we continue to live. Purpose and meaning are the drivers *par excellence* of culture, and these are even tied in to our ongoing brain development. Ignoring such a complex relationship and substituting for it an idiosyncratic meme theory, as is the wont of the cranies, is simply an attempt to impose a hypothesis on the facts. The "evolutionary algorithm" is the Apostles Creed of the new atheist fundamentalism.

The materialistic world-view on which the new faith rests is the ultimate death knell of purpose and meaning. We have already seen in passing a number of reasons why this view is predominant in some influential parts of our culture. I should now like to focus on what I see as the main cause of this influence. Unsurprisingly, our quest is now to be assisted by another stroll around the *Philosophical Forum*, starting from where we left off at the end of our last visit.

CHAPTER 14

Return to the Philosophical Forum

You may remember that poor old Descartes (1596–1650) always gets it in the neck for plaguing the world with dualism and posing the problem of how mind and body can possibly affect each other. I've argued that quantum understanding points to an underlying reality which is monistic, which we can experience as both mind and matter. There is only one reality—but a truly scientific view of it opens up more human possibilities than are allowed by one-sided materialism. These possibilities are related to culture, which includes the "-isms" I mentioned in my previous chapter and no doubt other features in which everyday life is embedded. Religion is a major part of most cultures, in fact a strong case can be made that in general religion forms cultures.

Monotheistic religion has been the strongest formative influence in our western culture, but materialism has now embedded itself in our midst, as somewhat of a cuckoo in the nest. I don't, of course, mean materialism in the sense of gross acquisitiveness, but in the sense of believing that the material world is all that there is and all that there can be. We saw briefly at the end of Chapter 10 that this outlook was picked up by rogue elements in the Catholic church in the seventeenth century, and then passed on to the French materialists, with whom David Hume was familiar, and into English-speaking culture through him. There were, of course, many other streams, including those that influenced Karl Marx so strongly. Even though we have had a century of quantum mechanics, and its potential for more holistic world views, such views still only hover in the background. We need now to ask why this is.

On this visit to the *Forum* we're not going to hang around the "Mind and Matter" room; rather, we're going off to a separate gallery which looks altogether more used. Arranged along the gallery are three statues titled "Locke", "Berkeley", and "Hume". Here we shall try to establish why materialism is predominant. We shall also sort out our epistemology once and for all.

The Brits Fight Back

Descartes set up a model of the person in which mind and matter are separate but connected. In addition, he set up a theory of knowledge—epistemology: "I think therefore I am" was his famous dictum. Although he did not deny the usefulness of observation within the scientific method, the real foundation of things, of truth that *cannot* be doubted, was to be found solely in the realm of thought by the application of reason. This is the view known as *rationalism*.

The opposite view was given a huge push forward in 1690 by the English philosopher John Locke (1632–1704). He started the ball rolling with his *Essay Concerning Human Understanding* in which he denied that we have any innate ideas of logic, self, God, morality, or anything else. Everything we know is gradually acquired through the senses, so inner cogitation without such knowledge is a waste of time. This *empiricism* was consonant with the growth of science, and his political writings also had enormous effect, particularly on the founding fathers of America. We noted in Chapter 2 that the colonial preacher Jonathan Edwards was a great admirer of his work. Locke was, incidentally, a staunch defender of Christianity, though departing a long way from the Puritanism in which he was brought up.

Moving along the gallery we reach a rather more portly statue, that of the Irish philosopher, Bishop George Berkeley (1685–1753), an empiricist, but also a true full-blooded idealist. As far as he was concerned, material objects don't exist at all in their own right. The only actual evidence we have is that of our senses, and only that which is observed can be said to exist. This makes it difficult to explain why things that are not observed are still there once we start observing them again. Berkeley's answer was simple: God observes everything all the time, so they continue to exist. It's a neat twist, seemingly rather outrageous at first, and treated as such by his contemporaries. Berkeley's view has some resonances with modern physics, including the observer effects we have discussed.

The third (even more portly) statue is that of David Hume (1711–76). Unlike Locke and Berkeley he was probably an atheist, although he had to be cautious about expressing that view in some quarters, especially in his native Scotland. As I have mentioned in various contexts already, he was the ultimate sceptic, denying that one could prove the existence of God, material objects, the self, cause and effect, and any objective morality. He also tended to say that we had to go on believing in some such things because they are part of our human nature and necessary to our lives. Hume spent much time in France and was highly regarded by Voltaire—presumably they enjoyed a good laugh about poor old Leibniz and the "best of all possible worlds" theory.

Empty Minds?

This tale of an Englishman, an Irishman, and a Scotsman, when put in such a brief way, does no justice to the depth of all three and their huge influence, but it's not my purpose to go into detail. Their major importance for us was in defining empiricism as a strong philosophical influence in the

English-speaking world. The core of that philosophy is that there are no innate ideas—we are born with empty minds—and that all knowledge is acquired through the senses, the scientific method being a clear example of this process.

We should not assume, though, that all three of these great thinkers were the same—far from it. Locke retained some elements of rationalism. Berkeley, on the other hand, was utterly consistent. To be is to be observed, a blatant re-run in a way of the argument from first cause, and open to the same kind of objection: who observes the great observer? More importantly, though, it is extremely difficult not to think of everyday things without thinking of a material existence.

Berkeley's view seems to be the kind of philosophy that would attract a mathematician—and he was such, as were Descartes and Leibniz. They too espoused forms of idealism. Perhaps this trend is inevitable given that mathematics is the ultimate set of non-material realities. By contrast, Locke was most interested in medicine and politics, while Hume was a formidable historian and much more famous for that, in his own day, than for his philosophy. The latter was in some need of popularisation by the late nineteenth century, a process duly carried out by T. H. Green, T. H. Grose, and T. H. Huxley, who extended his bulldog activity to match*.

Like Berkley, Hume was also very consistent, but in a rather different direction. His sceptical views were a rejection of those European philosophers who had followed Descartes down the rationalist route rather than the empiricist way proclaimed by Locke. Rationalists fall back on pure thought because they believe that sense perceptions are unreliable—everyday experience tells us that. Things look different if the light changes, they sound different if we are underwater, and they feel different if our hands are numb from cold. How can we trust such variable qualities to tell us anything about ultimate reality? In contrast, truths arrived at by reason, such as mathematical proofs, are always true. The internal angles of a triangle drawn on a flat surface always add up to 180 degrees, even if there's a funny smell in the air or we're sitting in the dark.

Unfortunately, rationalists like Descartes, Leibniz, and Spinoza had different starting points and therefore reasoned their ways to somewhat different conclusions, which tended to discredit their method. Leibniz started from seven basic principles, including the pre-established harmony that we briefly encountered in the "Mind and Matter" room. Unsurprisingly, he came to different conclusions from those of Spinoza. Leibniz's theory of monads (don't ask) seems to be unique to him, and not taken up seriously

---

* I am indebted to a comment on *www.evolvingthoughts.net* to the effect that in the Victorian era the initials "T. H." obviously stood for "Towards Hume"—although it was Huxley that was the real advocate as far as I can see, while Green was at least ambivalent about Hume, even though he and Grose edited and republished his works. It seems like an astonishing example of fair play.

by anyone else.

Baruch Spinoza (1632–77) believed in a version of double-aspect monism, but reached that conclusion, being a rationalist, just by thinking very hard, starting from the nature of substance. That's the kind of thing that drives empiricists to distraction. They prefer to observe and draw conclusions from their observations. If the *Philosophical Forum* were located on mainland Europe, Spinoza would have a lot more space; as it is, he has a little cubby-hole in the basement.

The difficult thing about rationalism is to establish a starting point, something which is held to be indisputable or *self-evident*. I have previously complained about this use of the idea of the self-evident as being a coded way of saying "evident to me". With the advance of science it's obvious and understandable that empiricism seemed much less cluttered with dubious notions. It also had the advantage of removing the justification for many power structures, both ecclesiastical and secular. It's not surprising that empiricism was a breath of fresh air.

However, empiricism has some skeletons in the cupboard. These are outlined in the *Forum* in a modest multimedia presentation which, after an appeal for donations, runs through four fundamental issues for the empiricist. You may remember from Chapter 2 that there is an evangelical Christian booklet called *The Four Spiritual Laws*. There should be another called *The Four Empiricist Flaws*.

Problems for Empiricists

The first problem is that the basic belief of empiricism is itself a statement with no empirical support. What evidence could there be that truth can *only* be found through sense-experience? One would have to prove, from sense-experience alone, that *all* other claims to truth are false.

Even without going further into the logic behind the claims of empiricism, let's just take the view that we are each born with an empty mind, the famous *tabula rasa* or "blank slate". We cannot directly examine the mind of a new-born infant and show that it's empty; but inasmuch as there is evidence it points the other way. Instincts, for example, are not learned. Certain abilities to categorise seem likely to be inbuilt. We have already looked at the remarkable innate ability we have to learn languages. Some other puzzles are also coming to light; for example, very young children have an awareness of the danger of a precipice, even though they have never experienced the pain of falling. This can be objectively observed.

The second tricky point about empiricism is that it is actually impossible to escape Hume's scepticism as we have noted at several points, extending beyond simply the existence of God to the existence also of material objects, the self, cause and effect, and any objective morality. It seems that getting rid of God carries an overhead of getting rid of much else with which we are familiar. Logically there are no half measures. Yet, as I have said, even Hume himself allowed that we have to go on believing in some things out of practical necessity, responding to aspects of our humanity that are separate from reason. That sounds like a half measure to me.

The third problem is that having devoted ourselves to sense perceptions, what, in the end, do we know? We obviously don't perceive objects directly, because light waves, sound waves, or other communications have to be received by our senses, travel to the brain and be processed by the brain. Therefore we are only perceiving a bundle of sense data. We cannot know to what extent this has been mangled or modified along the way.

Finally, there is the problem that we cannot have empirical knowledge of everything, and we cannot investigate everything, therefore we have to choose in which area our knowledge will lie. There is no empirical method for determining this. As a result, the empiricist has to make a decision about where to look, just as the rationalist has to decide what is self-evident. Who knows, if we had taken a different path of exploration our conclusions might have been very different. Of course, as our knowledge increases there will be some self-correction, but we are still faced with the often-complex decision of where to look next.

It seems, then, that this question of how we know things is quite complicated. The rationalist and the empiricist are equally tied to arbitrary judgements.

At this point the Germans throw their towels onto the philosophical deckchair. Immanuel Kant (1724–1804) accepted the reality of sense perceptions, but believed that we are not aware of them "raw" so to speak, rather we have within us concepts (for example, time, cause and affect) according to which we integrate diverse data, so that external objects appear to us as a reality. This "reality" *represents* real objects, but we cannot know what they are like *in themselves*. This is a kind of synthesis of empiricism and rationalism, for sense perceptions *and* innate concepts in our minds are equally required for knowledge. Needless to say, there are many differences of interpretation as to what he meant.

The Great Confidence Trick

Today, on the "how we know things" front, empiricism appears to rule the roost because, at least in popular perception, it is regarded as the philosophy that brought us science. Unfortunately, this is a major misunderstanding. Many principles of the scientific method are found in the medieval theologians that we've mentioned before (Grossteste, Occam, Roger Bacon, and so on), in classical Muslim and Rabbinic scholarship, in Aristotle, and, of course, in the work of Sir Francis Bacon (1561–1626). Science was well founded long before Hume's views became popular.

What empiricism did was to elevate the practical principles of science into universal rules—rules for the acquisition of *all* knowledge—ignoring the four problems I have outlined.

If we *define* the only true knowledge as that which is obtained through the senses, then since the senses can only perceive the material world we are bound to be materialists—unless of course we take the dramatic route of Bishop Berkley, but not many do. By the end of the nineteenth century science saw the entire universe as more or less explained. The fact that many features of our existence—particularly morality and aesthetics—were simply ignored or taken for granted was kept in the background. Such features were therefore left rather defenceless during the twentieth century.

This discussion is not just about religion defined in some narrow sense, it is about our whole culture. We have been the victims of a cultural confidence trick which has moved the goalposts not only of religion but also of morality, aesthetics, and public life as a whole. It is certainly unfair to demean the ingenuity of individual philosophers who, I believe, are diligent and committed to their discipline, and I have no intention of doing so. But there does seem to be a failure in the philosophical enterprise as a whole, for although it lays out the options it has never been able to create a definitive body of truth that would stand the test of time.

Within professional philosophical circles total materialism is not by any means held unanimously. It is a view, however, that has become widely popularised through its link with empiricism, which in turn benefits hugely from the false assumption that a *universal* empiricism is the driving force behind science.

Since this is an absolutely critical point, allow me to express this false logic in steps:

- Science is successful in establishing knowledge.
- Science works through observation.
- Only the material universe can be observed.
- Therefore only the material universe can be known.
- Therefore only the material universe exists.

If you have a spare moment you might find it interesting to analyse the occurrence of undistributed middles and illicit process in this sequence of statements. Referring back to my illustration of Chapter 2, this could become known as the red train / green train form of analysis.

Why should it not be the case that pure reason gives us valid knowledge in areas such as logic and mathematics, but observation gives valid knowledge of the material world on our everyday scale of things? Why should it not be that reality is monistic with two aspects and not exclusively material or mental? Why should there not be a universal mind with which our minds can communicate? Many credible philosophers have pursued such lines.

The principle that we live by is not defined by a single one-sided philosophical opinion. The principle we live by is that of *coherence*—we make sense of things. My suggestion is that it is this making sense of things that defines us as human, and it is a process that might well involve in-built concepts as well as observation and deduction.

What is Coherence?

To explain coherence, let's start by being a bit rationalistic and declaring that two plus two equals four, and lo behold! for every example of two plus two we've ever come across this idea is confirmed. We know what the word "round" means, and amazingly just about every human being we know agrees that certain objects are round and others are not. Does this not show that we have minds already primed with truths, from which we can then reason our way to other truths?

Probably—but this only really seems to work for maths and logic. It's customary at this point to raise questions like, "How do you know that what you call red is the same as what I call red?" This is the sort of question that gives philosophy a bad name. But, fair enough, to a colour-blind person red may mean the same as green, while husbands and wives in clothes shops frequently dispute what more subtle colours actually are. It would seem that the only way to define a colour would be through stating its wavelength—we can trust numbers more than we can trust our internal categories such as "red".

Yet every day millions of drivers across the globe successfully negotiate traffic junctions controlled by lights on the basis of red being red, apart from the exception of the colour-blind, who have to rely on the positions or brightness of the lights. Such variabilities don't show that the principle has failed, only that sometimes we make mistakes. We know that there is mental processing going on, maybe even a pandemonium of competing thoughts in each of us. Even so, there are not multiple traffic pile-ups on account of using colours as signals. Somehow those competing thoughts get their act together with remarkable speed and come up with the right answer, just about every time.

Another example of variability occurs in the extremely gifted—prodigies who learn Latin at the age of three, for example—and in the *savant* who is able to perform incredible feats of memory or calculation beyond even the prodigy. Yet the fact that we cannot say in a moment which day of the week it was on 14th February 1862 doesn't mean that we are generally likely to be wrong about which day of the week it was yesterday.

Variability also applies to the assessment of probability. At some point it becomes impossible to conceptualise the difference between one chance in a trillion trillion as compared to one chance in a trillion trillion trillion. Our assessment of such numbers is subjective—but that does not equate to "wrong" or "meaningless". If it came to taking a risk that might involve losing your life, you would draw a line somewhere and say that after this point—maybe one in a million—you're not going to worry about it. Exactly where the line should be drawn would be subjectively debated, and some may not be comfortable until the risk reduced to one in ten million, but I don't think anyone would argue about the *Golden Grain* level of improbability being the same as impossible, for all practical purposes.

Human knowledge is subjective—whether we start from pure thought or from observation. The "mirror problem" shows as much. We may formulate a perfect mathematical model of the universe, but we cannot know whether that corresponds to actual reality. We might be able to verify some parts of that model with tools like the Large Hadron Collider, but we cannot know what our conclusions might have been if we had set up different experiments within it, or if the whole mighty machine had been conceived differently. What we call fact is actually *coherence* between these different sources of knowledge.

Simply put, coherence is a word we use of ideas that fit together according to certain principles that we consciously or unconsciously apply. Somehow or other ideas of redness, motion, meanings of words, numbers, probability and a whole lot of other things work sufficiently well to make sense of our experience of ourselves, other people and the world in general. There are three main principles of coherence, as outlined below.

Consistency

It goes without saying that two statements that contradict each other are incoherent, but that also applies to one statement that is self-contradictory. Sometimes this contradiction is obvious—for example, if I were to say that the world was created by a giant dwarf. Sometimes it's more subtle, but contradiction can always be shown by use of a hypothetical situation. Take the statement, "God always grants whatever any human being asks in prayer". What is supposed to happen if two opposing sportsmen pray that they will win the same trophy, or two enemy governments that they will win the same war? Use of a hypothetical situation is easier than analysing the use of words like "always", "whatever" and "any", which would produce the same verdict using formal logic. Consistency is the first test of coherence.

Convergence

You may remember that William of Occam was the thirteenth-century thinker who laid down the rule that we should not unnecessarily multiply explanations of things (Occam's Razor). For example, we know that unsupported solid objects fall to the earth—we might propose that this is because of some affinity between solid objects and the earth. We also know that the motion of planets is elliptical, so we might propose that there is a kind of invisible bungee rope attaching the planet to its star. But we have the gravitational explanation of these phenomena, making both of the other suggestions redundant—they converge on the theory of gravitation. The application of Occam's razor reveals the convergence—they are two sides of the same coin.

Comprehensiveness
Bertrand Russell famously disagreed with the whole idea of coherence as a source of knowledge because any statement can be made consistent with some belief system somewhere. Therefore a belief and its opposite could both be designated coherent, which is absurd. A good example of this is the difference between atheism and deism. Often they are treated as similar, varying only in degree, but in fact they are total opposites. You can't get much more opposite than saying "there is no God" or "there is a God".

However, atheism and totalitarianism could conceivably form a coherent set of ideas. So could deism and "green" politics. It might also be possible to construct a kind of coherent green totalitarianism—sandals replacing jackboots perhaps, and green shirts instead of the conventional brown or black. But that would not make atheism and deism any more coherent with each other.

The fairly obvious principle here is that the word "coherence" is applied to a set of beliefs, not as an absolute description of one belief. Russell is quite right, and the answer is to regard coherence as a matter of degree. So, for the sake of argument, if there were three competing theories of everything, and if each theory were coherent within itself, would that make each theory equally valid on the grounds of coherence?

Well, it would depend on the *comprehensiveness* of the three theories. We may find an important example of this in physics one day, for as is well known, relativity and quantum mechanics are coherent within themselves but not entirely with each other. Any new theory such as "m-theory" that was coherent with both would obviously be more comprehensive than either one individually, and would therefore be more coherent than either one individually.

I believe we need an understanding of knowledge that is not tied to one philosophical idea but offers a wider coherence. We are so steeped in materialism and empiricism, and have been told so many times that nothing else is valid, that it will be a big struggle to take a more balanced view. Where might it all lead? Well, it might start to loosen up our cultural gridlock, and I should like to move towards a close by examining this possibility.

CHAPTER 15

The Theological Theme Park

I had a dream the other day. It was of a cross between a theme park and some kind of open-air festival with a colossal rollercoaster. People alight from the roller coaster and grab their ice creams and hot dogs before entering the theme park proper. In the distance—but outside the park—there is the big yellow crane, standing on the horizon.

Within my theme park it's all pretty broad minded. The *Philosophical Forum* has an interactive learning centre (the appeal for donations succeeded) which is surprisingly popular. The agnostics are considering opening something similar, but aren't yet certain about it. The beer tent has its own organic brew, "Aquinas Lite", and hosts mini-lectures which specialise in natural theology made simple. The "all you can think and drink" package always draws a good crowd, and has been franchised to other locations, subject to local byelaws.

Among the side shows some historical re-enacters are doing the trial of Galileo—it's rumoured that they're going to do the Spanish Inquisition just when no one expects it. There's even a "meme dream" tent, but once the technology took off a bunch of American fundamentalists got cracking and now produce most of the good titles, all with feelyvision of course. As usual, they've also cornered the merchandising.

Most of the park is taken up with the pavilions, where small groups support particular themes such as those we've looked at in this book. The main activity among all these colourful people may not sound exciting. Apart from normal social activities, they simply talk to each other, share ideas, look at each others' exhibitions, and set their stalls out. Literally.

However, it's not just a free for all. The task is to produce coherence. There are mechanisms, based around special communication software, through which "coherent connections" are circulated. By the way, anyone that has anything to say is warmly received, not just theologians. Occasionally cranies turn up and are welcomed, but mostly they stand at the gates giving out leaflets for rival attractions opening soon at their place just up the road, which is a giant mock up of a space station crammed with virtual reality rooms. They're using their crane to help with the construction, and many of them see this as a living parable.

If ever the theological theme park opens, I'll be there. I'd love to know from a Jewish scholar what it might have been about Spinoza's liberal faith that led him towards a double-aspect monism. I would like to discuss with a Christian fundamentalist a few modifications to the *Four Spiritual Laws*. I would like to hear from different schools of Muslim thinking how they view

Christianity in the West. All the time the question should not be simply "what do you think?" but "where's the coherence?"

Perhaps it's fairly clear what my daydreaming is trying to tell me. I think it's a conviction that has grown with the writing of this book, namely, that the issues that have been raised ought to be the subject of public discussion.

It seems very odd that although so many of those asked in surveys regularly admit to belief in God, we rarely hear such belief mentioned in the political or cultural arena. A high level of debate is encouraged about other matters, ranging from politics to science, from interpretation of history to the Booker prize, from fashion to global economics. Why not discuss religious beliefs? Why not discuss "the meaning of life" instead of mocking the whole idea? Why not look for coherence within the wholeness of human culture, with science and religion both included? This all sounds like an enormous task, but with today's communication and digital knowledge base the raw material is already there.

Coherence and Belief

I should like to give now some examples of "coherence thinking". These are, of course, my personal views, but even for those who disagree I hope they will illustrate the principle involved.

My first proposal is that if we consider the most ancient belief, polytheism, there is incoherence with the most fundamental truths of science. The idea that there could be more than one all-powerful being is self-contradictory and therefore incoherent. Of course polytheism does not require all-powerful beings, but even weak gods must have *some* detectable influence on the universe. If they don't, then they can only be hypothetical. If the proposed gods do have influence on the universe then we should expect to detect routine contradictions in the laws of nature as conflicting wills pull one way and then the other. We simply do not see that.

One way for polytheism to resolve this problem is to allocate strict spheres of influence so that each god is a god of something. Alternatively, we could think of these beings as so weak that they are scarcely gods at all, but more like spirits that can frighten people in the dark or speak through an Ouija board—shades of the ancestor worship found in many ancient traditions and in the claims of mediums today.

If we were to believe in these weak gods we would also need to have a supreme God who keeps all the others in line in an organised pantheon of divinities; alternatively this supreme God might emanate sub-deities who are dependent on him. This is, of course, all grist to the mill of the varied polytheistic traditions of Greece, Rome, the Near-East, India, and China. But then we seem to have arrived at a type of "deism plus"—the lesser deities are not necessary and fall foul of Occam's razor. I don't see how pure polytheism can be redeemed from this incoherence.

At the other end of the spectrum, atheism is coherent. Unlikely as it may seem to the rest of us, it is still *possible* that the universe came into existence from nothing and developed entirely by chance. Therefore there is no spiritual dimension, no external basis for morality, no basis for aesthetics, and no reality other than the material. As I expounded in Chapter 1, when taken in that narrow—but coherent—manner, the results can be frightening.

However, what we have on offer from Dawkins and other writers is "atheism plus", which becomes incoherent. "Atheism plus" attaches values to things which, according to the atheist's basic principle, should be dismissed as mere whims. We see this most in ethics. Hume was very sceptical about any objective basis to ethics, posing the famous question: how can you get an "ought" from an "is"? That didn't stop him from adopting the principle of utility, which was a direct influence on Jeremy Bentham and his utilitarianism, which we considered in Chapter 1. But there is no real convergence.

Of course, there is nothing to stop an individual atheist from also believing in utilitarianism. Such a person may be very coherent, in the popular sense of the word, able to explain clearly both atheism and utilitarianism, but there is no real reason to connect the two. They are not coherent in the sense of putting together a bigger picture. There is a similar problem when Dawkins waxes lyrical about aesthetics as if there were some great value at stake, since for the atheist beauty is simply in the eye of the beholder and vanishes when the beholder vanishes or, for that matter, nods off to sleep. Total scepticism is coherent, but partial scepticism is not.

Deism could at first sight be coherent if it stuck to a basic claim that God created the universe and its physical laws and then left everything to run its course—this is "classical deism". The atheist and the deist look at the same evidence—all that we have said concerning probabilities in cosmology, evolution and so on—and come to opposite conclusions. For the strict atheist God is an unnecessary hypothesis. For the strict deist God is a necessary hypothesis as some kind of cause or designer of everything there is, but not in any other capacity—he is not a personal God in the sense of a deep involvement with the world that moulds our daily experience, or in the sense of providing a revelation through religious texts.

However, there is also the possibility of a "deism plus", which historically has been developed in a number of directions, deriving moral and aesthetic values from belief in God. Often these additions are no more *necessary* to deism than to atheism, and they create the same incoherence, unless deists tweak their understanding a little in the direction of monotheism, which they sometimes do.

Pantheism is another, rather different, attempt to define the relationship between God and the universe. Dawkins describes pantheism as "sexed-up atheism"—an odd take on the subject, since pantheism holds that the universe is God. Indeed, for the atheist it is simply giving an alternative name (God) to the universe and therefore has no real relevance.

This kind of belief has a long history going back to some of the Greeks and Romans and many strands of Eastern religion. Spinoza is often credited with founding a form of more modern western pantheism, although it is doubtful whether he meant to *limit* God to the universe, he may have just meant that everything is *in* God, a view sometimes known as *panentheism*. His critics regarded him as an atheist, while his later admirer Moses Mendelssohn (grandfather of the composer) claimed him as a theist.

The reason for this confusion is simple. God is normally regarded as infinite, the universe is not. Therefore the theist would say that God and the universe cannot be the same thing. On the other hand, if the universe is somehow *contained* in God, there is no limitation on God. But then the theist would point out that there is very little difference between that view and the traditional theistic understanding of God as immanent; that is to say, permeating the whole universe. Pantheism seems to be an unnecessary add-on. It fails in the coherence stakes not through lack of consistency or comprehensiveness, but through lack of convergence. It falls victim to Occam's razor.

Agnosticism

When T. H. Huxley wasn't barking as "Darwin's Bulldog", complaining about the lack of evidence for natural selection, promoting Hume, or making his phenomenal contributions to science and education, he mused on the subject of whether knowledge of God is possible. He concluded that we cannot know whether there is a God, referring to this view as "agnostic". There were others before him, notably *Protagoras* (490–420 BCE), but Huxley first coined the term in the modern world.

Agnosticism sometimes appears to be an easy way out, but it seems to me incoherent to claim that there could be a God who is all powerful and wishes to reveal himself, but the existence of whom is uncertain. An all-powerful God surely cannot fail in such a way. By the same token, an all-powerful God who does not wish to reveal himself will be totally undetectable, therefore belief in such a God would be purely speculative. Any number of such undetectable entities could be proposed, so such a belief would also be incoherent. It could of course be that the allegedly possible God is not all powerful, but if that were so there could easily be more than one such God, which takes us back to polytheism and its own problems of incoherence already outlined.

I don't entirely share Dawkins' verdict on agnosticism as poverty stricken. In my experience there are two types of agnostic. There are those who simply don't want to engage with the issues, or feel that if there is a God then it's his exclusive job to cater for their needs 24/7. But there are other agnostics who are more like theists beset by doubt, often due to suffering and the historic failures of the Church. Broadcaster John Humphrys in his book *In God we Doubt: Confessions of a Failed Atheist* gives a very convincing and human picture of this type of agnosticism, engaged with the issues and admirably humanitarian. This is certainly not poverty stricken, and as I have already pointed out "doubting Thomas" has always had a recognised place in the Christian faith. That does not, however, make agnosticism a coherent way of thinking in its own right.

It seems to me that the word "agnosticism" should be abandoned, while "agnostic" should be retained as a description of a person who cannot, or will not, come to a decision on the choice between atheism and deism (or theism). People can similarly be agnostic about political parties, the likely course of the national economy, or the benefits of TV talent contests. I can see potential benefits in being agnostic about all three. Even in the field of religion the agnostic could simply say that it is not necessary to make a decision. Yet that does not make agnosticism into some kind of movement or a set of beliefs.

If you were in a strange town and asked a native for directions to, say, a hotel, you might get a helpful response, or a "sorry, don't know" response, both equally unsurprising. But if the native said cheerily, "Sorry, don't know mate, I'm an agnostic you see", you would be puzzled. Since you have been driving all day, you ask whether there is a reasonable restaurant nearby. "Can't tell you, I'm afraid. I'm an agnostic." Or perhaps a pub? "Could be, it's just that being an agnostic I don't know..."

I don't recollect a *Monty Python* sketch in this vein, but the material is all there, with Michael Palin in the lead role. Agnosticism is not a belief system, even though it may be fashionable to call oneself an agnostic. It is not a reasoned third way.

Incidentally, if our helpful native affirmed that there is indeed a hotel close at hand, we should naturally enquire "where?" If he then responded "everywhere" we should find that rather difficult. He might further explain that, if we consider the essence of the hotel concept, then a shop doorway, a derelict house or a cardboard box all show the presence of hotel. The bird in its nest makes its own hotel...

As we accelerate away to the strains of, "Wherever I lay my hat, that's my hotel", we reflect on how much our culture owes to the sixties. As I have already suggested, pantheism often seems to me like a metaphor. If we say that God is everything and everything is God, what new claim have we actually made?

Humanism

According to the website of the *British Humanist Association* (BHA), "Humanism is the view that we can make sense of the world using reason, experience and shared human values and that we can live good lives without religious or superstitious beliefs. Humanists seek to make the best of the one life we have by creating meaning and purpose for ourselves. We choose to take responsibility for our actions and work with others for the common good."

I have always had some respect for humanism. However, it lacks coherence; for example, the word "good" is too vague. Does it refer to prosperity, altruism, some kind of communitarian spirit—or what? There are many similarly-undefined words in the passage quoted, and even the phrase, "religious or superstitious beliefs", which seems clear, is not. In the news section of the BHA site at the time of writing there is a joint statement issued with Buddhists, for whom there seems to be some sympathy within humanism. It seems Buddhism is no longer considered a religion. If that is so, what *is* the humanist definition of religion?

The focal point of the humanist statement appears to be "by creating meaning and purpose for ourselves". But some find meaning and purpose in watercolour painting, while others find them through mass murder. It all seems extremely ill-defined, which I suppose creates the distinctions that exist between humanists, for example between the optimistic and pessimistic.

Curiously, I imagine there are deists who hold similar values to many humanists as part of their belief system, but would be excluded from the BHA definition of humanism as quoted above, whereas atheists, who have no rationale for holding humanist views, are welcomed. This is somewhat of an irony since two of the earliest founders of humanism are generally recognised as the devout Italian Catholic poet Petrarch (1304–74), and Desiderius Erasmus (1466–1536) who was highly influential on the Reformation but remained a Catholic priest. Humanism developed during the Enlightenment largely as part of the broader deistic religious trend.

Later, in the nineteenth century, Unitarians were instrumental in the promotion of humanism in the USA and in Britain, largely through the formation of the "Ethical Societies", which left religion as an open question. The *South Place Ethical Society* in Bloomsbury, London, is, as far as I know, the only remaining society outside the United States. It is only in the twentieth century, with key figures like T. H. Huxley's grandson Julian Huxley (1887–1975), that humanism acquired a distinctive anti-religious status as exemplified by the BHA. The *South Place Ethical Society* now supports secular humanism.

Protagoras opined that "man is the measure of all things"—but which man exactly are humanists talking about? Nietzsche's superman? The proverbial "man in the street"? The foetus in the womb? An abstraction that basically means "mankind"? I suppose most frequently we think of it as the latter, but what does that abstraction mean in practical terms? Humanism could be made coherent, and possibly a strong cultural force, if it could define itself more exactly.

Secular humanism and atheism are often allied but do not in fact add anything to each other. They do not contradict, but both parties ought to cut the other's throat with Occam's razor. There is no real convergence, and the impression that there is arises only from mutual antipathy to monotheism.

Edging Towards Monotheism

The deistic humanism which spurred the formation of the Ethical Societies does offer a more compact world view than either of its components considered separately. Yes, this is a version of "deism plus", which I have declared incoherent, but it can redeem itself by retaining the link between God and the values of humanism. The creative spark is in some way intelligent and moral, therefore our own natural morality would match with his, hers, or its. This in turn gives an ideological basis for humanism. All that the BHA statement says about shared values, responsibility, the common good, and so on is now rooted in the universe itself, as part of the natural order. It is quite easy to extend this basis to aesthetics—beauty is still subjective to some extent, but there is now a basis for using the word, because beauty is inherent in the universe.

This idea can quite easily be extended to our scientific understanding. It has often been pointed out what a coincidence it is that our ability to understand the universe is so appropriate. It didn't have to be like that; we could have been built in such a way that although we were uniquely equipped for survival we simply could never have a clue about the nature of reality. In other words, we have an intellectual side to us that is related, through the universe, to the intelligence at work in the creative spark.

There is an increase in coherence in such views because the creative spark has not only intelligence but is also the source of values—moral, aesthetic, and intellectual. In other words, there is an element of idealism here. As a reminder, that is the assertion that mind is as real as matter. In my double-aspect world there is only one reality, and it is a reality in which values are just as real as galaxies. The materialist, of course, does not accept this epistemology because morality, beauty, and understanding are, for him, merely mental constructs arising from the material structure of the brain, and have no existence beyond that.

Although this type of belief is very different from secular humanism, it is still only *edging towards* monotheism as normally understood. There is still a chasm between the deistic God and the human race, with no special revelation through a book such as the Bible, no additional revealed morality and no point in prayer, except perhaps as a self-improvement exercise of some sort. Even though the highest aspirations of humanism may be seen as having divine approval after a fashion, there is no day-to-day personal relationship with God such as monotheism envisages.

Monotheism

The crucial step towards monotheism is to recognise that God is personal, in the sense of a being with whom one can have a day-to-day relationship.

Let us suppose that our deistic humanist wakes up one morning with the uneasy feeling that follows a bad dream. In that dream there featured a massive computer, the size of a ten story office block. At ground level there is a small manufacturing area at which deliveries of common chemical elements are made from time to time. At the other end of the building a roller shutter opens every few minutes and a newly manufactured human being walks out. These newly manufactured people gather at a coffee shop next door, introduce themselves to each other, gradually get their bearings and decide what they are going to do next. Occasionally laughter is heard.

Such a dream might be the result of over indulgence in science fiction, or of eating cheese before retiring to bed. Or it might be an unconscious conviction struggling to emerge, namely, that it does not seem possible for a *something* to make a *someone*. I think this may be an archetypal instinct, but it is not difficult to support logically. The development of a person from a fertilised ovum requires a 40 week re-run of evolution within a womb that is itself a product of evolution, followed by a pattern of continued mental stimulus and response while brain development and cultural development are taking place. The amount of information that has to be focused into this gargantuan effort is unimaginable—we have dealt with this previously—but most importantly the end result is not a computer, it's a person. If our giant computer contained the necessary information for this, surely it must itself be personal?

Materialists, of course, would deny this disparity, indeed, their model of the person (aided and abetted by Ryle's wheelbarrow) is often explicitly that of a giant computer. For them, artificial intelligence is more or less identical (at least potentially) with human intelligence. It is a common assumption that computers are rapidly catching up with us so that, within a matter of a few years, we will be able to produce a computer with intelligence like ours.

This position is famously argued against by the "Chinese Room" thought experiment, which can be found on numerous web sites if you wish to follow it up. My version is this. On the next night, our dreamer keeps off the cheese, but still dreams. This time he is invited into the office block because the processing unit has malfunctioned. Fortunately, all the instructions that used to be followed by the computer are also written down and can be executed manually. He does this as instructed and eventually produces a human being.

On awakening, our deistic humanist realises that something profound is going on here. He is able to execute the person-producing programme just as successfully as the computer can, even though he really has no understanding at all how to make a person. It is now obvious that the computer, when operational, was also simply following instructions, with no real intelligence. So where do the instructions come from? Well, the first response is bound to be that they come from a programmer. But could they not have been written, alternatively, by another computer, a bigger and better model?

This mighty super-machine must surely be the size of a small town, but, even so, why should it write a programme to enable other computers to produce people—unless it is programmed to do so? This chain could go on until all the atoms in the universe were consumed in the making of higher and higher level computers and you would still need a programmer—a very clever programmer—to set the whole sequence going.

Fundamentally, even if this immensely complex computer existed it would lack the crucial attribute of *intention*. We do not see intention in the cosmos or in any inanimate earthly matter. We see it developing, possibly, in higher life forms and we see it at a phenomenally high level in ourselves. It is one of the defining characteristics of a person.

Computers do not have intentions. If we thought they did, we should have to be very careful about that huge network of computers connected in some way to the Large Hadron Collider, the whole network comprising in many respects a massive computer with the LHC itself at its heart. If such a machine somehow acquired intention, it might start to flex its muscles by vindicating Eloi Cole and creating a small black hole. That wouldn't be much fun, by all accounts.

The small step from deistic humanism to monotheism brings further opportunities for coherence, especially since the grand intention to create is regarded in monotheism as a supreme act of love, which is thereby elevated to a principle for humanity.

Comprehensiveness

The type of progression I have sketched out appears quite coherent. Additional concepts are not added arbitrarily and the result is more comprehensive than the individual elements considered in isolation. I fully admit that pure atheism is coherent within itself, but it does not imply anything meaningful beyond its limited bounds. It stands in splendid isolation, and therefore is less coherent than monotheism or even deistic humanism, because it is less comprehensive.

The atheist would respond angrily that this is nonsense because there is no coherence between science and monotheism—with the assumption in the background that there *is* coherence between atheism and science. I think the atheist is wrong because atheism does not add anything to science. We have seen that getting rid of God and attributing the universe to a mere lucky fluke is not necessary as a foundation for science. More importantly, it does not function as such. You may remember Hume's point that the true sceptic should doubt the consistency of the laws of nature, cause and effect and so on. Atheism is not the foundation for science that it sometimes likes to pretend.

Monotheism and Science

If we consider only out-dated "classical science", limited to Newtonian mechanics and based on a materialistic view of the universe, then certainly that is not coherent with monotheism. However, if we mean twenty-first-century science the situation is quite different.

One gets some surprises—for example, I have often thought that the popular idea of resurrection is based too much on the brilliant 1920s painting by Sir Stanley Spencer, *The Resurrection in Cookham Churchyard*, with lids removed from tombs, bodies rising out of the ground, and so on. Of course, the belief in resurrection is found across many religions, but I have often thought of it in terms of transformation rather than those literal images used in religious art. This seems more relevant in the light of modern physics. I was glad to find that physicists Frank Tipler and John Polkinghorne, eminent authorities in the fields of particle physics and quantum mechanics, support the transformation concept.

Similarly, the concept of restoration that we looked at in Chapter 3 links with the idea of the mind taking part in the formation of the universe. One of the main proponents of such views was the late (and much revered) John Wheeler, who during his long life was part of all the main steps forward in theoretical physics and was the first to use the term "black hole". Wheeler's ideas are taken up, with variations, by John Barrow, Frank Tipler, Paul Davies, and others, who occasionally link their ideas to Bishop Berkeley. Michael Frayn also pursues the participatory theme with great perceptiveness in *The Human Touch: our Part in the Creation of a Universe*.

The basic concept is that of the *noosphere*, which may be defined as the sum of human consciousness. Wheeler's view is that the effects of the noosphere can extend backwards in time. Intriguingly, cosmologists also arrive at this concept through mathematical models, the main one of which seems to graph out as a giant inverted thimble. Some claim that the noosphere, ultimately, will extend to the whole universe. Those who were paying attention in Chapter 3 may recognise some coherence with *Lux Mundi;* those who make the further link to St Athanasius get a gold star.

There is, however, an even more profound implication here, because human consciousness is a very mixed blessing. We have seen how the "dark side" of that consciousness could destroy humanity, therefore there is a moral dimension to it. Would we not need some way in which the bearers of consciousness—individual people—could turn away from the negative and destructive? If there is also a universal mind, would we not also need some way in which conflicts between our consciousness and that universal consciousness could be reconciled? We could refer to these moral elements as re-birth and atonement respectively. Without such elements we might create universal hell, not heaven.

Atheists like to minimise the coherence between science and any kind of religion. Yet one of the most interesting aspects of the progression of monotheism is that it has, for the most part, sought to preserve not only its own tradition but also the wisdom of antiquity and the great phases of discovery since then. It has also sought to contribute to those periods of discovery.

I find it intriguing to read of St Augustine pleading that the Bible should not be interpreted against the established facts of science. Or to learn that Bishop Grossteste laid down the principles of the telescope centuries before they could actually be implemented. Or to think of St Thomas Aquinas trying to figure out questions of substance and location that still intrigue physicists. I like to imagine Newton working fervently (even if neurotically) on the principles of Biblical interpretation, and Bishop Berkeley successfully correcting some of Newton's theory of calculus. I find it interesting that the first person to prove the Big Bang theory mathematically was Georges Lemaître, a Belgian Roman Catholic priest.

If faith and science are in conflict I wonder why William Thomson (Lord Kelvin) attended chapel daily even while pursuing his ground-breaking work in thermodynamics. How did the mathematician Kurt Gödel retain a monotheistic belief? Why did Sir William Bragg speak so warmly of his faith in Christ? Why did Max Planck regard religion and science as equally necessary to human progress? Why did the devout evangelical Asa Gray support Darwinism? How did David Lack, Ronald Fisher, and Theodosius Dobzhansky maintain their distinctive versions of Christianity while contributing so much to evolutionary theory? Many others could be cited.

Dawkins claims to be mystified as to how contemporary scientists like Francis Collins, Russell Stanard, John Polkinghorne, and the late Arthur Peacocke could believe in a personal God. Again, other names could be added. The answer is simple—like their predecessors above, they have found that their belief creates greater coherence across the diverse elements of life than does atheism. Charles Townes, the 1964 Nobel Prize winner in Physics and inventor of the laser, put it like this in a talk reported in the *Harvard University Gazette:* "I look at science and religion as quite parallel, much more similar than most people think and that in the long run, they must converge."

Seeking coherence has always been the way of the best theology and the best religion—recognising that all truth is equal, by whatever route it is attained. That tradition has, more often than not, been voracious in the pursuit of truth in all spheres—it is no coincidence that science in the form that we know it developed supremely within monotheistic cultures. I cannot think of any other force that seeks to create such coherence across science, the humanities and the common human experience of life. Drawing out the coherence across science and diverse beliefs is an urgent task. I would cite it as my fourth suggestion if we are to break the "Post-Enlightenment Gridlock".

CHAPTER 16

Significance

There is one final key point, without which all else may prove futile, and it is this. Atheists, and others who wish to deprecate religion, often make an assertion along the following lines: before Copernicus human beings believed they were at the centre of the universe, which was a relatively small place. Now, especially after Hubble, we know that we are not only far from the centre of things, we are merely a tiny speck in one arm of a galaxy which is one among billions in the vast expanse of time and space. We are totally, eternally and irretrievably *insignificant*.

This kind of thing is particularly rife in television documentaries because it allows stunning images of galaxies, super novae and so on to be shown, perhaps also with some archaic images of Galileo, all of which are easily obtainable. Yet in every aspect it is false.

There is no centre of the universe. Almost all of us think of the Big Bang as involving a tiny volume of matter that exploded from one point *into* space, but in fact the Big Bang was an explosion *of* space. On the common picture of an explosion we would be able to detect, from the lingering heat radiation, a point from which it all started, but the lingering radiation from the Big Bang is pretty uniform and points nowhere. The ancient and medieval world did of course envisage the earth being at the centre of the universe, which was wrong, but the picture of the earth being somehow right on the edge of the universe is also wrong. With our modern understanding, the statement that we are not at the centre of the universe is just as meaningless as the statement that we are.

Being at the centre of the universe was probably not as important for ancient and medieval people as we sometimes think. It was not an assertion they made to establish human significance, although it might have confirmed that belief. It was a conclusion reached on scientific grounds: at night, one could *see* the whole universe revolving. That fact was obvious, not something that needed a theological reason. Further, there were only two possible ways of explaining this observation; either the universe revolved around the earth, or the earth revolved on its axis. To look at the obvious facts again, we don't feel the earth rotating. Many of the more thoughtful also pointed out that if the earth were rotating at the huge speed necessary to account for the movement of the stars, we would feel a very strong draught all the time as we moved through the atmosphere. The earth must therefore be static; that being so, it must be at the centre of the universe because the stars rotate in circles. This may seem naive perhaps, but it is quite understandable—and scientific—given the information available at the time.

Regarding the size of the universe, astronaut Yuri Gagarin is reputed to have jested as he orbited the earth that he couldn't see any God up there. (The words may well have been invented by Russian premier Nikita Khrushchev, but they have passed into space folklore.) Yet if a medieval monk had been with Gagarin on board *Vostok 1* he would not have been surprised at the lack of any sign of God, because it was well known, at least from Ptolemy onwards, that the universe was a very big place.

The medieval natural philosophers reckoned that the universe was about 140 million miles across. If size is the main issue, that seems quite big enough to convey the insignificance of humanity—I doubt that adding more zeros really makes much difference. From Ptolemy onwards the earth was perceived as small compared to the size of a star, and a tiny speck compared to the whole universe.

Size is a rather two-edged sword if we want to measure significance. It's interesting that those who want to detract from religion focus so much on how small we are compared to the universe, rather than on how large we are compared to the sub-atomic scale of things. In any case, we tend to measure significance not so much in terms of size but in terms of function. A leg is much bigger than a heart, but if we had to choose to live without one or the other we should be foolish to jettison the smaller item.

Both in science and life in general it is the thing that is different that is considered significant—the unexpected experimental result, the uniquely odd building, the inexplicable coincidence—these things cry out for our attention. It is not ridiculous, therefore, to argue that the same applies to life on earth, which appears to be unique in the universe. The rest of the cosmos is, for the most part, fairly boring—when you've seen one hydrogen atom you've more or less seen them all.

Now add in the notion of complexity, about which much has already been said. I remarked earlier that the human brain with its associated neural network is probably the most complex system in the universe. Why should we not take complexity as the ultimate measure of significance?

Functionality, uniqueness and complexity are positive indications of the significance of things, much more so than location or size. To these three positive indications I would add a fourth: relationship. I can stand on a busy thoroughfare and see thousands of people walking past, of which one might be my wife. Who is the most significant to me out of all those thousands? Relationship brings significance, regardless of how many other people walk past. In monotheism relationship with God makes us significant, a point understood in all generations through the medieval to the modern, and not dependent on our position in the galaxy or the size of the universe.

There are good reasons, then, to regard the earth, its life and its human occupants as the most significant feature of the universe as we know it. There is, however, one final lingering question, because the size of the universe taken together with the speed of light implies, as we have seen, a huge age of the universe—approximately 13.7 billion years. Even the earth is around 4.6 billion years old. Human beings have been evolving for around 2 million years, and *homo sapiens* for about 200,000 years.

The implied question is this. If there is a God, why did he choose to achieve his purposes in such a roundabout way? Why not just get to the point and create everything as it is today, but in a moment—an instant and obvious creation? Why go through those aeons of cataclysm? Why go through those billions of years involved in evolution?

Well, I think that even atheists would agree that *if there were* a God it would be reasonable to suppose he had a purpose for human beings. It would also be reasonable to suppose that he wanted us to live in certain ways that tied our wishes in with his, and allowed his purpose to be carried out. In other words, there would be a certain morality binding on us as created beings. There would be other aspects to his will for us in addition, such as enjoying life, love, developing cultures and communities, exploring the universe, and perhaps achieving things of which we have no idea as yet; but some kind of morality would be essential as a basis, if only to stop us destroying each other and forgetting our purpose altogether.

In order to fit with this divine purpose, therefore, we would have two essential requirements.

Our first essential requirement, as I argued earlier, would be a general regularity in which our choices make sense. That seems like a tall order when we bear in mind that the very fabric of the universe, at the smallest level of detail we know, contains an element of randomness, the exact opposite of regularity. Nevertheless, regularity is what we gain when vast numbers of sub-atomic particles interact and form the structures of atoms, molecules, planets, stars, and galaxies. Whatever complex random activities may be going on behind the scenes, everything on the scale to which we relate as human beings follows the laws of nature. Putting it rather simplistically, the trillions of quantum transactions average out, so that on a larger scale there is a general regularity.

Our second essential requirement would be the ability to make real decisions—in other words, an element of free will. Do we make real decisions or not? I believe that we do. We have real intentions which we execute as far as we can. That is a severe problem for materialism, for if all thoughts were ultimately due to the arrangement of atoms in the brain, then our decisions would be just as much determined as the movements of the planets. The only way out is to re-assert the reality of our minds. This is not to suggest a ghost in the machine, but it is to suggest that the pile of chemicals cleverly arranged to make a human being has to it a mind dimension, including free will. We do not entirely understand how this might work, but we have seen that quantum transactions have a role in the functioning of our brains and other parts of the nervous system, and these transactions have an element of randomness about them. Whatever the intricacies involved, it seems inherently likely that such randomness is one necessary component in an organism possessing free will.

The great process from Big Bang to modern man, then, has created a moral universe, a context for human life that follows Newtonian rules, and an element to human beings that does not. One could definitely call that a fairly neat trick. I suggest, however, that it takes 13.7 billion years and a very big universe to carry it out.

The puzzle is why this great process should take so long when it would seem that divine intervention could have sped things up—at the same time possibly avoiding the need for evolutionary, animal, and human suffering, which also seem to be part of the process.

To get anywhere near a solution to the puzzle from a scientific point of view would need extensive knowledge of thermodynamics in relation to the phases of the universe from Big Bang to the present. The amount of time and energy needed to form the elements in the stars would be particularly important, since life depends on these. We would also need to understand more about our own functioning and how quantum transactions fit in with that. Yet even within our present state of knowledge, it seems to me likely that the enormity of time and space are necessary to allow both general regularity and genuine randomness to coexist in the same universe.

My particular hypothesis could, of course, be wide of the mark, for we find ourselves close to the thought horizon of both science and theology. Yet the fact even of possible answers to such matters means that the size and age of the universe are not the problems for the monotheist that atheists would like them to be.

One day we may know more for certain. In the meantime, our human functionality, uniqueness, complexity, and potential for relationship with God will continue, for me at least, to make our planet the most significant place in the universe.

This belief explains, perhaps, the somewhat ambiguous title of this book. We often use the phrase "the age of science"—just as we refer to other historical periods such as "the age of discovery", "the age of reason", or "the age of empire". In that sense, atheists very clearly want us to have faith in the age of science to deliver a good future. I think it will be no surprise when I declare that, despite a positive attitude towards science, I do not have such a faith.

Atheists also tell us that in the age of science it is unreasonable to have any faith, as religions understand that concept. No surprise here either. I have spent most of my chapters arguing that faith, rightly understood, does not contradict reason.

The result of my meandering, then, is a matter of punctuation. It relies upon one humble comma. For I do not believe that we can have faith in the age of science. But I do believe that we can have faith, in the age of science.

Glossary

Terms in italics are also to be found in this glossary.

Abiogenesis
The process by which life arose from non-living matter.

Agnostic
A person who does not know whether there is a God, or who claims it is impossible to know whether there is a God.

Anglicanism
The worldwide association of churches that developed historically from the *Church of England* due to missionary work, the growth of empire, and the settlement of ex-patriots. It is the third largest Christian grouping, following the Roman Catholic and Eastern Orthodox. It contains 34 provinces, of which Canterbury and York are two, and ten other province-like bodies.

Anthropic Principle
The idea that our observations are all determined by our current situation as a carbon-based life form existing in a particular time and place, so that we tend to see ourselves as the goal of everything. We select those aspects of the universe as significant that give us meaning.

Atheism
The belief that there is no God, and that any ideas such as purpose or morality cannot therefore be derived from belief in God.

Atom
The smallest unit of matter that can join together with other atoms to form the chemical substances that make up the universe. Atoms were originally thought of as solid objects, then as miniature solar systems with *electrons* orbiting a *nucleus* made of *protons* and (usually) *neutrons*. Today the nucleus is known to consist of many *sub-atomic particles*, and electrons are considered as clouds of probability rather than solid objects located in one place.

Atonement
The religious view that *sin* has separated human beings from God and that some act on the part of humans or God is necessary to overcome that separation.

Baptists
Christians who do not accept the validity of the baptism of children (sometimes known as 'christening'). They emphasise individual decision, which is normally followed by baptism.

Bible
Collection of ancient writings originating approximately between 1000 BCE and 100 CE forming in different ways the foundations for the major faiths that make up monotheism. See *Old Testament* and *New Testament*.

Big Bang
A term given to the event which created the universe through the mas-

sive expansion of space-time. It was originally coined by Fred Hoyle in a slightly derisory manner.

Catholic
'Universal' or 'according to the whole' depending on context. So the phrase 'catholic church' means universal church, while 'catholic faith' means the beliefs established by the whole church, particularly through its early councils. In common usage the term mostly refers to the *Roman Catholic* Church, even though many other Christians would claim to be catholic in the broad sense.

Charismatic
A description of Christians from all denominations, especially the Pentecostal churches, who believe that practices such as prophecy and speaking in tongues are intended by God to be carried out in the present-day. This sometimes involves extremely extroverted worship.

Coherence
In *philosophy*, a theory of knowledge (*epistemology*) that claims statements are considered true if they cohere with a body of other statements that are held to be true, thus avoiding the problems of *rationalism* and *empiricism*.

Complementariness
In *quantum theory*, the fact that we need two complementary pictures to describe very small scale phenomena (e.g. light sometimes appears to act like a wave, at other times like a particle).

Consciousness
Level of awareness in animals such that they act rationally in relation to their environment beyond reflex and instinct. Developed in humans to include *symbolic reasoning*.

Consequentialism
The view that the morality of beliefs or actions should be established on the basis of their consequences, rather than in the light of a higher law.

Convergence
In *evolution*, the observation that many features of plants and animals (e.g. organs, body layout) develop separately, but eventually become very similar.

Cosmological Argument
The argument that the existence and energy of the universe imply a creator, normally referred to as God.

Creation
Foundational event in all *monotheistic* faiths, based on the account given in the first book of the *Bible*, Genesis, in which it is stated that God created the heavens and the earth.

Creationism
In extreme forms, the view that God created each *species* of animal and plant as a specific act, following the order of the book of Genesis, within the timeframe suggested if read literally. In less extreme forms the generally held views of cosmology and evolution are accepted, but it is still held that God intervened to form individual species, particularly mankind.

Culture
The features that social groups such as tribes and nations develop that go beyond the strict needs of survival, although some of these may indirectly aid survival.

Darwinism
The view that *evolution* took place in small steps because of minor variations in succeeding generations; those that favoured survival continued while others died away. Eventually the

changes would accumulate to form a new species.

Deism
The view that there is a God who created the universe and determines the laws of nature, but does not intervene in the universe now, thereby excluding the possibilities of *miracles* and *revelation*.

Determinism
The view that everything is determined by what has gone before and could, in principle, be predicted.

Deus ex machina
A God brought in or invented simply to solve a problem—a 'God of the Gaps'.

Dissenters
Although anyone can dissent from anything, the term is used more specifically of Christians who refused to conform to the discipline and structures of the *Church of England* from the sixteenth century onwards. Dissenters set up their own churches and organisations.

DNA
The double helix ('twisted ladder') *macromolecule* found in all living cells which carries the genetic code for the *species* and the variants within it. This code controls all the chemistry of the cell. When the cell reproduces it splits the ladder apart and rebuilds the missing halves so that the code is carried forward into both daughter cells.

Double-aspect monism
(sometimes known as 'neutral monism') In *philosophy*, the view that there is only one ultimate substance which underlies both *mind* and matter.

Dualism
In *philosophy*, the view that there are two ultimate substances, *mind* and *matter*, giving rise to the problem of how they could affect each other.

Electron
Negatively charged *sub-atomic particle* normally thought of as orbiting around the *nucleus* of an *atom*, but its position is more accurately described in terms of probability. *Atoms* can share electrons, which binds them together into *molecules*.

Emergence
The originating of something which is totally novel, for example in *abiogenesis*.

Empiricism
In *philosophy*, the view that truth can only be discovered through observation and reasoning about that which is observed. Nothing is self-evident.

Enlightenment
Broad movement approximating to the seventeenth and eighteenth centuries, during which the major foundations of physical science were laid on the basis of observation and reason.

Entanglement
In *quantum theory*, two particles such as photons or *electrons* which are entangled affect each other, whatever their distance apart. Sometimes referred to as 'non-locality'.

Epistemology
In *philosophy*, the subject of how we know things.

Eukaryotic
Description of a living cell that has a *nucleus*. All cells come under this category except bacteria and archaea, which are called 'prokaryotes.'

Evangelicalism
Umbrella term for churches and organisations within *Protestantism* that place most emphasis on the *Bible*, atonement, and individual faith.

Evolution
When used on its own the term generally refers to *Darwinism*. It can also be used in a more general way of any theory of development such as those proposed, for example, by Jean-Baptiste Lamarck and Robert Chambers.

Exaptation
The re-use of genetic material in ways different from its original use. The word is technically the opposite of adaptation, which normally refers to changing towards fulfilling a new function. Exaptation means changing from a function that was previously present.

Extinction
Complete elimination of a *species* due to adverse circumstances such as famine, drought, the rise of new predators, or natural catastrophes.

Fine tuning
The idea that the universe has certain physical characteristics (e.g. the strength of gravity) the values of which are crucial to the existence of intelligent life. The universe is finely tuned to make our existence possible.

Front loading
The theory that much or all of the genetic information needed for the progress of *evolution* was somehow loaded into *DNA* very early in the evolutionary process. Supporters of *Intelligent Design* claim that God put it there, but in principle it could have arisen by chance or by processes not now detectable.

Fundamentalism
Although now used in a general sense of people who accept an infallible basis for any kind of belief, the term originated with American Christians who wished to restore the fundamentals of Christianity against the new views of *liberal theology*. Upholding the authority of the *Bible* was seen as one way to do this, but over time this came to imply literal interpretation.

Gene
Unit of inheritance made up of one or more sections in a *DNA* molecule. Genes have different variations known as 'alleles' which account for variation within species (e.g. eye colour—although most of the variations are less visible and more important).

Genome
All the *genes* found in the DNA of an organism. Discovering this is known as 'sequencing'.

Genotype
All the alleles (see *Gene*) found in the *DNA* of an organism. These alleles are alternative versions of each gene. In a *species*, therefore, all members of the species have the same *genome*, but have different genotypes.

Goldilocks zone
(or 'habitable zone'). The range of distances from a star within which an orbiting planet may have liquid water and therefore support life as we understand it.

Holism
The idea that we should try to understand the whole, not merely the parts that make it up. At the physical level, *entanglement* indicates that all parts of the universe are potentially connected. At the biological level, *evolution* and the effect of organisms on each other indicate connections between them.

Chemistry connects the physical and biological. In *philosophy* the existence of *mind* (if accepted) indicates the possibility of an intelligent force at work at some or all levels. Holism attempts to look at this whole connected picture.

Hominids

Also known as the 'great apes': gorillas, chimpanzees, orangutans and humans, with the chimpanzees being our closest ancestors still living today. Modern humans can be termed hominids, but discussion is usually about how we developed from hominids, because we are a new development in many ways.

Homo sapiens

Latin for 'knowing man' who developed over about the last 200,000 years. We are technically a sub-species called 'homo sapiens sapiens', distinguished by complex speech, thought, and cultural activity compared to predecessors. The first evidence for 'homo sapiens sapiens' originates from about 80,000 years ago.

Humanism

Belief that we should focus on the potential and value of humanity, either alongside belief in God (religious humanism) or without belief in God (secular humanism).

Idealism

In *philosophy*, the claim that *mind* is the ultimate substance.

Intelligent Design

Belief that although *evolution* may account for much of the life that we see around us today, there must have been critical points at which God imposed design. *Irreducible complexity* is normally taken as the main evidence for intelligent design.

Irreducible Complexity

Observation that some complex organs and biochemical processes only function to the advantage of the organisms to which they belong because of their complete form; therefore it is difficult to see how they could have evolved in very small steps.

Liberal Theology

Movement which began in Germany in the eighteenth century, based on the belief that the *Bible* should not be accorded any special privileges as alleged revelation, but should be analysed like any other book to discover dates of authorship, editing, historical errors, and so on.

Macromolecules

Large *molecules*, some, such as *DNA*, containing thousands of *atoms*.

Materialism

In *philosophy*, the belief that the ultimate substance is material and *mind* is a spin-off of the material, probably temporary and probably an illusion. The material world includes energy.

Meme

A unit of memory held to replicate like *genes* and pass on ideas.

Metaphysics

Literally 'beyond physics'—in *philosophy*, the study of what ultimate reality is made from.

Methodism

Movement originating with eighteenth century revival, notably through the Wesleys and George Whitefield. Following rejection by the *Church of England*, Methodism became a denomination in its own right.

Mind

In *philosophy*, a non-material substance. Can refer to a universal mind or to individual minds that we believe we possess.

Molecule
A combination of two or more *atoms* bonded together by sharing *electrons*. The atoms concerned can be of the same chemical element or different ones.

Monism
In *philosophy*, the view that there is only one ultimate substance.

Monotheism
The belief that there is only one God.

Moral Argument
An argument for the existence of God that starts from the commonly held moral principles of mankind, taking them as given and pointing to a universal lawgiver.

Multiverse
Hypothetical conglomeration of universes in which ours is only one.

Mutation
A change in a *gene* due to a change in its underlying *DNA*.

Natural Selection
The widely held view of the mechanism of *evolution*, also known as *Darwinism*.

Natural Theology
Statements about God based only on the universe and nature, without reference to any proposed *revelation*.

Naturalism
The belief that only the natural exists, so that the miraculous is either impossible or else a meaningless concept.

Neo-Darwinism
The principles of *Darwinism* extended to include the knowledge of genetics gained during the first half of the twentieth century.

New Testament
Documents written in common Greek between approximately 50 CE and 100 CE which were subsequently organised into the collection we have today, normally bound into one volume and often combined with the *Old Testament* to form the Christian *Bible*.

Neutron
Particle with no electric charge found in the *nucleus* of most *atoms*. Variation in the number of neutrons results in different isotopes of the same element.

Newtonian
Relating to Sir Isaac Newton, nearly always referring to his theories of mechanics, often known as 'classical mechanics'. The Newtonian universe is the model of the universe that was accepted until *quantum theory* and relativity were discovered.

Non-locality
In *quantum theory*, the fact that particles separated by a huge physical distance can affect each other through *entanglement*.

Noosphere
The sum total of all human thought, parallel to 'biosphere'.

Nonconformists
Later name for *Dissenters*.

Nucleotides
Four types of *molecule* containing Carbon, Hydrogen, Oxygen, Nitrogen and Phosphorous. The *molecules* link in pairs to form the 'rungs' of the *DNA* 'ladder'. Their order conveys the code contained in the *genes*. *RNA* uses three of the same nucleotides plus a different fourth one, in a single chain.

Nucleus
In the cell, contains *DNA* (coiled into the chromosomes), *RNA*, proteins, *nucelotides* and other materials dissolved or held in suspension in water. The nucleus controls the day-to-day functioning of the cell and also its replication. In the *atom*, the nucleus is made up of the *protons* and *neutrons*, around which the *electrons* can be conceived as orbiting.

Observer Effects
In *quantum theory*, refers to the fact that observation and how we do it affects the reality of what is being observed.

Occam's Razor
The principle that we should not invent unnecessary theories to explain observations. The explanation requiring the fewest assumptions is always to be preferred. Originated with the fourteenth-century Franciscan friar William of Occam.

Ontological Argument
First stated explicitly by St Anselm of Canterbury in the eleventh century and disputed ever since. Argues that if we can conceive of a being greater than which cannot exist, then that being must exist in reality as well as in our thoughts. Existing in our thoughts and in reality is clearly greater than existing only in our thoughts. Therefore such a being must exist in reality.

Old Testament
(also called the 'Hebrew Bible' out of respect for Judaism). Recounts the history, religion and devotion of the Israelite people in a collection of books, written probably between 1000 BCE and 400 BCE, although the earliest books may well rely on previous oral and written sources.

Orthodox
In general means following the received traditions. Used specifically of the Eastern Orthodox Church which divided from the *Roman Catholic* Church in 1054.

Panentheism
The belief that the universe exists in God, but God is not the same as the universe.

Panspermia
The theory that life originated on earth from microbes brought here from elsewhere in the universe, possibly on meteorites.

Pantheism
The view that God is the universe and vice versa.

Pentecostalism
A diverse group of *evangelical* Christian denominations that believe in the 'Baptism of the Holy Spirit', an intense personal experience which often includes speaking in tongues. Originated in the US in the late nineteenth century, now global.

Phenotype
The bodily form and functions of an organism that are created when its *genotype* is expressed by development in a particular environment.

Philosophy
Literally 'love of wisdom' and comprising the discussion down the ages of fundamental problems such as *metaphysics*, *epistemology*, ethics, and human nature.

Pluralism
In *philosophy*, the belief that there is more than one ultimate *substance* making up the universe.

Polytheism
Belief in more than one god.

Presbyterianism
Types of church that are ruled by elders (presbyters) as distinct from priests and bishops. The minister is considered 'first among equals' rather than superior.

Protestantism
The various denominations and independent churches that broke away from the *Roman Catholic* church at the *Reformation*.

Proton
Positively charged particle in the *nucleus* of an *atom*. The number of protons determines what element the atom is. For example, hydrogen contains one proton, carbon contains six.

Providence
The idea of God at work behind and through the laws of nature.

Quakerism
(Religious Society of Friends) A group of seventeenth century *Dissenters* founded primarily by George Fox. Emphasised individual experience and testimony to God's work, rather than formal teaching; very diverse today.

Quantum Theory
(also known as quantum mechanics) Describes the behaviour of *sub-atomic particles* in terms of probability, including the effects of observation and the level of uncertainty involved. *Matter* and energy sometimes appear to act as particles and sometimes as waves. (*Complementariness*).

Rationalism
In *philosophy*, the view of *epistemology* holding that truth is established only through reason, not through observation.

Reformation
Broad sixteenth and seventeenth century movement in which northern-European churches broke away from the *Roman Catholic* church, forming, for example, the Lutheran Church and the *Church of England*.

Reformed
All *Protestant* churches are broadly reformed, but the word is also used more specifically of those who followed John Calvin and his associates, which take a more rigorous line on *sin* and predestination. Strongest among the English puritans, the French Huguenots and in Switzerland, the Netherlands, Eastern Europe, Scotland, and Northern Ireland. Today there are also numerous smaller Reformed groupings throughout the world.

Replicators
Natural elements of information transfer, of which the *gene* is the only proven example and the *meme* is a hypothetical example.

Revelation
In religion, refers to any information or vision held to be given by God to humans. In Christianity, primary revelation is through the *Bible*, though not necessarily dictated or to be taken literally.

RNA
Made of *nucleotides* like *DNA* but in a single strand, much shorter and structured like a loose ball of string instead of the DNA 'ladder'. There are many types of RNA with different functions in the cell, mostly connected with information transfer.

Roman Catholicism
The oldest western Christian church, dating back to the New Testament pe-

riod, and based in Rome for most of that time. Divided from the Eastern *Orthodox* church in 1054 and the *Protestant* churches at the *Reformation*.

Scepticism
Doubting everything except that which can be positively established by science.

Scientism
Belief that science can explain everything and thereby resolve all the problems of humanity.

Secularism
View that religion should form no part of public life e.g. in the media, education, or judiciary.

Sin
In religion, generally any departure from what God requires in human conduct. It is not linked particularly to sex, as in common usage. In Christianity, sin is also seen as an underlying condition of human nature.

Species
A group of organisms that can breed to form further fertile members of the same species and not hybrids.

Sub-atomic Particles
Electrons and the particles that make up *neutrons* and *protons* in the *nucleus* of an *atom*.

Substance
In *philosophy*, that which is the basis underlying all reality. Not to be confused with 'material'.

Symbolic Thought
Human ability to manipulate symbols in order to reason, communicate, and interpret/interact with the environment. The symbols used include words, mathematical and scientific notation, numbers, and visualisations such as diagrams and icons.

Synapses
The junctions between the neurons, which are the basic building blocks of the brain and nervous system. The synaptic gaps between neurons have to be crossed by chemical or electrical means, which makes them critical in the transfer of information.

System
Two or more parts that interact to produce a result that could not have been achieved by the parts in isolation.

Teleological Argument
The argument that the purpose inherent in things demonstrates the existence of God. Generally taken as the same as the argument from design, since design is the most frequent indicator of purpose.

Theism
Belief in a God who is involved in the universe and with human beings, and is to some extent personal. Could in theory be applied within *polytheism*, but generally used within *monotheism* in contrast to *Deism*.

Theistic Evolution
Belief that *evolution* and *monotheism* do not contradict each other. Rather, God can work through evolution to achieve his purposes.

Theodicy
Arguments that reconcile the reality of suffering with the belief in a personal God. Literally, justification of God.

Theology
Discussion and reasoning about God.

Transmutation of Species
The creation of a new *species* from a previous one.

Utilitarianism
Belief that moral principles should be decided on the basis of creating the greatest possible happiness for the greatest possible number of people, not on the basis of any higher law.

Bibliography

Appleyard, Bryan: *Aliens: Why They Are Here* (Scribner, 2006)
Appleyard, Bryan: *Understanding the Present* (BCA, 1992)
Appleyard, Bryan: *How to Live Forever or Die Trying* (Simon & Schuster, 2007)
Aquinas, Thomas: *Summa Theologica Online (First Part, Question 53)* http://www.newadvent.org/summa/1053.htm
Athanasius of Alexandria *On the Incarnation of the Word* (http://www.ccel.org/ccel/athanasius/incarnation.txt)
Baggini, Julian *Atheism: A Very Short Introduction* (OUP, 2003)
Barrow, John D.: *New Theories of Everything* (OUP, 2007)
Barrow, J. D. and Tipler, F. J.: *The Anthropic Cosmological Principle* (OUP, 1996)
Beattie, Tina: *The New Atheists: the Twilight of Reason and the War on Religion* (DLT, 2007)
Beauregard, Mario and O'Leary, Denyse: *The Spiritual Brain* (Harper Collins, 2007)
Behe, Michael J.: *Darwin's Black Box* (Simon & Schuster, 1998)
Behe, Michael J.: *The Edge of Evolution* (Free Press, 2007)
Blackmore, Susan: *The Meme Machine* (OUP, 2000)
Blackmore, Susan: Video lecture (http://www.ted.com/index.php/talks/susan_blackmore_on_memes_and_temes.html)
Campus Crusade for Christ: *The Four Spiritual Laws* (http://www.campuscrusade.com/fourlawsflash.htm)
Carey, George: *The Gate of Glory* (Hodder, 1986)
Collins, Francis S.: *The Language of God* (Simon & Schuster, 2006)
Cornwell, John: *Darwin's Angel: An Angelic Riposte to The God Delusion* (Profile Books, 2007)
Davies, Paul: *God and the New Physics* (Penguin, 1990)
Davies, Paul: *The Goldilocks Enigma: Why is the Universe Just Right for Life?* (Penguin, 2007)
Davies, Paul: *The Mind of God: Science and the Search for Ultimate Meaning* (Penguin, 1993)
Dawkins, Richard: *The Blind Watchmaker* (Penguin, 1991)
Dawkins, Richard: *The Extended Phenotype* (OUP, 1999)
Dawkins, Richard: *River Out of Eden* (Phoenix, 2004)
Dawkins, Richard: *A Devil's Chaplain* (Phoenix, 2004)
Dawkins, Richard: *The Ancestor's Tale* (Phoenix, 2005)
Dawkins, Richard: *Unweaving the Rainbow* (Penguin, 2006)
Dawkins, Richard: *The Selfish Gene* (OUP, 2006)
Dawkins, Richard: *Climbing Mount Improbable* (Penguin, 2006)
Dawkins, Richard: *The God Delusion* (Bantam, 2007)
Dawkins, Richard: *The Greatest Show on Earth* (Bantam, 2009)
Dennett, Daniel C.: *Consciousness Explained* (Penguin, 1993)
Dennett, Daniel C.: *Darwin's Dangerous Idea: Evolution and the Meanings of Life*

(Penguin, 1996)
Dennett, Daniel C.: *Breaking the Spell: Religion as a natural phenomenon* (Penguin, 2007)
Eagleton, Terry: *Review of The God Delusion*, London Review of Books, Vol. 28 No. 20, 19th October 2006
Edwards, Jonathan: *Sinners in the Hands of an Angry God* (http://www.ccel.org/ccel/edwards/sermons.sinners.html)
d'Espagnat, Bernard: *On Physics and Philosophy* (Princeton University Press, 2006)
d'Espagnat, Bernard: *The Quantum Theory & Reality*, Scientific American, November 1979
Flew, Antony with Varghese, Roy Abraham: *There is a God* (Harper Collins, 2007)
Frayn, Michael: *The Human Touch: our Part in the Creation of a Universe* (Faber, 2007)
Graham, Billy: *Peace with God* (http://www.ccel.us/PeaceWithGod.toc.html)
Gray, Asa: *Darwiniana* (http://www.manybooks.net/titles/grayasaetext04drwna10.html)
Gray, John: *False Dawn: the Delusions of Global Capitalism* (Granta, 1999)
Gray, John: *Black Mass: Apocalyptic Religion and the Death of Utopia* (Penguin, 2007)
Green, Toby: *Inquisition* (Macmillan, 2008)
Greenfield, Susan: *The Private Life of the Brain* (Penguin, 2002)
Handy, Charles: *The Empty Raincoat* (Arrow, 1995)
Hannam, James: *God's Philosophers: How the Medieval World Laid the Foundations of Modern Science* (Icon, 2010)
Harris, Sam: *Letter to a Christian Nation* (Bantam, 2007)
Hawking, Stephen W.: *A Brief History of Time* (Bantam, 1988)
Hawking, Stephen W. and Mlodinow, Leonard: *Grand Design* (Bantam, 2010)
Hitchens, Christopher: *God is Not Great: the Case Against Religion* (Atlantic, 2007)
Hitchens, Peter: *The Rage Against God* (Continuum, 2010)
Humphrys, John: *In God We Doubt: Confessions of a Failed Atheist* (Hodder, 2008)
James, Willliam: *The Varieties of Religious Experience* (Fontana, 1971)
Jastrow, Robert: *God and the Astronomers* (Norton & Co, 1992)
Justin Martyr: *Dialogue with Trypho the Jew* (http://www.ccel.org/ccel/schaff/anf01.viii.iv.lxxx.html)
Kellogg, Vernon: *Headquarters Nights* (http://www.archive.org/stream/headquartersnig00kellgoog)
Lennox, John C.: *God's Undertaker: Has Science Buried God?* (Lion, 2007)
Lewis, C. S.: *Miracles Harper* (Collins, 1998)
Lewis, C. S.: *The Great Divorce* (Collins, 2011)
Lewis, C. S.: *Mere Christianity* (Collins, 2011)
Lewis, C. S.: *The Abolition of Man* (Harper Collins, 2011)
Lewis, C. S.: *The Problem of Pain* (Collins, 2011)
McGrath, Alister: *Suffering* (Hodder & Stoughton, 1992)
McGrath, Alister: *Dawkins' God: genes, memes and the meaning of life* (Blackwell, 2007)
McGrath, Alister and McGrath, Joanna Collicutt: *The Dawkins Delusion* (SPCK, 2007)
Margulis, Lynn and Sagan, Dorion: *Acquiring Genomes: A Theory of the Origins of Species* (Perseus, 2003)

Nadeau, Robert and Kafatos, Menas: *The Non-local Universe* (OUP, 2001)
National Academy of Sciences: *Science and Creationism* (http://download.nap.edu/catalog.php?record_id=6024)
Nietzsche, Friedrich W.: *Thus Spake Zarathustra* (http://www.gutenberg.org/cache/epub/1998/pg1998.txt)
Nilsson, Dan-E. and Pelger, Susanne: *A pessimistic estimate of the time required for an eye to evolve*, Proceedings of the Royal Society London B, Vol. 266, 22nd April 1994
Paley, William: *Natural Theology; or Evidences of the Existence and Attributes of the Deity* (http://www.archive.org/details/naturaltheology00pale)
Polkinghorne, John: *Quantum Physics and Theology: An Unexpected Kinship* (SPCK, 2007)
Radin, Dean: *Entangled Minds* (Simon & Schuster, 2006)
Radin, Dean: *The Conscious Universe* (Harper Collins, 1997)
Rees, Martin: *Just Six Numbers: The Deep Forces that Shape the Universe* (Phoenix, 2000)
Ringgren, Helmer and Ström, Åke V.: *Religions of Mankind* (Fortress, 1967)
Rowson, Martin: *The Dog Allusion: Gods, Pets and How to Be Human* (Vintage, 2008)
Ruse, Michael: *Can a Darwinian be a Christian? The relationship between science and religion* (CUP, 2006)
Ruse, Michael: *Science and Spirituality: making room for faith in the age of science* (CUP, 2010)
Russell, Bertrand: *Why I am not a Christian* (Routledge, 2004)
Ryle, G.: *The Concept of Mind* (Univ. Chicago Press, 1984)
Sheldrake, Rupert: *A New Science of Life* (Icon, 2009)
Sheldrake, Rupert: *The Presence of the Past* (Icon, 2011)
Stenger, Victor J.: *God: the Failed Hypothesis* (Prometheus, 2008)
Sterelny, Kim: *Dawkins vs. Gould: Survival of the Fittest* (Icon, 2007)
Swinburne, Richard: *Is There a God?* (OUP, 2003)
Tipler, Frank J.: *The Physics of Christianity* Doubleday (New York, 2007)
Torrey, R. A. (ed.): *The Fundamentals* (http://www.xmission.com/~fidelis/)
Townes, Charles H.: *Laser's inventor predicts meeting of science, religion: Townes sees more parallels than disparities*, Harvard Gazette (http://news.harvard.edu/gazette/2005/06.16/05-laser.html)
University of Geneva Department of Physics: *'GAP-Optique'* web site (http://www.gap-optique.unige.ch)
Voltaire: *Candide* (http://www.literature.org/authors/voltaire/candide/)
Wald, George: *Life and Mind in the Universe*, International Journal of Quantum Chemistry, Vol. 26, 15th March 1984
Ward, Keith: *What the Bible Really Teaches: A Challenge to Fundamentalists* (SPCK, 2004)
Ward, Keith: *Is Religion Dangerous?* (Lion, 2006)
Wolpert, Lewis: *Six impossible things before breakfast: the evolutionary origins of belief* (Faber & Faber, 2006)
Ward, Keith: *Why There Almost Certainly is a God* (Lion, 2008)

Index

abiogenesis 116, 122, 140, 155, 172f, 227
Agnosticism 51, 214f, 227
Albigensians 23
Amish 39, 53
Anabaptists 4, 39
Anglo-catholic 47, 62
Anselm of Canterbury, Saint 54f, 136, 175, 233
Anthropic Principle 59, 124, 132-137,154, 170, 177, 195, 227
anti-Semitism 12-17, 28
Appleyard, Bryan 70, 171, 191f
Aquinas, Saint Thomas 56f, 148, 211, 221
Aristotle 6, 206
Athanasius of Alexandria, Saint 62, 221
atonement viii, 33, 42-45, 64, 170, 189, 221, 227
Augustine of Hippo, Saint 54, 61, 221
Bacon, Roger 27, 58, 206
Baggini, Julian 1, 6, 10, 13, 16-18
Baptists 31, 47f, 50, 227
Barrow, John 59, 220
Bartlett, Robert 19, 148
Bede, Venerable 21, 58
Behe, Michael 24, 82f, 89-94
Bentham, Jeremy 5f, 10, 12, 213
Berkeley, Bishop George 177, 202-204, 220f
Big Bang 56, 111, 123f, 127, 141, 155, 184, 221, 226, 227
Blackmore, Susan 190f, 197
Blessitt, Arthur 33, 47
Brahe, Tycho 108
British Humanist Association 2, 216
Carey, George 34
Cathars 23
Catholic 13f, 17, 20, 23-25, 33, 47-52, 53, 59-62, 157f, 172, 202, 216,221, 228
Charlemagne 20f, 58
Church of England 31, 34, 46-50, 54, 57, 63, 157, 164
co-evolution 95
coherence 208-210, 211-222, 228
Collins, Francis 40, 221
Communism 11, 17f, 39, 194
complementariness 145-148, 154, 156, 228
conceptual thinking 184-186
consciousness 75, 77, 86, 88-92, 107, 111, 120-123, 140, 153-156, 172, 177, 185f, 198f, 220f, 228
consequentialism 6-10, 19, 27, 43, 51, 152, 228
convergence 97, 102, 209f, 213-217, 228
Copenhagen Interpretation 147, 152, 179
Copernicus, Nicolaus 108, 139, 223
cosmological argument 67, 175, 228
cosmology viii, 72, 107, 109, 170, 177, 182f, 213
Creationism vi, 30-35, 40, 50, 82, 228
Crusades 22f, 26, 31, 75
cults, religious 37, 70-72
culture vi, ix, 1, 6, 14, 26f, 36, 43f, 58, 60, 65-67, 68, 72f, 111, 120, 136, 154, 158, 163, 166, 186-195, 200f, 202, 207, 212, 215, 222, 228
Darwin, Charles vi, 12, 16, 21, 57f, 60f, 63-65, 67, 77f, 83f, 97, 104, 107,136, 155, 169
Darwiniana 58
Darwinism 2, 30, 51, 77f, 155, 172, 184, 190, 221, 228
Davies, Paul 110, 121, 173, 220
Deism v, 4, 46, 49, 53-55, 60, 76, 108, 138, 184, 210-217, 229
Dennett, Daniel vii, 2, 124, 135, 155-157, 183, 190, 197-199
Descartes, René 149f, 198, 202-204
design ix, 56-59, 66, 82, 84, 99, 112, 124, 133-136, 139, 170, 172-174, 177-181, 180, 184, 188, 229
determinism 151, 229
DNA ix, 97, 102f, 107, 112, 115, 117f, 120-123, 140, 153-155, 159, 172, 184, 188, 229
dualism 147-150, 153, 197-199, 202, 229
Edwards, Jonathan 37, 44, 47, 203
Einstein, Albert 14, 79, 107
electron 142-146, 180, 197, 229
emergence 140, 186, 229
empiricism 203-207, 210, 229
Enlightenment 1, 15-17, 27f, 46, 50-52, 53f, 57f, 60, 63, 67, 68, 73-76, 78, 84, 107, 108, 137, 156, 172, 216, 229
entanglement 144-148, 153-155, 229
enzymes 113-118
epigenetics 97
epistemology 50-52, 57, 76, 149, 173, 202-210, 217, 229
Erasmus, Desiderius 216
Essays and Reviews 60-63, 75, 78
eugenics 12, 16f, 78
euglena 90
eukaryotic cell 111, 119-121, 126, 172, 229
evangelicals 31-52, 53, 58f, 61-63, 73, 157, 172, 205,

240

INDEX 241

221, 230
exaptation 83, 102, 118-121, 230
extinction 96, 230
Fascism 13-18
Finney, Charles 30
Flew, Antony 184
Fox, George 53
Franciscans 39, 58
front loading 102, 122, 230
Fundamentalism ix, 3, 28, 29-52, 67, 73, 157f, 189-191, 200, 230
Galileo 108, 139, 211, 223
Galton, Francis 12, 15f, 78
gene 83, 96f, 103-107, 114, 181, 182, 184, 188, 230
gene duplication 96
Genesis (biblical book) 60f, 165
genome 113, 118, 140, 230
gnosis 70, 72, 74
Gödel, Kurt 56, 221
Goldilocks zone 109-111, 115-117, 126, 135, 173, 177, 230
Goldschmidt, Richard 96
Gould, Stephen Jay 2, 81, 95f, 107, 190
Graham, Billy 31, 33f, 44, 47
Gray, Asa 58, 60, 221
Gray, John 26, 39f, 194
Greenfield, Susan 90, 154, 173, 185, 199
Grossteste, Bishop 58, 206, 221
Haldane, J B S 199
Hameroff, Stuart 154
Hamilton, W D 66
Handy, Charles 194
Hannam, James 59
Harris, Sam vii, 2, 8, 20, 38
Hawking, Stephen 56, 149, 173, 179, 183
hedonism 193
Hegel, Georg Wilhelm Friedrich 11, 17
Heisenberg, Werner 142
Hilbert Space 128
Hitchens, Christopher vii, 1f
Hitchens, Peter 158
d'Holbach, Baron 1, 5, 156
holism 156, 171, 181, 184, 202, 230
Holy Club 46f
Holy Roman Empire 20

hominids 105-107, 112, 118, 120, 123, 155, 185, 231
homo sapiens 104, 111, 120-123, 155, 185f, 192, 225, 231
Hooker, Richard 54
hope 171
Hoyle, Fred 81, 110-114, 117, 121, 184
Humanism 51, 216-220, 231
Hume, David 139, 163, 202-208, 213f
Huxley, T H vi, 78, 94, 204, 214, 216
hybridisation 96
Ibn Jubayr 22
Icke, David 69f, 72, 74
idealism 150-153, 156, 203f, 217, 231
illuminati 16, 74, 197
immanence 170
Implicit Design 107, 181
Inquisition 20, 23-26
inspiration 76
intelligence 97, 105f, 121, 130-132, 191, 195, 217-219
Intelligent Design vi, vii, 31, 82-84, 89f, 101, 107, 124, 231
intention 219, 225
intervention, divine 54, 123, 138, 166f, 226
Irreducible Complexity 82-84, 87-90, 101, 103, 107, 114, 120, 231
James, William 41, 75
Josephson, Brian 154
Justin Martyr 39
Kant, Immanuel 6, 64, 206
Kellogg, Vernon 12f, 51
Kepler, Johannes 108, 139
Kimura, Motoo 96
Krebs Cycle 119
Lamarck, Jean-Baptiste 29, 77
language 111, 185-188, 195, 200, 205
Large Hadron Collider 178, 209, 219
law, natural 4, 6, 46, 54, 64-66, 84, 97, 107, 108-111, 121-123, 127-129, 138-140, 141, 153, 155, 159f, 164-167, 172-176, 181, 183, 212f, 220, 225

legend 195f
Leibniz, Gottfried 4f, 152, 168f, 171, 203f
Leroi, Armand 97
Lewis, C S 34, 64-66, 157, 167, 169
Locke, John 47, 202-204
Luther, Martin 14-16, 27
Lux Mundi 62f, 75, 221
macromutations 96
Many Worlds Interpretation (MWI) 128, 147, 179
Margulis, Lynn 95,119
Maslow, Abraham 187, 194, 199
materialism 54, 73, 151-158, 159, 172, 197-200, 202, 207, 210, 225, 231
membrane, cell 83, 114-125, 126
meme ix, 155, 188-200, 211, 231
Mendel, Gregor 78, 107
metaphysics 149-151, 231
metasystems 93
Methodism 43, 46, 48, 54, 231
Michelson-Morley experiment 79,138
Mill, John Stuart 6f
Miller-Urey experiment 115f
mind-body problem 151f, 155, 197, 199
miracles 60f, 137, 139, 159-171, 172, 182
monastery 21, 55
monism 149-156, 197, 199, 205, 211, 232
Moody, Dwight L 30
moral argument 64-67, 136, 172, 232
multiverse 126-137, 147, 154, 232
mutation vii, 77, 84, 85-94, 96, 102f, 118-123, 132, 153-155, 159, 181, 182, 184, 232
myth 12, 51, 60, 71, 76, 195-197
narcissism 193
National Secular Society 2
natural theology 57-63, 73, 136f, 211, 232
naturalism 164f, 232
Nazism 11-17, 28, 39, 192
neo-Darwinism vii, ix, 84,

90-95, 101, 105, 172, 232
neutral theory of molecular evolution 96
Newton, Sir Isaac 4, 46f, 54, 74, 108f, 139, 148, 220f, 226, 232
Niagara Bible Conference 30, 45
Nietzsche, Friedrich W 11f, 16f, 48, 78, 200, 216
nonconformists 46, 50, 53, 232
non-locality 145, 232
noosphere 220f, 232
nucleotides 115, 232
nucleus 111, 119, 142f, 233
observer effects 146-148, 203, 233
Occam, William of 27, 58, 206, 209
Occam's Razor 2, 31, 162-165, 209f, 211, 213f, 217, 233
occult 12, 69-74
ontological argument 55f, 67, 175, 233
orrery 108f, 139, 180
Oxford Movement 47
oxygen catastrophe 118, 126, 133
Paley, William 56-62, 83f, 104, 136
panentheism 214, 233
panspermia 131, 233
pantheism 213-215, 233
Penrose, Roger 121, 154, 173
phlogiston 79
photon 80, 144-146
photosynthesis 87, 119
Pietism 46
Planck, Max 80, 91, 107, 141, 221
Planck's constant 80, 91
plasticity (of brain) 185f, 199
pluralism 149f, 233
polytheism viii, 191, 212-214, 234
post-enlightenment gridlock 76, 84, 107, 156, 172, 222
prayer 21, 109, 159, 171, 180, 200, 209, 218
pre-established harmony 152, 204
Presbyterian 25, 32, 48, 50, 234
protocell 117-124, 126, 140,

155
protozoa 93
providence 166-170, 234
Ptolemy 178, 224
punctuated equilibrium 95
Puritans 46, 54
Quakers 39, 53f, 234
quantum theory 80, 91, 107, 109, 128f, 135, 141-149, 153-156, 158, 159, 162, 165, 172f, 177-181, 182, 184, 199, 202, 210, 220, 225f, 234
Radin, Dean 144, 154, 163
rationalism 203-206, 234
Rationalist Association 2
Rees, Martin 110,121
Reformation 21, 23f, 32, 39, 47f, 50, 53-55, 60, 73, 172, 216, 234
relativity 79f,107, 109, 152, 210
Renaissance 108
replication (RNA/DNA) 118
restoration 62f, 220
resurrection 164-166, 220
revelation 45, 50, 53f, 57, 61-64, 74, 76, 159, 164, 171, 172, 213, 218, 234
revival 31, 33, 40, 44, 47f
ritual 68, 74f, 195f
RNA 97, 112-118, 140, 234
Romanticism 75f, 193
Russell, Bertrand vii, 2, 5, 55f, 127, 210
Ryle, Gilbert 155-157, 198, 218
salvation history 196
Schleitheim Confession 39
Schrödinger, Erwin 142-148
Scientism 159, 171, 192, 199, 235
Scopes, John vi, 31, 51
secularism 158, 159, 235
Sheldrake, Rupert 154
signs 167
singularity 56, 111
Society for Psychical Research 75
Socinianism 54
South Place Ethical Society 216
Spinoza, Baruch 204f, 211, 214
spiritualism 74f, 77
Stenger, Victor J 2, 82f, 169,

173-175, 179, 184
suffering, problem of 5, 19, 26-28, 39, 41, 60, 158, 159, 167-171, 180f, 182, 187, 215, 226
symbiogenesis 95
symbiosis 95, 104
synapses 85, 152, 154, 185, 235
systems 88-98, 100f, 103f, 109-111, 113, 118, 136, 172, 194, 199, 224, 235
Tegmark, Max 129f, 179
teleological argument 56-61,67, 177, 235
telepathy 162-164
temes 190
Theism v, 46, 215, 235
theistic evolution vii,31, 40, 235
theodicy 169f, 235
Tipler, Frank 220
tradition 194, 196, 221f
transhumanism 171, 190
UFOs 70f, 75, 160, 191
uncertainty 142f, 147f
Unitarianism 54, 74, 216
viruses 8,90, 95, 103, 197
void 126, 174f
Voltaire 4f, 15, 18, 26, 48, 53f, 124, 168, 203
Wagner, Richard 12, 15f, 28
Wahhabism 44f
Waldensians 23
Wallace, Alfred Russel 75,77f, 155
Ward, Keith 25, 41
Warfield, B B 30, 32, 40
Wesley, Charles 43, 47
Wesley, John 46-48
Wheeler, John 220
Whitefield, George 47
Wilberforce, Bishop William vi
Woese, Carl 95
Wolpert, Lewis 1, 10, 182f
Young's double slit experiment 145

EU GPSR Authorized Representative:

LOGOS EUROPE, 9 rue Nicolas Poussin, 17000 La Rochelle, France

contact@logoseurope.eu

www.ingramcontent.com/pod-product-compliance
Lightning Source LLC
Chambersburg PA
CBHW070548160426
43199CB00014B/2412